THE HIBEES

Picture session at Easter Road for season, 85–86.
Back row: J. Stirling, W. Irvine, A. Sneddon, A. Rough, C. Harris, R. Rae,
B. Rice, B. Thomson, A. Brazil. Middle row: J. Blackley, T. McNiven,
A. Peters, P. Kane, K. McKee, G. Hunter, G. Durie, S. McElhone,
J. McBride, G. Neeley, T. Craig. Front row: D. Lennon, C. Milne, E. May,
I. Munro, G. Rae, D. Fellinger, J. Collins, P. McGovern, M. Weir.

THE STORY OF HIBERNIAN FOOTBALL CLUB

John R Mackay

Foreword by
KENNETH WAUGH

JOHN DONALD PUBLISHERS LTD
EDINBURGH

ISBN 0 85976 144 4 (Paper)
ISBN 0 85976 152 5 (Cloth)

Phototypeset by H.M. Repros Ltd., Glasgow
Printed in Great Britain by Bell & Bain Ltd., Glasgow.

Foreword

Having been brought up not far from Easter Road Stadium, Hibernian Football Club has been an important part of my life. It was with some pleasure that I read through the page proofs of this book, taking a trip down memory lane as the players from the past once again came to life. It is important to have such a history, documenting both the glory days and the times, perhaps no less memorable, when the club's back was up against the wall. Leafing through the pages, though, it is quite clear that the club has led the way in many aspects of the modern game. Hibernian was the first Scottish side to play in the European Cup, the first to instal undersoil heating and, more recently, was the first club north of the border to offer an electronic scoreboard for the enjoyment of its supporters. As a club, we will continue to make innovations and break new ground as football must always be seen to be progressing and leaving behind outdated spectator accommodation.

Reading through this book, the golden days are vividly conjured up. Which forward line in Scottish football history, for example, could match the Famous Five? — Smith, Johnstone, Reilly, Turnbull and Ormond. There have been many great players parading our colours since — the likes of Joe Baker, Pat Stanton, Alan Rough and, indeed, George Best, and many more, too numerous to mention. And who can forget the European matches here when the likes of Barcelona, Leeds and Liverpool graced the famous 'slope'?

An up-to-date history of the club is long overdue, in my mind, and it is essential reading for any true Hibernian supporter. That is not to say that it is necessarily a good thing to dwell on the glories of the past. We have been taking significant steps both on and off the park recently to build for a future which I hope will be every bit as significant as the last 110 years. My years as chairman have already seen a great deal of change at the club and there will inevitably be changes to come if we are to keep Hibernian Football Club at the forefront of Scottish football.

Reading through the book, may well provide many fans with treasured memories — the great Hibs teams of the past, the players they have watched come and go down through the years. However, it is also a time to look forward — at the chapters that have yet to be written.

Kenny Waugh,
Chairman Hibernian F.C.

Sources

The main source of information has been *The Scotsman*, but reference has also been made to the following newspapers and football encyclopaedia:

(Edinburgh) *Evening News*
Edinburgh Evening Dispatch
Dundee Advertiser
Edinburgh Courant
Glasgow Herald
Glasgow Evening Times
Glasgow Observer
Glasgow Daily News
Sporting Post (Dundee)
Scottish Umpire
Scottish Referee
Scottish Sport
Dundee Courier
Scottish Football Annual
Rothmans Football Yearbook (Queen Anne)
McKinlay's A to Z of Scottish Football (Macdonald)
Encyclopaedia of British Football (Collins)

The following books were also interesting and useful:

100 Years of Hibs (Docherty & Thomson–John Donald)
One Hundred Years of Scottish Football (Rafferty–Pan)
Scottish Football — A Pictorial History (McCarra–Third Eye/Polygon)
The Old Firm: Sectarianism, Sport and Society in Scotland (Murray–John Donald)
The Story of the Hearts (Reid)
The Hearts — The Story of Heart of Midlothian (Mackie)
Glasgow Rangers — The Story of Scotland's Greatest Football Club (Fairgrieve)

Acknowledgements

I wish to thank all those who have helped in any way in the production of this book, and especially the following:

Rikki Raginia, Phil Thomson and Jim Lawrie, whose contributions have been considerable, and Joe McMurray, on whose unrivalled first-hand knowledge of the club I have relied heavily.

The staff at the National Library of Scotland, the Scottish Section of the Central Public Library, and the Scottish Football Association, for their friendly assistance, and likewise Bill Brady of Scotsman Publications, without whose co-operation the illustrations might have proved a major problem.

David Heggie, Alan Murray, Jim Macgregor, Keith Harper, John White and John Anderson, on the textual side, Dave Simpson, Jimmy Stewart, Mrs. Rowena Taylor, George Staddon, George Liston and the New 50 Club for illustrations.

My thanks to Scotsman Publications Ltd., for their kind permission to reproduce the many illustations of theirs in this book.

John R Mackay

Contents

CHAPTER 1

The Irish Connection, 1875–78

The Hibernian Football Club was founded in 1875. Queen Victoria was on the throne; Disraeli had taken over from Gladstone as Prime Minister a year earlier when the Conservatives had ousted the Whigs (or Liberals) in the General Election, and there was as yet no Labour Party. Trades unions had been legalised in 1871, income tax was 3d in the £ and Forster's Education Act had brought elementary education to most children for the first time. There were 13,000 miles of railway around Britain, but the usual forms of transport were still the penny farthing and the horse-drawn carriage. The Tay Bridge was being built by men earning 8d a day, and was to be destroyed before the '70s were out.

In Edinburgh, it was an age of expansion, with the city spilling out in all directions. The New Town spread itself elegantly west of Queensferry Street, while the less fortunate migrated to the multiplying tenements around the town. Most of the surrounding villages that have lost all or most of their identity under the sprawling suburbs were as yet unscathed, and in particular the hamlet of Powburn still clustered round its tannery and its toll on the road to the south, where now stands the group of shops on Mayfield Road, and where much of the capital's early football history was made.

The Hibernian Football Club was in fact formed at a meeting of the Young Men's Catholic Association (YMCA) under the chairmanship of Canon Hannan, and the name was the suggestion of Michael Whelehan, a young man of about twenty-one years, and who was elected the first club captain. Hibs' centenary captain, Pat Stanton, is, interestingly, a direct relative of Whelehan. The YMCA had its own premises in a hall in St. Mary's Street.

The Secretary was Mal Byrne, and it was one of his early tasks to draw up a set of rules for the new club. The resulting document carried the club crest featuring the Irish harp, and the motto, 'Erin-go-bragh' (Ireland for ever). Members were required to furnish at their own expense 'Caps, White Guernsey with Harp on left breast, also White trousers with green stripes'. Monthly meetings were held in Buchanan's Hotel in the High Street, and the monthly subscription was 6d. Members missing the monthly meeting were fined a further twopence.

Practices were to be held in the Meadows every Tuesday, Thursday and Saturday, and regular attendance was looked for. And in the event of actually playing a match against someone else, 'Members are expected to

1

leave all disputes to be settled by the Umpires, without giving any opinion on the matter at issue'. It was all too often to be shown that the players of the nineteenth century found that last one as hard to uphold as their present-day successors.

The Origins of the Game

Forms of football had been played for centuries. King Robert the Bruce and more than one of the Stewart kings had outlawed the game because archery seemed a more useful line of defence against the regular incursions of the English, but a few traditional games do survive to the present day. Other versions of football were practised on the playing fields of Eton and other public schools. But an early *Scottish Football Annual* had no doubt where lay the credit for the popularisation of the association game: 'in Scotland the game seems to have nearly died out. The modern game, we may say, belongs to England'.

The first football club was Sheffield FC, founded in 1855, and still operating in minor grades. Notts County, the oldest league club, started in 1862, a year before the Football Association. Scotland's first club, Queens Park, was formed in 1867 and supplied all the players for the first international with England in 1872, a year before being instrumental in founding the Scottish Football Association.

Queens Park were also instrumental in bringing the association game to Edinburgh, putting on an exhibition game in December 1873. Rugby was already the establishment game in the capital, being played by such clubs as Edinburgh Accies, Edinburgh Wanderers and Royal High School FP, on whose ground the game was played. Following this demonstration, Edinburgh's first association football club, Third Edinburgh Rifle Volunteers, was founded in early 1874 and Thistle, who had played for a year or so under different rules, threw in their lot with the association code. In the next eighteen months or so, there was a mushrooming of clubs in the capital, including Heart of Midlothian, Hanover, Swifts — and Hibernians.

Meanwhile, the Scottish Cup was first competed for in 1873–74 by sixteen teams, all from the West, and Queens Park won it without losing a goal. They retained the trophy in 1875, beating Renton 3–0 in the final, but the signs were there that their supremacy was becoming less pronounced — Vale of Leven had actually scored against Queens in a friendly in January, the first Scottish side so to do, and Queens had only managed to score against Renton in the last fifteen minutes. 3rd ERV entered the 1874–75

The Hibs team of 1876 in their hooped strip of that time. Back row (l to r) Hall, Quinn, Gilhooley, Beveridge, Candlin, Rourke, Creamer and McGrath. Middle — Byrne, Donelly, Whelehan, Hughes, Browne and Keegan. Front — Meechan, Watson and Flynn.

competition, losing 3–0 to Helensburgh in the opening round, and also tackled teams like Alexandria Athletic and the Rovers from Glasgow, without taking on any of the West's big guns.

In Edinburgh, some of the rules of the game were interpreted rather loosely. Commentators from the West noted that players in the capital still had a tendency to pick the ball up, and in a game between the second XIs of 3rd ERV and Rovers, ends were exchanged three times. The game as played in the West of Scotland was hardly one for cissies, but matches in the capital were criticised for their rough play and unnecessarily heavy charging. In early 1875, a game between a scratch 3rd ERV side and Thistle ended seven minutes early owing to a 'struggle' among the players.

An Unfriendly Welcome

By the start of 1875–76, considerable progress had been made in the capital. The Edinburgh FA has been formed and the Edinburgh Cup subscribed for. It was not surprisingly 3rd ERV who won the first final, beating Thistle 6–0 in the spring. 3rd ERV went further afield for their opposition, meeting Towerhill, Rovers, Abercorn, Northern and Western Wanderers while Heart of Midlothian, Swifts, Hanover and Thistle expended their energies mainly upon one another. Hibernians found things rather more awkward.

Hibs spent most of the season trying to join in the fun. They applied to join the Edinburgh FA but were told they would have to join the national association first. The *Scottish Football Annual* of a few years later recalled their problems: when Hibs applied to join the SFA, 'that body, thus early displaying a spirit which has all along marked their dealings with the Hibernians, *refused them admission.* 'The Association was formed for Scotchmen' said they in effect, and the Hibernians had to return and knock at the doors of the EFA for admission'. Member clubs were advised not to play them, but fortunately they found more sympathy among the footballers of Edinburgh. A petition was started on Hibs' behalf and signed by all the prominent players in the area, and when this was finally presented to the SFA in the autumn of 1876, Hibs were reluctantly admitted into the SFA.

It seems likely that many Saturdays in late 1875 were spent by Hibernians' players playing against each other, but by the end of the year, they had met Heart of Midlothian at last, losing by the only goal on Christmas Day when 'the Mid-Lothian played three men short for the first 20 minutes. Cavanagh and Byrne played well for the Hibernian, J. Wylie and Laidlaw for the Mid-Lothian'.

Hearts were one of three Edinburgh clubs in the 1875–76 Scottish Cup. They drew twice with 3rd ERV in the first round so that both teams went through under the rules of the time. Ramsey or Herrara would have thrilled to such a rule. 3rd ERV went on to beat Thistle and lose to Rovers while Hearts lost to Drumpelier in the second round.

January 1876 saw 'the first meeting of the 2nd XIs of Thistle and Hibernians, at the East Meadows, and resulting in a win for the latter by a goal, the ball being carried through in a maul on the goal-line'. None of the city clubs yet had a ground of its own, and most of the games took place at the Meadows. Pitches varied from 100 to 200 yards long, 50 to 100 yards wide, and with goals topped by a tape rather than a crossbar. Crowd encroachment was a problem as it could often influence the outcome of a game, as could the tactic of pushing the upper parts of the posts towards each other, thus lowering the tape. January 1876 also saw a curious game at Sheffield. The goals were 'forward of four miles apart', and the kick-off took place halfway between them. Not surprisingly no goals were scored and 'when time was called, the ball was in the vicinity of Wadelay'.

On February 5th came Queens Park's first defeat, by 2–1 to the Wanderers at Kennington Oval and nearly nine years after the club was formed. It also saw the meeting of Hibernians and Thistle 'for the first time, at the East Meadows. The Hibernian succeeded in getting several tries but the match eventually ended in a draw. The match was played under Association rules'. It is not clear whether 'tries' is used in the rugby sense or just means 'attempts', but the last sentence says a lot about the public awareness at the time. Later in the month, Wick beat Thurso in a rugby

An old print of Hibs — winners of the Edinburgh Cup 1894. Second Division Champions in season 1893-94. Holders of the Rosebery Charity Cup 1894-95.

match that lasted 4½ hours, Glasgow beat Sheffield (at association football) before 6,000 spectators, 'a huge number', and Hearts took part in the first ever match at Dunfermline.

The next mention of the Hibernians in *The Scotsman* is March 4th, when their 2nd XI drew with their Hanover counterparts. In the same month, Queens Park completed their first hat-trick of Scottish Cup wins, this time against 3rd Lanark Rifle Volunteers, later known as Third Lanark.

Season 1876–77 effectively started in the last week in September, with the Scottish Cup draw and a preview of the season in *The Scotsman*. The Edinburgh area had seven entrants in the national competition, including Hearts, who scratched at once owing to 'deficiency of membership', Dunfermline, Fife's first entrant, but still no Hibernians, who were not yet SFA members. 'The Hibernia,' said the preview, 'a club in connection with the Young Men's Catholic Association, has also joined the East of Scotland Association, and promises to be an acquisition for the district. They have entered with all the other clubs mentioned for the East of Scotland Challenge Cup', i.e. the Edinburgh Cup, and mention was made of the petition to the SFA.

The early rounds of the Scottish Cup were regional, as they continued to be until the introduction of the Qualifying Cup. The Edinburgh District has seldom extended so far — it included Dundee St. Clements, Bonnybridge Grasshoppers and Lenzie. St Clements did well to reach Round 3 but Swifts went one better, losing to Lennox in the round of the last twelve.

Meanwhile Hibs opened the season by beating Hanover 1–0 at the Meadows, arousing less interest than Thistle and Swifts at the same venue. Two days later, the Edinburgh FA held its first meeting of the season in Buchanan's Hotel. Dunfermline were admitted, Heart of Midlothian were reported to have 'broken up', and the Edinburgh Cup draw took place without them. Hibs' first cup-tie was to be against Thistle, and, like the other ties, it was played on October 14th.

Thistle and Hibs put on 'one of the best and stiffest matches of the day, and play in the East Meadows was witnessed by several hundred onlookers, the majority of whom persisted in going within the touch and goal lines, so splendid runs were repeatedly spoiled, and led to the last goal being disputed by the Hibernians who maintained that the ball had passed the goal and bounded off the spectators'. With the wind in the first half, Hibs had achieved only a goal disallowed for offside, and thereafter, although 'the back play of Donelly and the Hibernian captain neutralised many fine runs', the Thistle forwards 'shot through' following a corner. 'Kelly was next to be conspicuous with an excellent run before the Thistle backs came to the rescue, but later he shot one through for the Hibernians and was carried shoulder high'. Both sides redoubled their efforts, but the only goal directly followed the disputed incident and fell to Cochrane with 'a good shot'. The Hibs team was McGraw; Whelehan and Donelly; Quinn and Watson; Byrne, Hughes, Kelly, Rourke, Cremar and Mehan. Michael Whelehan, Hibs' first captain, turned out as goalkeeper, back and centre-forward on occasion. It does not seem as though the skipper lacked a voice in team selection meetings.

On October 28th, Hibs played out a goalless draw with St. Andrews, yet another new team from Edinburgh, not Fife, and a week later met Swifts. This was the first time that Hibs had been included in *The Scotsman's* Saturday list of fixtures — it usually mentioned only association games involving the major Glasgow teams and Edinburgh rugby games, all mixed in together and it turned out to be 'the best and most enjoyable match these clubs have yet had', a clear indication that it was not the first such meeting; Swifts won 2–0. The only first-half incident was 'a good shot by Sutherland that struck the tape and bounded over', but in the second, 'Swifts' forwards worked better together and repeatedly assailed Hibernians' goal. After nice passing, Walker shot through and 10 minutes later a splendid shot by Hogg secured the second goal'. Hibs 2nds beat Swifts 2nds 4–0, while in London Queens Park defeated Wanderers 6–0.

November 18th was the last big match day of 1876 — bad weather saw to that. Hanover beat Hibs 1–0 and the Edinburgh Cup semi-finals took place. Swifts led 3rd ERV 1–0 but the game was abandoned because of darkness, while the other tie was drawn.

On January 13th, 3rd ERV defeated Swifts 5–0 in their replay, and St. Andrews, who had by this time taken the name of the defunct Heart of Midlothian club to become the present Hearts, beat Hanover 2–1. Vale of Leven beat Ayr Thistle in the only Scottish Cup semi-final; brilliant organisation had left three clubs in the competition and Rangers received a bye into the final. Two weeks later 3rd ERV defeated Hearts by 'seven goals (two disputed) to none' and an indignant Hearts' secretary wrote in to explain that the score had been 5–1. On February 3rd, Swifts defeated Hibernians 1–0 at the Meadows; and on the 10th, Hibs 2nds beat Hanover 2nds 3–0.

On February 24th, Hibs defeated Hearts 1–0 at the Meadows, almost certainly their first victory over their great rivals. The East of Scotland Cup final was arranged for the same day, but 3rd ERV did not turn up and Thistle became holders. Two weeks later Hanover defeated 'the Hibernia' by two goals to none, and although the Scottish Cup final had still to be played, the season was 'virtually ended' and *The Scotsman* decided that a review of it was in order. Despite defeat by Vale of Leven in the Scottish Cup, Queens Park had maintained its premier position, while in Edinburgh, 'dribbling and passing had taken the place of rough play', though 'the want of a proper ground was a hindrance as the Meadows was continually encroached on whenever there is a good match on'.

Mention was also made of the performance of the main local clubs, 3rd ERV, Thistle, Hanover, Swifts, Dunfermline and Hibernians, who 'had also been busy, their back play being the most noticeable feature of their play'. No mention was included of St. Andrews or Heart of Midlothian.

Hibs played at least two more games before the summer break. On April 7th they played Thistle again at the Meadows, and this time Hibs reversed their cup-tie defeat by the new cup-holders. Thistle scored in 'barely ten minutes which the wearers of the green equalised five minutes before half-time. Immediately upon changing ends, Quinn, by a good run and sure shot' obtained the deciding goal. By now Hibs' team was Brinn; Byrne and McGlynn; Wheleghan, Cavanagh; Rourke, Flynn, Quinn, Cremar, Donelly and McWhin. Michael Whelehan is said to have been somewhat annoyed by various mis-spellings of his name.

A fortnight later, Hibs defeated Hearts again by 1–0 at the same venue, while in between Vale of Leven had retained possession of the Scottish Cup by beating Rangers with a goal five minutes from the end of the second replay, the first replay having been terminated during extra time because of a squabble over a disputed goal.

Numerate readers will have calculated that of the ten Hibs matches reported above, four were won, five lost and one drawn. The *Scottish Football Annual* gave their record as played 12, won 6, lost 5, drawn 1. The records of Thistle, Swifts, Hanover and 3rd ERV are also given, and with that of Hibs give a net balance of about twenty wins. It therefore seems likely that this total was achieved against lesser clubs in the area, and that would excuse the lack of reports about them; one or both of Hibs' other two victories are probably accounted for in this way.

An Impressive Start

By the start of season 1877–78, the first step to move away from the Meadows had been taken by 3rd ERV, who had secured Powburn, 'one of the best grounds in the district' as befitted the city's top team. The others still shared the Meadows, though Hibs now had a club house at St. Mary's schoolroom in Lothian Street. Their colours were registered as green and white jerseys, white knickers, green cap and hose. The club had 'a strong membership, and splendid back play. The team is very heavy, they pass well, dribble fairly and are splendid kicks'. Swifts wore blue jerseys with a white Maltese cross, Hanover's strips were light blue and white, Thistle's dark blue with a single white band, and 3rd ERV used blue and white. Hearts, in red, white and blue, were to change to maroon a year later, and their share of the *Scotsman's* preview was 'The want of dribbling tells against Heart of Midlothian, most of whom kick too heavily'.

With an apparent advantage in kicking and dribbling ability as well as superior weight, it was presumably no surprise when Hibs won their opening tie in their Scottish Cup campaign by defeating Hearts 2–1, albeit after a goalless draw. They had already beaten Hanover by the only goal, and followed up this successful start by defeating Thistle by the same score. Hibs and Hanover next drew 1–1 in the second round of the Cup, but the event was overshadowed by the selection of an Edinburgh team to play Queens Park the following week, October 27th, in the Capital's most important match yet. Hibs were represented by M. Byrne, 'a very good back, both to tackle and kick', and Francis Rourke, 'a very good forward, unselfish and backs up the left wing well'. The venue was Powburn, and a large crowd of 2,000 attended. Edinburgh made a splendid fight, were highly satisfied in holding the premier club to the only goal scored just on time, and entertained their visitors thereafter in Young's Iona Hotel. Hanover were also represented by two men in the big game but seemed to miss them more, because Hibs won the cup-tie replay 3–0 on the same afternoon.

The third-round draw was also regional and paired Hibs with Swifts; again the Irishmen were successful, this time by 2–0. Meanwhile in Glasgow, Queens Park went out by the only goal to 3rd LRV, only the second Scottish club to beat them.

The Edinburgh Cup came next, and Hibs had yet another win over Hanover, this time by 3–1 at Powburn, and after that their first trip west to oppose Arthurlie at Barrhead. 'The first half play was rather in favour of the strangers, but on sides being exchanged, the Arthurlie showed superior play and scored two goals within the last ten minutes of play'. The 3rd ERV-Hearts game was abandoned owing to 'a dispute', and a surprising addition to the football columns was the Midlothian Bicycle Club.

Back to the Scottish Cup, and Hibs had now reached the 'all-in' stage, where they were paired with Thornliebank, the Renfrewshire village team who had reached this stage at the expense of Arthurlie, and two years later were to put their name firmly into the record books by reaching the final. The tie was played on 1st December at Pollokshaws, 'and resulted in a win for the Hibernians by two goals to one'. Further down the same column in *The Scotsman* there was a further report, this one crediting Hibs with a win by 'two goals to none'; which was correct proved immaterial when during the following week the SFA committee decided that the match had been a draw and should be replayed the following Saturday. Arrangements were hurriedly put in hand and the teams met again at Newington. This game was drawn too, the teams on this occasion scoring the same number of goals, and so both progressed to the next round. Hearts had a less profitable afternoon, losing 9–2 to Petershill.

The 15th of December brought 3rd LRV to Powburn to play Edinburgh, and Owen Quinn — 'plenty of weight and uses it to advantage' — joined colleagues Byrne and Rourke in the capital line-up. The result, a 3–0 defeat, was a big disappointment but no doubt spirits were revived in Young's Iona Hotel.

To reach the fifth round of the national competition at the first attempt was a considerable achievement, but Hibs' run ended there, with a trip to Copeland Park, Govan and a 3–0 defeat from South-Western.

Edinburgh was first-footed by Glasgow Rangers — there was also a club in Edinburgh called Rangers — who sent a scratch XI to play Brunswick, another recently formed Edinburgh club, at Powburn. The crowd was only 200, but they seem to have got value for money; Brunswick scored the only goal of the first 'half' which lasted an hour and a half, but the visitors replied with two goals in a further forty-five minutes.

If the first half of the season had been dominated by the Scottish Cup, then the remainder was no less so by the Edinburgh one. Having disposed of Hanover, Hibs next faced Thistle on January 12th in the semi-final. 'With the hill and a slight breeze against the Irishmen in the first half, they succeeded in scoring one goal, Donelly giving the ball the final touch. In the second half the Thistle were besieged during the entire game, and although trying to play the 'passing game', their exertions were fruitless, the ground and wind being against their doing so', and Hibs scored three times more, to win 4-0. Snow interfered with football during the rest of the month, but on February 9th Hibs met Hearts at Mayfield in what was the first final for both.

'A good number' witnessed the affair. In the first half, Hibs came closer, with a number of corners, and a goal resulted from one of them; however, 'a foul was proclaimed' and so it did not count. The second half 'was a repetition of what had already taken place with the exception that from the borders of the Heart's ground splendid kicks carried the ball over the tape twice' and a further goal for Hibs was disallowed. 'The Hearts forwards', was the conclusion, 'did not seem to be altogether in trim, but the Hibernians played exceedingly well.' The Hibs team was Brown; Byrne and Whelan; Whelehan and Cavanagh; Donelly, Donaghue, Quinn, Cremar, Flynn and Rourke. The same eleven turned out a week later at Mayfield for the replay.

So did upwards of a thousand spectators, despite the weather. The snow had gone, but instead there was rain and a stiff wind which 'completely upset the calculations of the Association players'. Against the elements, 'Hibernians played a capital defensive game' and play was so even that neither team scored, for half an hour. But at that stage there was 'a foul to the Heart, and out of the scrimmage that followed, the ball was headed through amid great cheering'. The second half was an exciting affair, with Donelly's runs prominent for Hibs, while Mitchell and Alexander 'took the ball to the mouth of the Hibernians goal before being collared'. Then with five minutes to go and Hearts 'seeming all but certain of victory', Donelly 'ran the ball prettily down the side; he centred it beautifully in front of the goal when Rourke shot it through amid a scene of the wildest enthusiasm, the Irishmen tossing their hats and jumping and cheering for several minutes'.

The Committee of the Association had 'somewhat unwisely' left the possibility of an extra half-hour to the two captains, and despite the lateness of the hour, the protest to be lodged about the equalising goal and the fact that Hibs had finished the stronger, Tom Purdie, Hearts' captain, was a brave man to refuse to play beyond the normal time 'notwithstanding the demonstrative appeals with which he was met by the followers of the green'. So the next week it was back to Mayfield.

The third game 'attracted upwards of 1200 people, but the wise action of the Committee of Management in raising the price of admission made the number within the field select for the greater part of the time, and thus the match was more enjoyable than on the former occasion' — but no more decisive. In the first half, Rourke scored with a smart shot following a corner. Rourke and Donelly were prominent as Hibs pressed, and in the middle of a scrimmage 'Donelly kicked the ball right through the posts, but in its passage it was fouled by one of the defenders. The foul was claimed by one of the Hibernians, and consequently the decision of the umpires was in favour of the Heart'. It was all very confusing.

In the second half, Burns equalised with 'a magnificent header' and this was followed by a break-in of nearly a thousand further spectators from outside the ground. After some debate it was decided to continue, but the late arrivals saw little of note, and the issue remained to be settled.

In the break before hostilities were resumed, Hibs met Swifts at the Meadows, where the 500 or so spectators 'kept the unfenced ground in better order than usual' and Hibs won an enjoyable match by 3–0.

The next instalment of cup action took place at Bainfield, Merchiston, by the kind permission of Mr. J.C. Hay. The 1500 crowd included many Rugbians, whose season had ended. Although the previous games had been rough, this one 'excelled in that respect — heavy and unnecessary charging, rash back kicking and an almost total want of dribbling and passing completely spoiling the beauties of the Association game'. Hibs kicked off against the hill and sun at 4 o'clock, and despite at least half a dozen corners in their favour 'Ross neatly headed Hearts into the lead at 4.30', so Hibs had one goal to retrieve in the second half. Confident with the wind and superior weight, Hibs pressed on, but at least four more corners were fruitless before Donelly headed through after a free kick 'amid a scene of the wildest enthusiasm, the Irishmen tossing their hats and caps into the air with delight' — again. An extra half-hour also failed to resolve the tie.

With the coffers of the East of Scotland FA fuller than the Hon. Treasurer could possibly have hoped for, the proceeds from the fifth meeting, at Powburn on 18th April, were generously donated to the Royal Infirmary; unfortunately bad weather limited them to £13 net. Hibs had lost Brannan, but were still favourites, though hardly overwhelmingly so, but 'the calculations of the knowing were upset and the Heart won after a grand fight by three goals to two'.

Hibs failed to use their initial advantage of the hill, and there were no first-half goals. But soon after the break Reid threw the ball out, and Whelehan intercepted and shot the first goal. Alexander levelled matters, Quinn scored as a result of another error by Reid, Mitchell equalised this time, and after a goalmouth scrimmage Alexander scored a goal that was disputed but allowed. Hibs put in a storming finish, but this time there was to be no draw, and the saga ended on a sour note when Tom Purdie 'was most discracefully set upon by a lot of roughs after passing Powborn Toll and had to take refuge in a house in Causewayside'. The reporter was relieved to report that none of the Hibernians players was involved in 'this cowardly outrage'.

CHAPTER 2

The Best in Town, 1878–82

The 1878 Edinburgh Cup Final was just what football in the capital needed; as the acts were played out, interest increased and the event was even noticed from Glasgow. It was true that the praise was not in all cases overwhelming, but at least the *Scottish Football Annual* was there to see Hearts take the trophy. 'Play was decidedly poor, not to say almost savage in the roughness of the often unnecessary charging, while it was obvious to the merest tyro that the teams overlooked almost entirely the beauties of the Association game.' However, as the same expert ascribed Edinburgh's greatest hopes to the game being taken up at Fettes, we can probably disregard his views.

The following season then saw a great expansion in Edinburgh football. There were bigger crowds and more teams, with Bellevue, Edina, Waverley and Aberlady (but not Fettes) joining the Edinburgh FA. The pressure on the Meadows and other public pitches was eased by some of the bigger clubs obtaining their own facilities. The 3rd ERV were the first to do this, at Powburn, but they had left the Association after a dispute, and by the start of the season Brunswick were established at Raeburn Place, Thistle at Grange Loan, and the University at Corstorphine, to which the North British Railway Company ran football specials for big games. Hibs had moved into the Powderhall Grounds, Bonnington Road '15 minutes from Waverley Station', and still had their club house in St. Mary's Street. Hearts were still at the Meadows but had a club house in Anderson's Coffee Rooms, 1 St. Patrick's Street and were now in maroon jerseys with a scarlet heart on them.

Despite all these moves, when Hibs entertained Airdrie (not the present club) in early September, the venue was Powburn, and the game provided a 'striking contrast' to the Hearts v. Stonelaw match which followed it, ' and not at all favourable'. 'Rough play and heavy charging was freely indulged in, and the game does not call for default.' With several reserves Hibs won 'by seven goals and a disputed one to nothing'. A further early friendly took Hibs to Copeland Park (five minutes from Ibrox Station) where the 'back play of South-Western being their strongest point', the black and orange stripes won by 3–0.

A week later, Hibs made their first appearance at Powderhall, against Dunfermline in the Scottish Cup. This was not the present-day Athletic who were not formed until 1885. Hibs won 5–2 and 'the victory, it appeared, might have been even more decisive but for the watchfulness of the

This picture of Hibs was taken around 1879. It is regretted that the names of the players are not available.

Dunfermline custodian'. The second round took Hibs to Powburn to meet 3rd ERV and 'the result was a complete surprise. Hibernians scored three goals in the first half-hour, and the match was stopped owing to two of the Volunteers having to retire through illness'. The goals were scored by Heron, Quinn and Donelly, and thereafter 'a mixed friendly was played until the call of time'.

In between a rare midweek game took place in the capital when Our Boys, from Dundee and later to amalgamate with East End to form Dundee FC, 'taking advantage of the Dundee Fast' lost 5–1 to Hearts. The next important visitors to the capital were 3rd LRV, on October 26th, and they defeated the Edinburgh FA team 6–1 which was not surprising as the home side included no players from Hibs, Hearts, University or 3rd ERV, although these clubs do not seem to have been very heavily committed. Hearts beat John Elder, a Glasgow shipyard team, 5–0; Hibs 2nds beat Swifts 2nds 10–2 and were in action a week later too, beating Thistle 2nds 4–0.

Bright Stuff at Powderhall

Two days later, the curious were attracted to Powderhall to witness 'Hibernians v. an Association team (by electric light)'. 'Electric light was given by three Siemens' dynamo-electric machines, under the management of Mr. E. Paterson of London. A few hundred people assembled, more to witness the light than the match. A light equal to 6,000 standard candles was placed at the west end of the ground, and two equal to 1,200 at the east end. The engine attached to one of the latter was unequal to the occasion, but play was conducted with good advantage for about an hour under the fitful beams of the other two. A strap connecting the larger machine and its engine then broke and the rest of the game was played under difficulty. So far as the game went, Hibernians won by three goals to nothing.' A similar experiment had taken place at Cathkin (3rd LRV) a week or two earlier, but another the next night at Powderhall was called off 'for some unexplained reason'.

Back in daylight, Hibs had cruised into the third round of the Edinburgh Cup, having beaten Bellevue 13-0 and Waverley 7-0, and the next opponents were University in the Scottish — the students received byes to this stage because their term had not started. The supporters crowded out to Corstorphine courtesy of the North British Railway Co. and saw Hibs kick off against a stiff wind, but nevertheless establish a territorial ascendancy, when 'Grant raised the siege on the University goal, dribbled prettily up the field and finished with a long shot that went under the bar amid great cheering'. Whelehan, in goal on this occasion, saved another attempt with 'a timely kick', but then Grant, at the end of another run, 'centred prettily and Tulloch with a splendid shot earned the second goal'. 'Hibernians were now put on their metal' and Rourke scored one before half-time, and the Irish supporters do not seem to have been too worried. 'The friends of the green were sanguine that with the wind they would score rapidly' and so it turned out. Flynn equalised in a scrimmage, Rourke scored in a similar situation, and 'the scene that followed baffles description, cheer upon cheer greeting the success, and caps tossed in the air by the followers of the green and white stripes'. Flynn and Rourke each got another and Hibs won 5-2.

The fourth round paired Hibs with Rob Roy — from Callander, not Kirkintilloch — and Hearts with Helensburgh. The latter tie came off first, at Helensburgh, and was drawn, but the SFA Committee decided that the replay should also take place at Helensburgh. Hearts protested that this was unfair, whereupon the Committee decided that they had scratched! On December 7th, Hibs beat Rob Roy by nine goals and one disputed to none, and were drawn against Helensburgh in the next round.

Frost and snow caused a lot of trouble in December, but on the Saturday before Christmas 'with probably more valour than discretion, these clubs agreed to meet to play off their tie. The Helensburgh men arrived in the forenoon and by half past two several hundred spectators had assembled in the ground of Hibernians at Powderhall, but after stripping and entering the playing ground, the Helensburgh men refused to play, the reason being the condition of the ground. A friendly was proposed, but the adherents of the green stripes would not hear of it, so sides between the Hibernians were formed and play engaged'. Then in the New Year came 'a decision which coming on the back of the Heart of Midlothian-Helensburgh one will probably cause some surprise among the Association players in the east'. This was that, as no match had actually taken place, the tie was yet to be decided. By an oversight, it was to be played in Edinburgh.

Because of the severe weather the Helensburgh game did not take place for some weeks, and not much local football escaped either, but Hibs did play Brunswick on consecutive Saturdays in February as well as win the 2nd XI Cup by defeating Hanover 2–0 at Powburn. Brunswick were expected to provide stiff opposition, but Hibs beat them 6–0 in the President's Trophy — a one-off tournament arranged because so many new teams had joined the Edinburgh FA too late to play in the Edinburgh Cup. It was therefore less of an upset when the score seven days later in the East of Scotland semi-final was 6–1.

That brought them up against Hearts again in the final at Powburn, with a crowd of 4,000. After a 'capital match', the result was another draw.

Hibs failed to take advantage of the wind in the first half, so in the second, 'the followers of the maroon were confident they would soon score, but the wearers of the green dashed these hopes, as Donelly came right away from his oppenents and shot for goal, the ball going through amid a scene of the wildest excitement. It is but fair to Reid to state that the disgraceful way in which spectators pressed within his goal line completely prevented his stopping the ball'. Hearts were still making determined efforts amid cries of time when 'the ball bounded off Alexander, Burns and Nelson giving it the final touch through'. The crowd now broke in and carried the fortunate Alexander shoulder high, but the less lucky captain, Purdie, was lamed by a kick as he left the field. Police arrested one of his assailants, O'Reilly by name, but which team he supported was not disclosed!

A week later, Helensburgh made their long-awaited re-appearance, and again there was controversy. It seems that Hibs did the early attacking, but 'the besieged not only drove the enemy back but by a succession of beautiful passes stormed their goal, when one of the visitors directed the ball between the posts — but it seemed that something disallowable had taken place, for the west was not credited with a goal'. Donelly put Hibs in front; McLeod equalised before half-time.

On resuming, 'when Hibernians were about to storm the opposite goal, the keeper of it ran far out to check the course of the ball and before he could get properly set again, one of the 'Hibs' sent the ball between the posts. A dispute arose as to the legality of the goal and the matter was compromised with a corner' which seemed scant reward, especially as Boyle soon scored a second goal for the visitors.

Champions of Edinburgh

A snowstorm and a 3–0 win over University took up the next two Saturdays, after which the North British Railway Co. shareholders benefited again from the replay against Hearts, at Corstorphine, and 'after one of the best passing games yet shown by Hibernians, the cup has at last fallen to them by two goals to none, which their play all round in this match thoroughly deserved'. First, Purdie missed his kick, 'a grand shot of Whelehan's sending the ball through' — the versatile captain was at centre this day — then 'after the Irish fort had been saved several times by brilliant back play ... Rourke and Lee took the ball from one of their opponents who had fallen on it and shot it through amid great cheering'. Further success was not forthcoming but the winning line-up was Brown; Byrne, J. McKernan; Waugh, J. McKernan; Quinn, Donelly, Whelehan, Flynn, Rourke, Lee. Michael Whelehan accepted the cup at the Association's AGM and noted 'with gratification that it had been played for with less party spirit and feeling than in former years'.

The *Scottish Football Annual* was still less than impressed: 'the second half of the game may be quickly disposed of as neither side did anything effective with the exception of heavy charging, in which they indulged all round'.

There was still the President's Trophy, and Hibs met Thistle, having a good run including a win over Hearts, and 'one of the best Association matches seen in the district this season' ended 0—0. The replay was quite different. This one was 'noticeable for rough play and unnecessary charging and the way in which the umpire's decisions were ignored'. Lee scored in three minutes, Thistle soon made it level, and two goals by Donelly made it 3-1.

The semi-final was with Hearts at Powderhall. 'The contest was pretty fast and well spiced with collisions which generally resulted in a 'spill', frequently a double one, with rather grotesque-like evolutions, which pleased the onlookers immensely'. The game itself was still anybody's into the second half when 'the 'Hearts' forged their way near the line on the left, and the ball being nicely passed towards the goal, a short but active struggle in front of it ended with the reduction of Hibernians' fort'. That was the only score and Hearts went on to beat Hanover in the final by 5–4 after an extra half-hour.

The final act for the season was an away game with Kilmarnock Athletic, in aid of the local Fever Hospital. *The Scotsman* credits Hibs with a 4–3 win, but the report throws some doubt on which side actually got the four.

Hibs Move to Mayfield

When cricket again reluctantly gave way to football, by now at the start of September, there were yet more clubs ready for the fray, and twenty-two entrants for the Edinburgh Cup. The most significant new name was that of St. Bernards, while the inclusion of Bathgate and West Calder indicated that the word had been heard in wildest West Lothian. A major cause of concern was the imminent spoiling of the East Meadows, and the authorities were looked to to take steps to prevent their over-use.

Hibs had left Powderhall and acquired a pitch at Mayfield 'two minutes' walk from Mayfield car terminus'. It seems likely that this ground was the same as had previously been known as Powburn, since it was about this time that the old village and its toll were demolished as the city expanded along what became Mayfield Road. It was more convenient for the spectators than players, because the changing rooms were in the Catholic Institute in St. Mary's Street. The new ground was to be opened on September 6th by 'the popular Glasgow Rangers who will doubtless get a good reception', and more games with western teams had been arranged than hitherto. But 'it is to be hoped that the unnecessary charging for which the club has become noted will be conspicuous by its absence'. The club colours were now plain green jerseys in place of the horizontal stripes, Michael Whelehan and Pat Cavanagh were captain and vice-captain respectively, and the club had 121 members. Hearts, who had followed Hibs into Powderhall, had 120.

The popular Glasgow Rangers were unfortunately unable to raise a team on September 6th. It is not known what they thought of the changing facilities or the heavy charging, but apparently their players were involved in the Queens Park sports. The honour of opening Mayfield thus fell a week later to Kilmarnock Athletic, but it was a bit of an anticlimax. Early on 'A. Watson of the home team was disabled and had to retire which was very detrimental to Hibernians and they scored only one goal to their opponents' six'. Meanwhile Hearts had been ambitious enough to tackle Vale of Leven and only lost 2–1, which was a tremendous result as shown during the *après football* in the Cafe Royal when Vale admitted to having 'anticipated a victory of six goals at least'.

Hibs started another good cup run against Hanover at Mayfield. Donelly (2) and Lee put them three goals to the good before McDonald scored to give

Hanover some hope when they had the wind in the second half. However, the wind kindly dropped and Donnelly and Cox added two more for Hibs, whose next tie was with Dunfermline. The Fife men started on the offensive but before long were 'completely outmatched' and did well to keep the score to 4–0. Without any Hibs players, Edinburgh tackled Ayrshire at Kilmarnock and lost 7–2.

After a friendly with Hanover (won 6–1) Hibs were drawn to meet Hearts in the Scottish Cup third round, at Powderhall on November 1st. Hearts had reached that stage by beating Brunswick in a game that started late and finished in darkness owing to 'the failure of the Heart to have a ball'. For the tie with Hibs, their arrangements were even less successful. 'At 12 o'clock the Heart, to a number of forty, took possession of the ground and the various money boxes but at 2 o'clock the manager with a posse of policemen ejected those present.' There had been some problem about the lease.

So the tie was rearranged for Mayfield one week later. Hearts arrived at one o'clock, kicked the ball through the goal and claimed the tie. Shortly after three o'clock, Hibs did likewise and also claimed the tie. That it was a dispute rather than a misunderstanding was evident when immediately after Hibs had enacted their part of the juvenile charade, St. Bernards emerged from the wings to play Hibs in the Edinburgh Cup, the Irishmen winning a good game by 3–1.

The SFA ordered the teams to meet at Mayfield on November 15th. Hibs' crowd arrangements left something to be desired and the referee turned up twenty minutes late, but despite all the previous bickering, the game itself was conspicuously free from the extravagant charging. After fifteen minutes a combined rush brought Hibs within shooting range and Byrne scored the opening goal. Hearts retaliated but, displaying 'capital defence', Hibs held out till the interval. In the second half Cavanagh scored in a melee, then with the light failing fast and five minutes to go, 'a ringing cheer let the majority know that Hearts had scored their first goal'. Then with the ball in the possession of the Hearts goalkeeper Reid, in some danger however of being forced bodily through his goal, spectators broke in and 'prevented either side getting fair play'. A dispute arose, no goal was the decision and it was some time before the remaining minutes could be played out in pitch darkness.

With the delays, the fourth round was now due, and Hibs drew 2–2 at Mayfield with Park Grove, an unlikely name for a team from Govan, and as the replay a week later at Trinidad Park also finished level, both sides progressed to the fifth round which for Hibs meant a visit to Mauchline in Ayrshire. Again they were successful, by two second-half goals from Owen Quinn, after an even opening period. In the end only first-rate goalkeeping kept the margin to two. Snow restricted play in December, but Hibs did beat

Brunswick in the Edinburgh Cup, though only 4–3 after being three down with twenty minutes to go.

Hibs' Cup run ended at Dumbarton on January 3rd, despite a fine start. They opened the scoring in five minutes, then 'Rourke managed to get the ball in the centre and with his usual good judgement brought it carefully up and shooting was again successful'. Dumbarton then settled down and scored four times before the interval; second-half play was 'a little loose' but the home team finally won by 'five goals and one disputed to two'. It might have been more: 'Browne in Hibernians goal deserves special mention. Having caught the ball in his arms at one time and before he contrived to get rid of it several of the opposing team rushed upon him and attempted to push him through the posts. Seeing there was no chance of escape, he hurled himself to the ground, keeping good hold of the 'leather' and was almost immediately pounced upon by both sides. Pushing out and pushing in lasted more than five minutes, during which poor Browne and the ball were entirely invisible, but Donelly came to the rescue, scattering the enemy and setting the plucky goalkeeper at full liberty'. We are not told exactly how Donelly achieved this.

The weather in January was no improvement, but at the end of the month Hibs met Hearts at Powderhall in the Edinburgh semi-final. This game was free of incident. Hearts were superior in the first half and led 2–0, but the roles were reversed in the second and goals from Byrne, Quinn, Cox, Cavanagh and Rourke gave Hibs a 5–2 win.

Thornliebank proved attractive visitors in what was Hibs' last game at Mayfield. The visitors scored against the wind in the first minute, and twice more in a hard and plucky second-half display to win 3–0. A week later Hibs opened their new ground at Hibernian Park, Easter Road. This ground was not on the site of the present Easter Road stadium but on what is now Bothwell Street, between the bend in that street and the footbridge to Albion Place. Hanover were the first visitors — Hibs won 5–0 — and a fortnight later met Rangers at the same venue. This time Rangers were able to raise a team and a good one at that because they won 4–1.

Dunfermline had reached the East of Scotland final and met Hibs at Powderhall on March 6th. Against the strong wind, Hibs made good use of fewer chances and were level 3–3 at half-time. With the wind they got three more and won easily 6–3, but a protest about crowd encroachment was upheld, so they had it all to do again two weeks later. This time 'nearly the whole of the game was played in the Dunfermline territory' and Hibs won 5–0.

A large crowd assembled on April 3rd to see Vale of Leven, and Hibs did well to gain a draw with their illustrious visitors. The next two weeks were set

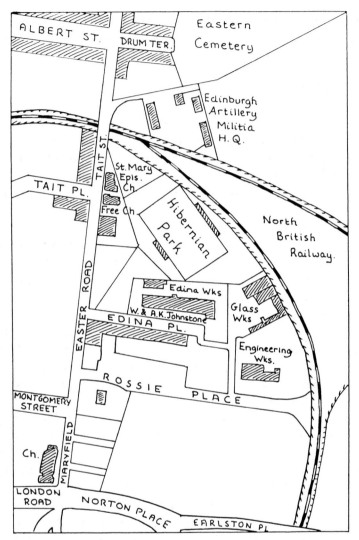

Map showing the position of the first Easter Road Park, drawn from a map published in 1888 by near neighbours W. & A. K. Johnstone.

aside for district games ; Edinburgh lost 16–0 to Queens Park — happily for those involved the team was not reported — then beat a Sheffield XI 3–1, so the sensible solution that the district side should not play club sides was proposed.

The season ended with a number of friendlies. Hibs lost 3–0 to the touring Scottish Canadian team, one of the strongest sides seen in the Capital with many internationalists, and 5–2 to the Pilgrims from Glasgow, who had some help from Rangers players, but they finished on a winning note away to Kilmarnock Athletic, Cox being responsible for the game's only goal.

A Cup to Keep

For 1880–81, Pat Cavanagh had replaced Whelehan as captain, and Donelly's departure meant promotion for the promising young centre McFadyen. Otherwise it was as before. Hibs were poised for the first hat-trick in, and thereby perpetual possession of, the Edinburgh Cup, while Hearts in particular were intent on preventing that from happening. Their first move in securing this aim was a motion to the Edinburgh FA 'that the Edinburgh FA request Hibernian Football Club to withdraw from the said Association in consequence of the unfair and brutal play exhibited by them on the field and the rough usage that the players are subjected to after the game'. The motion was thrown out — but only after a vote of 10 for, 10 against and 5 abstentions.

Small wonder then that Hibs looked further afield for their opening games. John Elder of Govan were beaten 6–2, then on their first visit to Hampden to play Queens Park 'Hibernians played a very good defensive game' and restricted their opponents to a single goal kicked by A. Smith. September was rounded off with a visit from Blackburn Rovers, and attracted 1500 spectators.

In the first half the English 'throw-in' was used — similar to the present one. In the second, the Scottish rule was followed, which meant that the first player to reach the ball threw it in at right angles to the line. This rule exaggerated the advantage of a partisan crowd but lessened time wasting, and was soon abolished. In the game itself, Hargreaves scored for Rovers fifteen minutes in, then 'Hibernians knit themselves well' and McFadyen scored twice. 'Rovers fought back magnificently but Hibernians' backs baffled them' until McIntyre shot under the goalkeeper's legs to equalise. In the second half, Rourke and Cox (2) gave Hibs an impressive victory.

After a bye, Hibs met Dunfermline in the Scottish Cup for the third year in a row and there was much excitement before Hibs won 3–1. In the first round 'the Heart being the luckiest won by three goals to one' against Brunswick; their good fortune continued with a bye and they drew Hibs at Powderhall in the third round.

The 5000 crowd was rewarded with 'a really good exhibition of association football with the almost entire absence of rough play'. Hibs were favourites, especially as the ground was heavy, but 'the result was a surprise and illustrated the uncertainty of football'. Hearts scored in twenty minutes, and though Hibs responded, a foul against them 'for a hand' led to Hearts scoring again and Lee made it three in a scrimmage. On the change of ends there was 'hard fighting' in Hearts' goalmouth, Rourke scored twice in a minute, and Hearts 'strove to maintain their advantage'. But while they were disputing the straightness of a throw-in, Hibs stole upfield and equalised, and an argument ensued. After that little was seen of Hibs, and Hearts scored two more goals for the victory they so badly wanted.

Friendlies in the autumn included Kilmarnock Athletic (2-0 at home), Portland also from Kilmarnock (1-1 at home), Rangers (1-5) in their first visit to Kinning Park, and Vale of Leven (1-3) in Alexandria. Then at the end of November Hibs held Rangers to a draw at Easter Road, Byrne and Rourke scoring for Hibs.

In the Edinburgh Cup, wins of 10-1 over Caledonian and a club record of 15-0 over Burntisland Thistle led to another showdown with Hearts at Powderhall on 4th December. Seven thousand spectators paid, and more broke down a gate when the game started. Hearts again scored first — Edwards smartly netting a rebound — but eventually Hibs asserted themselves. Cox made 'a capital run on the right and Lee with great cleverness kicked through'. Second-half play was even but Rourke scored twice in a minute near the end, and 'the Irishmen were carried off shoulder high by their friends'. But still Hearts were not finished with the Edinburgh Cup. They protested that Hibs had a player who was not a local — the Committee decided against them — and for good measure their President wrote to *The Scotsman* to say it had only been 2-1 anyway.

Safely over a difficult hurdle, Hibs lost 4-2 in a friendly to St. Bernards who were using the new defensive formation of three half-backs and only five forwards before Christmas brought unusual visitors to Easter Road, the Holmes Zulus.

Two thousand people came to see them, but though 'they appeared to kick well, they were deficient in passing' and Hibs won easily by 6-0. Jake Reid of Hearts was in goal for Hibs, while the visiting line-up for the benefit of their supporters was: Umlathoosi; Cetewayo, Dabulamanzi; Sirayo, Methlaguzulu; Umcityu, Ngobamalrosi, Maquenda, Jiggleumberrgo, Muyamani and Amatonga. This team purported to come from Sheffield.

January and February were all but wiped out by frost and snow. Hibs were luckier than most, beating Kilbirnie 5-2 at Easter Road and Cartland 3-1 at Kilmarnock, as well as the University 6-1 at Corstorphine in the snow to reach another Edinburgh Cup final, this time with St. Bernards.

The Scotland-England rugby international at Raeburn Place was postponed a week from March 5th, so the Edinburgh Cup final was put back a week from March 12th. Then the rugby was postponed again because the

These magnificent trophies were presented to the Hibernian Football Club by the Edinburgh Football Association in recognition of their being the outright winners of the first ever Edinburgh Cup and the Second Eleven Cup in three successive years, 1879–1880–1881.

English were unable to get their team together, so both games took place on the 19th. 'The passing of the St. Bernards being very neat', they were four goals up with an hour gone but Hibs made it level. Two weeks later Hibs won the cup outright by 1–0 after an extremely fine game.

Following this success, Hibs made their first tour to England and in particular Lancashire. They lost the opening game 4–2 to Blackburn Rovers then gained their only win against Bolton Wanderers. Hibs were pegged back to 3–3 from being 3–1 up but Flynn snatched the winner in an exciting finish. They finally lost 2–0 to Blackburn Olympic before 400 spectators on a miserable afternoon.

It is tempting to end the story of 1880–81 with that tour, but honesty dictates mention of a further visit by Rangers. The Glasgow team had scored five when Rourke headed Hibs' first goal 'amid the wildest enthusiasm which was dampened immediately when a long shot struck the post and earned Rangers' sixth goal'. Hibs did better in the second half, but lost 9–3, further losses only being prevented by McKernan 'who played a grand defensive and offensive game'. Just as well someone did!

A definite pattern had emerged in the football season. The Scottish Cup ties were played through the autumn and local ties were scheduled to interleave with them, although the latter were inevitably delayed by postponements, draws and disputes in the premier competition. With only these two tournaments, it was important for the bigger clubs to stay in them to keep interest alive.

It was in 1881 that Hibs erected their first grandstand at Easter Road. Dean of Guild approval was obtained in September, and the stand was ready for use at the cup tie on October 8th, just three weeks later. Around the same time, the Edinburgh FA chose a shield, with crests top and bottom, to replace the Edinburgh Cup, and it is now known, of course, as the East of Scotland Shield.

With thirty-six sides competing, there was a strong case for seeding the Shield competition, but that was an idea that had not yet germinated in 1881, and so Hibs met Hearts in the first round in the latter's new ground at Tynecastle, but across Gorgie Road from the present park. Unfortunately the large crowd was treated to 'one of the roughest games ever seen between these clubs', with fouls galore and 'several players got into fighting positions'. Rourke equalised Hearts' early goal and Flynn scored twice in a minute late in the first half. Lee put the game beyond Hearts on resuming, so the result having been determined, there was peace to get on with the feuding.

Hearts made a quick exit in the Scottish Cup too, to St. Bernards who were as a result Hibs' visitors on October 8th, with a crowd of 5,000 and the new grandstand well filled. Saints were getting a reputation for scientific play, and it was a good tie. Rourke scored twice for Hibs and Arthur once for St. Bernards, and so Hibs just got through.

Cox, Byrne, Flynn and Rourke all played for Edinburgh against Ayrshire, then, with byes in both tournaments Hibs undertook some ambitious friendlies, defeating Bolton Wanderers 3–0, Dumbarton 2–1 and Lancashire cupholders Accrington Stanley 6–2, all before large attendances at Easter Road.

With the Scottish Cup now at the all-in stage, Hibs had to travel to the village of West Benhar which was, and reportedly still is, near Shotts. Contrary to expectations, they could only draw 4–4, but managed to get all eight of the scores in the replay a week later.

Immediately the fifth round was due and 4,000 turned out to see

Dumbarton at Easter Road. The ground was soft and slippery but 'the strangers, remarkably swift footed and exceptional at long kicking', led 4–1 at the interval. They won 6–2 overall but 'for the latter portion of the game seemed to play against time, repeatedly kicking out over the ropes and over the hoarding onto the railway'. Also, both teams protested about their rough treatment at the hands of the other. Hibs' appeal fell on sympathetic ears because they were granted a replay, but little good it did them because they lost it by 6–2 as well, although 'a tougher fought match ... has seldom been witnessed'.

But in the east Hibs had no peers. They beat Dunfermline 5–2, Hearts 3–2, Hanover 6–1, University 4–1 and West Calder 7–1 before meeting St. Bernards again in the first Shield final at Tynecastle. Hibs were well on top in the first half and scored four goals to none, and seemed to have taken something from their tussles with Dumbarton because in the second, while St. Bernards scored twice, 'dissatisfaciton was expressed at the attempts of Hibernians to waste time and on two occasions the referee had to intervene and lift the ball'.

March was again the time for representative games, and McKernan, Cox, Rourke, McFadyen and Cavanagh were involved in Edinburgh's wins over Sheffield by 8–1 and Ayrshire by 5–2. Thereafter Hibs embarked on another tour to Lancashire.

Blackburn Rovers were their first opponents and were preserving an unbeaten home record. 'Good breaking' was responsible for their leading 3–1 at half-time, but a hat-trick by Gillie Byrne therafter put Hibs in front. Then goalkeeper O'Brien slipped with the ball, apparently several feet out from goal, but Rovers were awarded a score. For a while Hibs were unsure about whether to continue, but eventually they did, doubtless feeling they now knew how their hosts had kept such a good record so long. Hibs next beat Bolton again by 3–1, with goals from Flynn, Cox and new signing McGee.

The season ended on a high note with no fewer than seven Hibs men, including Waugh and O'Brien for the first time, playing for Edinburgh in a 7–1 trouncing of Cleveland.

CHAPTER 3

The Scottish Cup, 1882–87

By 1882–83 season, Hibs were having to deal with the problem which comes to all successful clubs, rebuilding their side after the going of established players. As was often to be the case in Scotland, the problem was worsened by players leaving for England to earn a better living. This was despite professionalism still being outlawed in both countries, with the clubs who practised it as a matter of course voting, as members of their associations, to keep the game amateur. In 1882 William Cox and James McKernan joined Bolton, and Frank Rourke emigrated to America.

The first-round ties posed little problem, Hibs beating Brunswick 8–0 in the Cup and Glencairn 6–1 in the Shield, but in the second round of the former they only got through 3–2 against West Calder in a 'fast and for some time a pretty rough match' and without M. Byrne who 'was disabled by a kick at an early stage'. Their weaknesses were exposed in the first 'derby' at Tynecastle, 'the substitutes not being thoroughly trained as yet', and might well have been worse off than three down when McFadyen and Waugh scored late goals. The new Hibs line-up was O'Brien, Cavanagh, McIntee, Brannigan, Waugh, Flynn, Joyce, Byrne, Hannan, Fox, McFadyen.

With a Scottish Cup bye, Hibs beat Dunfermline 7–1, then Waugh, Flynn, Gillie and Byrne represented Edinburgh against Lanarkshire before Partick Thistle visited Easter Road in the 4th round and drew 2–2 in a rough match. Hibs won the replay 4–1, then a week later beat Thistle again, 2–0 in a friendly.

Arthurlie provided the fifth-round opposition and beat Hibs 4–3, the game ending in such darkness that the ball was invisible to the spectators around the ropes, but the match 'having been declared void by the SFA', the teams met again on December 23rd at Kinning Park, Glasgow; 'against a strong sun which contributed materially to their defeat', Hibs were one down in a minute, four at half-time and six at the close.

The Shield as usual was behind schedule, and Hibs beat Edina 6–0 and Rose 7–1 to reach the last three, where they received the bye and University beat Hearts 5–2 and qualified to meet Hibs on February 24th.

Meanwhile Hibs had team problems. Curran, Nolli, Philbin, J. Lee, Kirk and Taylor were among players tried in a 4–2 defeat from the students at Corstorphine and in a 1–1 draw at Tynecastle, and because of their difficulties, they asked for a postponement of the Shield final until March 10th. This was refused because Dr. Smith of the University would probably be playing for Scotland on that day — as indeed he was — and because with the students also competing in the Charity Cup, there was a need to play off the games during term time. Hibs then scratched and the students took the trophy by default.

The Edinburgh Charity Cup was presented by Lord Rosebery and is often referred to as the Rosebery Cup. Its inspiration was the succesful Glasgow Charity Cup, and its form a four-team knock-out competition. In its first tie, Hibs met Hearts on March 10th at Tynecastle and lost 3–1. St. Bernards beat University 5–3, then lost a disappointing final to Hearts by 2–0.

The Ayrshire Connection

By now Hibs were widening their net for available talent and came up trumps on a St. Patrick's church outing to Ayrshire; a scratch Hibs team played a local eleven in Lugar, and 'discovered' a whole new halfback line of McGhee, McGinn and McLaren. Jim McGhee soon became Hibs' captain, and can be likened to Pat Stanton of more recent times in terms of leadership by example, loyalty and great popularity. James McLaren had a genius for controlling a game that earned him the nickname of the 'Auld General' and more than compensated for his lack of speed. Better times were just around the corner with this trio, but their initial appearance left some doubts about that — Queens Park were Hibs' visitors and beat Hibs 10–2!

It was important for Hibs to reassert themselves in 1883–84. They started off well enough against South Western and settled an old score or two. 'Both sides made a creditable display and if the strangers were the weaker of the two they made the best possible appearance'. Which was just as well since they still lost 11–1. A more significant result was a 1–0 home success against Renton, who had recently eliminated Dumbarton from the Scottish Cup and had become a force to be reckoned with.

In that competition, after trouncing West Calder 5–0 and a second-round bye, Hibs showed that once again they were more than a match for Hearts, before about seven thousand spectators at Tynecastle. The game was 'rougher than usual' with several players concentrating more on opponents than the ball, and was generally a disappointment. 'A high kick from one of the Heart back division landed the ball dangerously near the goal' and gave Hibs their first goal, Brogan added another from a run from Lee and Flynn, then Wood reduced the Hearts' deficit. In the second half, McGhee scored within a minute and later made it 4–1 — the way it finished.

Hibs next beat Hamilton Academicals 6–3 at Easter Road, although 'play was by no means brilliant', and Hearts again, 3–2 at Tynecastle, before the biggest crowd yet seen in Edinburgh, then they had to travel to Dumfries to meet 5th KRV (Kirkcudbrightshire Rifle Volunteers) in their next Cup tie. 5th KRV played at Palmerston Park and were one of three clubs who joined to form Queen of the South after the First World War. Hibs beat them 8–1.

With another bye, it was a few weeks until there was any more Cup action. Hibs took on Queens Park again and the result was a 'distinct improvement' although the score was 5–1 to Queens after only an hour because of ground conditions. Hibs also lost 2–1 to Pilgrims at Copeland Park before meeting Battlefield, also from Glasgow, in the Cup quarter-finals. 'The Battlefield played a good game, but had hard luck in scoring', which to the reporter seemed adequate reason for their 6–1 defeat.

So Hibs were now in their first semi-final, but before that came off had some noteworthy wins against western teams at Easter Road. Flynn (2) and McGhee got the goals in beating Vale of Leven 3–2, Cowlairs lost 5–2 and Pollokshields Athletic 4–2. In between, Lundy, McGhee and T. Lee represented Edinburgh in a 2–2 draw with London, some revenge for a 9–2 hammering a year before (without any Hibs' men).

Cup semi-finals were still not played on neutral territory in 1884 and Queens Park came to Easter Road on February 2nd. Much the heavier team — no mean factor considering the style of play at the time — it was no surprise that Queens won with a bit to spare. 'At no period of the game can the contest be said to have been keen.' Dr. Smith, formerly of Edinburgh University, scored two, Christie three, and T. Lee obtained Hibs' solitary goal.

Next came a return with Hearts at Easter Road, where a hat-trick from James McGhee and a goal from J. Lee earned Hibs a 4–1 win and set them up nicely for another Shield final.

The Shield had provided Hibs with more problems off the field than on it. The infusion of new blood aroused the jealousy of their neighbours, and the EFA were persuaded to disqualify them from playing in EFA competitions. Hibs tried to canvass support, and assembled a sizeable lobby, but two general meetings of the EFA ratified the bans, despite the fact that two of the players concerned, McGhee and McLaren, had also represented the EFA in the meantime. The *Scottish Football Annual* later recalled how enterprise won the day.

'Now, at this time, the meetings of the committee of the EFA were very protracted, lasting generally till about midnight. The meeting room was small and badly ventilated, so that what between heated discussions and a stifling atmosphere, several of the members got thirsty on the verge of eleven o'clock. The Irish party noticed this and laid their plans accordingly. The discussion on the eligibility of McGhee and McLaren was kept up one night until the thirsty members retired for their cool and refreshing beverages. Not one of the Irishmen left their seats. Suddenly the debate collapsed, and the chairman had to put the motion, *viz.,* that McGhee and McLaren were eligible to play in Edinburgh Shield Ties. This was carried by a large majority. The drouthy members now returned, 'michtily refreshed', to carry on the fray, but, alas! like Lord Wolseley's expedition to the Soudan, they were too late.'

Hibs had not had much difficulty reaching the Shield final, beating Norton Park 4–1, Glencairn 5–0, and East Linton 10–0, and with their imported stars they had as little trouble winning it. McGinn scored four and McGhee two as Hibs routed St. Bernards 7–0.

There was more trouble in the Charity Cup. Hibs beat University 5–0 at Powderhall 'but in a number of instances the play of Hibernians was very rough and not regarded as legitimate', one of which presumably was when McLaren, trying to recover lost ground, struck a University man on the face and was immediately dispatched from the field of play by the referee and umpires. The University's appeal failed to get them a replay, but McLaren and McGhee were banned from the final — against St. Bernards, who had beaten Hearts 4–2.

The Charity Cup rules allowed guest players, and former Hib McKernan turned out for Hibs. The first half was goalless, but on one occasion the ball struck Hibs' bar and in the ensuing scrimmage, a second did likewise. McAuslane scored a 'pretty goal' for Saints but, with time running out, the ball went straight to goalkeeper Baillie 'who unaccountably let it slip, and M. Byrne scored one of the easiest and luckiest goals seen for a long time'. Lucky to get a second chance, Hibs were also lucky to survive it — Saints had them hemmed in for just about the whole game, but Flynn headed the only goal to give Hibs the trophy.

In other matches, Hibs beat Glasgow Northern 3–0 but for once slipped up by losing 4–2 to Hearts. April 19th was a day worth remembering, though — Lee and McGhee each scored twice to give Hibs their first win over Rangers by 4–1 and Hearts defeated Queens Park 2–1. For good measure, St. Bernards chose the same day to beat St. Mirren 4–2.

Professionalism

The autumn of 1884 was dominated by the question of professionalism. The problem was that while the general view was that professionalism would favour a few of the bigger clubs to the ruin of the rest, quite apart from its being unacceptable anyway from a moral point of view, not to introduce it would only increase the flow of the top players to England.

More column inches were certainly devoted to payment for football than to playing it, partly no doubt because of the early rash of fairly meaningless cup ties. Hibs reached the 4th round of the Cup by means of a first round bye and wins over Vale of Teith (from Callander) by 5–1 and Glengowan (from Airdrie) likewise. In the Shield they had one bye and beat Lorne Star 5–1 and Rose 10–0.

But if Saturday afternoons at Easter Road were tame, they were quieter still at Tynecastle. Hearts had beaten Dunfermline 11–1 in the Cup, but the latter protested that two Hearts players received payment from the club. This was upheld, so Hearts were disqualified from the competition and expelled from the SFA itself. Hearts' first appeal in November was rejected, but they were readmitted about a month later.

Meanwhile Hibs beat St. Bernards 4–1 and also made further progress in the Cup. Against Ayr at Easter Road, they were 'as usual conspicuously successful in their smart passing game', McGhee, McGinn and Lee put them three up at the interval and Hibs won by 4–1. Morton were the 5th round visitors, and though 'the way both goalkeepers conducted themselves was generally admired', the visiting one was beaten by Clark (2), McGrail and McGhee in a 4–0 result.

Somehow Hearts had retained their interest in the Shield competition until, that is, they visited Easter Road in the fourth round after their readmission to favour. Common put Hearts ahead in the second half, but 'excellent passing put Hibernians in the foremost position', though goals from J. Lee, Cox and McGhee served toward that end also.

Another well-known protest took place in December 1884: Rangers lost 4–3 at Arbroath and sent home the famous telegram 'Beaten on a back green'. The pitch was only one foot narrower than required, but Rangers were granted a replay and, revelling in the extra inches, won 8–1 on December 20th. A week later Hibs took advantage of another home tie to beat Annbank 5–0 to reach the semi-finals again.

Before this took place, Hibs beat Edinburgh Emmett 'by the long score of twenty goals to none'. Their opponents would have been grateful that most of Hibs' established players were playing at Renton, beating the local side 2–1, a good result in view of the forthcoming Cup tie.

So after defeating St. Bernards by 4–0 at Powderhall, Hibs met Renton again, this time with ground advantage, and before a large and expectant crowd. 'After a few minutes Hibernians got the ball through and this was followed by the Renton scoring out of a scrimmage.' Each side got one more in the first half, then in the second 'a third was put through by the strangers; Hibernians made every effort to follow suit but failed' and so for the second time went out at this stage.

But they came back to winning a week later in dreadful conditions at Tynecastle: 'both teams played well and in the end victory lay with Hibernians by seven goals to two' against Hearts. T. Lee and Cox scored early goals before Hibs had to hang on to beat Dumbarton 2–1, and this was followed by a 6–1 defeat of Partick Thistle. This took them up to the Shield final against University at Powderhall on 28th February. McGhee opened the scoring when an opponent missed the ball, but Chamberlain neatly levelled the scores before the break. Then one of several corners by J. Lee gave Hibs the lead again and soon McGuinn got the third, before Blades made it 3–2 in the last minute.

A month later there was a rare attraction for city enthusiasts. A number of Scottish clubs, including on occasion Hearts, also entered the FA Cup, and on this occasion Queens Park had reached the semi-final and drawn with Nottingham Forest at Derby. Now they had to replay and the venue was Merchison Castle School (now Napier College), perhaps a surprising choice with Easter Road and Tynecastle available as alternatives, and the need to erect a temporary grandstand over the cricket pitch for the occasion. Special trains came from Nottingham and Glasgow and the crowd exceeded 10,000. Queens won 3–0 but lost in the final to Blackburn Rovers. The SFA were soon to put a stop to their clubs entering English competitions.

During the year Edinburgh had beaten Lanarkshire 6–1 and lost to Dunbarton (county) by 4–1, and only four of the twenty-two positions had gone to Hibs men, which was surprising in view of their obvious superiority in the city. So when the game with Glasgow came off, Hibs would not release their players. The weakened captial team was further hit when some of those who had been selected failed to turn up, but fortunately Hibs' McLaren was in the crowd and took part in a surprise draw. Meanwhile, Hibs were losing 3–0 to 'a new combination of Airdrieonians'.

Premier Club in Scotland

The Edinburgh FA prizegiving took place in April although the Charity Cup was still outstanding. 'Judged by their scoring', remarked the Chairman after the loyal toasts, 'Hibernians occupy the position of premier club in Scotland, Cambridge University alone beating them in the United Kingdom', and he presented the Edinburgh Shield to Mr. Lundy and the Second XI Cup to Mr. Philbin. He was pleased to see that matches with Glasgow had got under way. Some Edinburgh players were certainly of international calibre and 'McLaren would surely have received international honours if the Committee had been certain he was a Scotsman'. The Edinburgh FA was toasted, Mr. McFadyen replied, and other toasts and songs followed.

Hibs' appeal by now extended far beyond the Edinburgh area and there was an increasing demand to see them in other parts of the country. They had the following of Roman Catholics all over Scotland and as a result were able to recruit from this wider population base. In return Hibs played more matches to help various Catholic charities. Their team showed two new faces in August 1885, the dependable goalkeeper Tobin, and inside-forward Preston, whose death was tragically only a few months away. On a happier note, and also a few months later, full-back Lundy and skipper McGhee became the first Hibs players to be 'capped' when they represented Scotland against Wales in April.

Hibs were especially popular in Dundee where they played five times, and they also played Airdrieonians thrice, winning twice and losing once by the odd goal. It might have been worse because in February the Lanarkshire team beat Rangers 10–2 at Kinning Park.

Hibs' first important result of the season was an encouraging 3–1 win over Renton, Preston, Clark and Cox scoring, and their second an even better one, winning 2–1 against Queens Park in a 'major surprise'. Hibs only just held out during the first quarter but then took heart when McGinn scored with a mis-hit shot off a post, and they got another when Preston centred and 'Philbin punted it through with his head'. They then managed to hold Queens to one goal in the second half. Further north, this was the day when Arbroath scored thirty-six times against the hapless Orion Cricket Club, in the Scottish Cup by mistake and playing under the name of Bon Accord.

With a first-round bye, Hibs' opening tie was in the second round against Hearts. They had beaten their rivals a fortnight earlier at Tynecastle before 'an immense gathering, estimated at nearly four thousand', with a dispute about a goal and plenty of rough play, so an unusually large crowd was attracted to the Cup tie. This time Hearts led at half-time by a scrambled sort of goal, but shortly after it Hearts' goalkeeper Gibson tossed the ball out straight to McGhee who dispatched it promptly back under the bar. The excitement became intense and in one struggle under Hearts' bar, McGhee again was successful. Hearts were undaunted but all their efforts failed to retrieve the position.

Progress therafter was easier against Bo'ness (6–0) and the high-scoring Arbroath (5–3), and then Hibs drew Dumbarton in Round 5. The venue

James McGhee. A sketch of the popular Hibs' captain which appeared in the 'Scottish Umpire and Cycling Mercury' in February 1887.

was the aptly named Boghead, but an early own goal and a late equaliser earned Hibs a replay at home. Five thousand people turned up and the pitch was a perfect quagmire. With this advantage Dumbarton took a quick lead, but then the veteran Paton missed the ball and McGhee heeled it through to the crowd's delight. Hartley scored his second for the Sons, then Clark replied for Hibs but the half-time whistle had gone and the goal was not allowed. The Irishmen made a big effort on resumption and one shot hit the crossbar, but then Brown sent a third goal spinning past Tobin. Dumbarton now settled in to defend their lead but Hibs kept at it and Preston then Clark got through to bring them level, amidst the wildest excitement. Dumbarton abandoned their negative style, but Hibs' staying power was becoming evident, and as the combatants became almost indiscernible in the gathering darkness, McGhee scored Hibs' fourth, which was disputed but allowed, and a famous victory was won.

Easter Road was well filled again a week later when Hearts contested the 4th round of the Shield. Again Hearts started well, scoring in five minutes, and as Hibs struggled, going two in front. Then Hibs began to show some form and drew level by the break. Two more goals from Preston saw them in a comfortable position, despite the occurrence of 'a misadventure on the part of Tobin, letting slip from his hand a very easy shot', making the final score 4–3.

The Ne'erday game with Third Lanark kicked off at one o'clock, to interfere as little as possible with the Powderhall meeting, and Hibs, below their usual form, were fortunate to win 4–1. A day later they played hosts to the famous Corinthians who fielded 'one of the strongest combinations ever seen in Scotland', and the result was 'a really scientific display of association football', especially on the part of the visitors who had the edge all through and won by 7–3. New names in the Hibs line-up were goalscorers Lafferty, another recruit from Lugar, and Mailley.

There were five teams left in the Cup, and in the only tie Hibs had ground advantage over Cambuslang. They made the most of it too, with two goals in a minute in the first half — McGinn scored in a scrimmage, then the goalkeeper saved from McLaren but he and the ball were unceremoniously bundled through the goal. Lafferty banged through a rebound early in the second half, so although the dark blues fought back with goals from Plenderleith and Buchanan, Hibs were in another semi-final.

This took place a week later, also at Easter Road, and the visitors, also in dark blue, were Renton. There was blinding snow and sleet, so the huge and expectant crowd was as uncomfortable as disappointed as the 'Rantin' won well. McIntyre and Thomson scored two quick goals, and as Hibs were under siege for most of the remainder, this lead was never threatened.

The Shield was also now at semi-final stage; Hibs met University again on a snowbound pitch and won comfortably. McGhee scored early on from a corner and Ings was beaten again when Lee 'sent in a warmer' — just the thing for a cold afternoon. Ings himself contributed the third into his own goal and Hibs won 3–0. So a fortnight later 2000 people went along to Powderhall to see if St. Bernards could loosen Hibs' grip on the trophy, and it looked possible briefly when Wight headed them ahead in ten minutes, but Hibs assumed command and goals from Clark, McGhee (2), O'Donnell and an own goal gave them success by 5–1.

The opening Charity Cup matches were again played off early because of the students' involvement and Hibs defeated them 3–1 at the start of April, before a short English tour at the end of the month. They lost 6–2 to Bolton, beat Padiham Hibernians 5–2 and lost at Stoke by the only goal in the heat wave. A month later Bolton returned the compliment and were again successful, by 3–1.

Not surprisingly, Hibs met Hearts in the Charity Cup Final and again there was controversy; Hibs were leading 2–0 at half-time at Tynecastle and were coasting along thereafter when a charge on Bell by McGhee brought a break-in by spectators. The game was abandoned and McGhee only with difficulty extricated from a hostile crowd. It was an unfortunate first visit to Hearts' new (and present) ground and the outcome was a

'Darlin' Willie Groves who played in the Cup Finals of both 1887 and 1896.

replay at Powderhall. This time Hearts went two up, and when Hibs protested about the second goal, a similar invasion took place. The referee was the target of this one, and ironically it was McGhee who was instrumental in the official's deliverance. A third and more peaceful game resulted in an only goal win for Hibs.

Willie Groves

Arguments are frequent about the relative merits of Hibs players of different generations, but no list of the greatest of them would leave out the name of Willie Groves. The goalscoring inside-forward had come into the Hibs team during the latter part of 1885-86 and within two years had represented Scotland. In W. Reid's *The Story of "The Hearts"* of 1924 Groves was 'bracketed with Robert Walker as the finest products of

Edinburgh football. A bewildering dribbler with a puzzling swerve, Groves was of the type of McMahon, a later Hibernian product, and Gallacher the Celtic expert, but more graceful than either'. Praise indeed from a book about Hearts, but Groves was inspirational in his club's successes of 1886–87.

An understrength Hibs side went to Dundee in August and lost 5–0 to Our Boys; but it was to be more than four months later before they were beaten again. They quickly avenged their defeats at Bolton and Stoke, beating the Wanderers 3–2 with goals from Smith, Groves and Clark, and the Potteries men 4–1 — Groves got two, then Reynolds scored with a 'daisy-cutter'; Tobin fisted into his own goal, but the margin was restored in a scrimmage. Two days later West Bromwich started a Scottish tour at Easter Road — Paddock put them in front at the interval but McGhee equalised 'with a lightning shot' and excitement ran high till it became too dark to see. Hibs then finished the week by trouncing Middlesbrough 10–2, after being level at 2–2. Groves, McLaren and McGhee each got two, and immediately after the final whistle Hibs took on near-neighbours Vale of Midlothian in a Shield tie and won that one 5–0.

The Scottish Cup ties were also under way. Hibs had already accounted for Durhamtown Rangers of Bathgate by 5–1 with another three for Groves, and now had the toughest draw they could get in the regional ballot, a trip to West Calder to meet Mossend Swifts who were having an incredible run of only one home defeat in eight years, even if not all of the top sides paid them a visit. Fern scored an early goal to the delight of the masses straining at the ropes. Hibs were generally well able to take care of themselves, but they were relieved when McGhee equalised from a scrimmage 'before the game reached its coarsest' and happy to gain a replay. This engagement was no picnic either.

'Never since the Irishmen took possession of Easter Road have they had such a struggle to hold their own, and not against skilful play but solid weight and promiscuous kicking.' They were glad to be on level terms at the break but gradually took command after it, and at last McGhee enabled Clark to score 'amid the most extraordinary excitement' even for Irish supporters. A minute later Hibs scored again and Groves made it three, and as their opponents' kicking became even wilder, Hibs were happy to reach the end, missing only O'Donnell who had retired with an arm out of joint.

The third-round tie with Hearts at Easter Road proved easier. Clark and Reynolds scored two quick goals in twenty minutes and McGinn got another with a grand shot just on the interval. Hearts played up a bit in the second period but Hibs won by 5–1. The enormous crowd of 7000 had been a bit disappointed by the contest. The fourth round brought Queen of the South Wanderers to Easter Road. The first half yielded Hibs five goals without reply, and so an open and enjoyable second half was indulged in in which the blue and white stripes reduced the arrears by one, losing 7–3.

And so to the quarter-finals on Christmas Day, where 'the surprise of the round was the deteat of 3rd LRV by Hibernians' at Cathkin. Rain and sleet had fallen all week and a sharp frost had turned the many pools to ice, but the teams were determined to play. Early in the game Clark counted with a fine shot and after some fairly dangerous play had been indulged in, Reynolds got another, but just before half-time Marshall had the best run of the game which ended with Johnstone scoring. 'The second half was largely a period of Volunteers pressure' and they were often within an ace of scoring but, especially in the last quarter, Hibs' defence stood up tremendously well for a notable win.

The Shield draws during the autumn had generally been kind to Hibs, with byes, but they did have to go to play West Calder on December 11th. The rain poured and 'the ground was in fearful condition, with players sinking in the mud. Run and counter-run characterised play for some time but the game was not far gone when Hibernians had to draw the attention of the referee to the rough play of their opponents. A run by the home forwards ended with one of their number clearly beating Tobin amid frantic cheers wherein the spectators worked themselves nearly to a frenzy. The crowd was very partial and Hibernians continued to be treated with filthy language. McGhee was threatened with a fair challenge'. But again Hibs refused to be cowed by the abuse and scored three times in the second half.

The other features of this long unbeaten spell were Hibs winning one of three silver cups at the Edinburgh Exhibition Football Tournament by beating 3rd LRV by 2–1, wins against Renton (4–1), Port Glasgow (2–0), Bo'ness (3–1) and Clyde (4–0) and drawn games with Vale of Leven and Airdrieonians. The run ended with a 3–2 reverse at Middlesbrough on Boxing Day, and then Aston Villa brought them right back to earth on New Year's Day.

The earth in this case was mud, several inches of it, and Reynolds missed one chance because he fell in it. Hunter and Brown put Villa two up and 'Hibernians were completely out of it'. McGhee did score but Brown immediately got another to cool the celebrations, and by half-time Villa led 4–1 and had had three disallowed. Then they scored two more and had another not given before Smith got Hibs' second, and Vaughan put in their seventh before Clark made it 7—3. Some Hibs players appear not to have taken their lesson too kindly, and their feelings spread to the crowd so that on time being called the Birmingham umpire, Mr. McGregor, was 'severely handled'. In addition, the *Evening Dispatch* reporter, taken unawares by an English player, was assaulted and, with blood pouring from his face, had to be rescued by the nearest spectators. Two days later a game between Queens Park and Aston Villa at Hampden was abandoned at half-time owing to the conditions and was followed by a riot. Villa were leading 5–1 at the time.

The weather had also delayed the Scottish Cup competition, but Hibs' tie with Vale of Leven finally took place at Easter Road on 22nd January. The teams had been under special preparation for the game and 6,000 people turned out to see what difference it made. Most of the early play was around the Vale goal, but their right wing was able to take advantage of a moment's slackness to get past Hibs' defence, and McNicol beat Tobin amid loud cheering. Strenuous efforts to recover the lost ground were for a while fruitless, but Groves put Hibs level a minute before the break. The second half was very exciting. Either side might have taken the lead but it was in a scrimmage during a spell of intense Hibs pressure that the Irishmen forced the ball over the line. This spurred Hibs on and Montgomery scored another for them. Vale of Leven were not, however, entirely finished because they lodged a claim that Willie Groves had accepted payment from the Hibs club and therefore they claimed the tie. With a curious sense of timing the SFA decided to consider the protest just after the final, which Dumbarton reached a week later by defeating Queens Part 2–1.

And so it was a day out to Hampden on February 12th. The crowd of 12,000 used vehicles of every description to get there, including a special train of freight wagons with two engines on the new Cathcart railway. 'Hibernians' supporters were identifiable by their green silk ties and hats with 'Hurry up, Hibs' on them.' James McGhee led Hibs out first on to the slippery pitch. The first half was evenly contested with near things at either goal, and the second followed a like course until from a centre from the right, Aitken sent an unsaveable shot past Tobin. Play became decidedly less exciting as Dumbarton resolved to hold their lead, a ploy that came to nought when McAuley muffed a good shot from Clark to make the scores level. The cheering lasted a couple of minutes and was shortly resumed; Groves 'rushed the ball down in a style peculiarly his own', and while Dumbarton were disputing offside, he passed right to where Lafferty pounced on the ball and sent it flying past McAuley to win the Cup. The Hibs team was Tobin, Lundy, Fagan, McGhee, McGinn, McLaren, Lafferty, Groves, Montgomery, Clark, Smith.

They and the rest of the Hibs party were entertained to a banquet in the East End, before being cheered on to their train which was met at Waverley Station by a crowd of several thousand and a brake and pair with 'Welcome Hibernians, winners of the *Scottish Cup*' on one side and 'God save Ireland' on the other. After a triumphal procession to St. Mary's Street Hall and another large gathering, a few congratulatory speeches were made and 'all retired to rest'. This last quote, from the *Scottish Football Annual*, is probably an exaggeration.

Largely forgotten in the celebrations was Vale of Leven's protest. When this was heard, the complainants had no evidence to offer other than hearsay, but it still took the casting vote of the chairman to clear Hibs.

Hibs were more popular than ever now with their Cup success and played more than twenty more games before a leg-weary side finally closed the season with a 2–1 defeat by Dundee Harp on June 4th. Apart from the local competitions, they lost 3–2 to Renton in the Glasgow Charity Cup, and drew 1–1 with them in the Glasgow East End Catholic Charity Cup before large attendances, and had four more games against English sides. They lost 3–0 to Aston Villa and 3–2 to Wolverhampton on an Easter weekend tour, and played Notts County (5–0) and Church from Lancashire (1–4) at home. They also met Hearts in the East of Scotland Shield and Rosebery Cup finals.

The Shield went to Easter Road thanks to a 3–0 win by Hibs; Groves, Rafferty and Smith got the goals, but Hibs only just made it to the Charity Cup final, having two 2–2 draws with St. Bernards before winning the third game 6–1. The final, however, was more decisive. Hibs had a goal disallowed in nineteen minutes, but by that time Smith, McGhee and Dunbar, a recent recruit who had been capped with Cartvale, had put Hibs five goals to the good. Cox soon made it six, then seven just after half-time and Hibs won 7–1.

CHAPTER 4

The Celtic Connection, 1887–91

It was only eight weeks later that the Scottish Cupholders started another season, and it must have been something of a shock to lose 8–2 to Queen of the South Wanderers, even if they arrived in Dumfries without a goalkeeper and had to recruit one at the ground. The 6–0 defeat by Renton which followed the East End Catholic Cup replay at Barrowfield was not a lot better, but they got back into winning form by beating Stoke 2–1 and then met Preston North End's 'Invincibles' in a match billed as being for the 'Association Football Championship of the World'.

The English professionals were a little below full strength, but the crowd was the largest yet seen at Easter Road and the game was fast and furious, and sometimes rough. First-half play was fairly even, but a goal fell to McGhee with a long shot. Three minutes after the interval, 'McLaren, getting a high ball as it descended, banged it past Trainor' and the celebrations held up play for a minute or two. Now the Englishmen attacked in earnest: Gordon hit a post and a scorcher from Dewhurst struck the crossbar. Goodall's shot was next to hit the bar, but then he got his head to a cross from Gordon and steered the ball past Tobin. McLaren and McLaughlin both had to head further attempts off the goalline, but eventually the final whistle saved the relieved defenders.

A measure of Hibs' achievement was that a week later Preston were in Glasgow to open Ibrox, where Rangers had moved on being told to quit Kinning Park. 'After Preston had scored eight goals, a section of the crowd, gradually becoming more and more irritated, invaded the pitch. The game was stopped. It is not recorded that the Rangers players raised any loud objections' (J. Fairgrieve). On the other hand, it was maybe as well that Hibs' opponents were not Aston Villa, who were in fact the FA Cupholders. While Preston were at Ibrox, Hibs were performing a similar function at the opening of Rugby Park, new home of Kilmarnock FC, in a 1–1 draw.

Nevertheless, the general impression was that Hibs were not playing as well as in the previous season. They lost 4–3 at home to Renton and 4–2 away to Dumbarton, and then fell to Hearts in the third round of the Cup. The first two rounds brought easy wins over Broxburn Thistle (5–0) and Erin Rovers (Durhamtown Rangers' new name) (6–0). The tie with Hearts took place at Tynecastle and the 1–1 result was a fair one. An enormous crowd was therefore present at Easter Road a week later, and they saw 'one of the greatest surprises that had yet been recorded'. Hearts scored the only first-half goal and then after resuming Common put them two up. Their goalkeeper Gibson was saving well, especially on two occasions from McGhee, but he was beaten at last by 'a long beauty' from Gallagher. The Tynecastle defence was then fully tested, but they held out and in the closing phase Hearts broke away and scored a third.

In the Shield, Hibs had had big wins against Polton Vale, Leith Harp and University, now much less of a force than previously, and then had the chance to avenge their Cup defeat by Hearts. Hearts protested that Hibs' newest recruits Gallagher, McKeown and Coleman were not local men and therefore not eligible, but the game went ahead and Hibs, leading 4–1 at half-time, won 5–2. McGhee (2), Cox, Groves and McLaren were the scorers and the match took place on Christmas Eve. McKeown was yet another product of Lugar Boswell.

In January Hibs lost 4–1 to 3rd LRV; the game was played in a downpour and a gale and one of the Volunteers' scorers rejoiced in the name of McLuggage. In February Queens Park made a long awaited visit to Easter Road and won an exciting game by 4–3.

The first Saturday in March was the date of the Shield final between Hibs and Mossend Swifts, and another surprise. Smith hit the post and Groves the bar in the first half but that was as close as Hibs came, and with twelve minutes left, Boyd beat Tobin for the only goal. A crowd of 5,000 welcomed the Swifts back to West Calder, a huge number considering the size of the place, the village band played 'See the conquering heroes come' and the players were entertained in the Masonic Hall.

Before the Charity Cup, Hibs' results included a 2–0 win against Derby County and a short Irish tour in which they beat Distillery 3–1 and Belfast United 4–1. They also reversed their 4–1 result with 3rd LRV.

In the Rosebery Cup, Hibs first met Hearts at Powderhall, where arrangements were not adequate for the huge crowd of over 8000 and palings gave way. A notable Hibs guest player was Kelly of Renton. The great game expected did not materialise — Dunbar scored in three minutes and Hearts were outplayed. Dunbar scored four and Groves and McGhee one apiece as 'play was monotonously round Gibson's charge. Hearts have certainly never played a worse game'. The final at Tynecastle was another tussle with Mossend Swifts, but this time the only goal fell to McGhee, after the goalkeeper had pushed out one of his shots. It was another hard game and it was the Hibs defence that took most credit.

Hibs also took part again in the Glasgow Charity Cup, and again lasted only one round, losing 3–0 to Cambuslang. They returned to Glasgow on May 8th when, with what turned out to be misplaced kindness, they played Cowlairs in a goalless draw to open the ground of the newly organised Celtic at Janefield.

Wolves in Sheep's Clothing

Celtic were formed in November 1887, largely by the efforts of a Glasgow priest called Walfrid who had watched Hibs and Renton contest the East End Charity Cup and had been impressed not only by the football but also by the revenue it generated. A handbill early in 1888 set out the aims of the club as principally to supply 'funds for the maintenance of the 'Dinner Tables' of our needy children' and to select 'a team which will be able to do credit to the Catholics of the West of Scotland as the Hibernians have been doing in the East'. 'Several leading Catholic football players of the West of Scotland' were apparently already engaged, and when the new club made their first appearance against Rangers on May 28th, they were strong enough to win 5–2. The only Hibs man involved was Mr McFadden, who refereed, though James Kelly, of Renton, had guested for Hibs in the Rosebery Cup.

When Hibs inaugurated the new season at Celtic Park in August 1888, things were very different. Apart from Kelly, McKeown, Gallagher, Groves, McLaren and Coleman were all in Celtic's colours, while Hibs not surprisingly had a totally unfamiliar line-up: Docherty, McVey, McKenna, McGeoran, White, Clifford, Naughton, Smith, McGhee, Mulvie and Clark. Celtic had the better of early play, but Hibs were as popular in Glasgow as anywhere, and when Smith opened the scoring there was great cheering. Groves equalised before half-time, and McGhee had to retire injured just after, but Naughton put Hibs in front again, though only for five minutes. Then Coleman equalised and Groves gave his new colleagues a slender win.

The next few results were not as bad as might have been feared, considering what had happened. Hibs beat Harp 3–1 in Dundee, and then, along with the Duntocher Brass Band, hanselled Clydebank's new home and won 3–0. Next came a visit to Ibrox where McGhee scored twice, but Rangers went one better, all in the first half. A one-goal defeat wasn't too bad, even if Rangers were having a lean time too, and a large support went with Hibs to meet Mossend in the Scottish Cup.

The Hibs defence looked decidedly weak, and Inglis scored against them in ten minutes, but they weathered the storm and were even having the better of things in the second half when Renwick broke away, ran the length of the field and set up a goal for Ellis, amid frantic scenes of celebration. McPhee pulled one goal back, but Hibs were out at the first hurdle, despite a protest about rough play. More new names on the team lines were Lyons, Molloy and Mack.

Smith and Clark scored the goals which gave Hibs a 2–1 win in their first home game, against Battlefield of Glasgow, but then they went out of the Shield at the first attempt too, in their first meeting with new neighbours

Leith Athletic at nearby Hawkhill. Yet another new centre McManus opened the scoring, but the ebullient Athletic hit back to win 3–2.

Hibs lost again a week later 4–2 to Partick Thistle in Glasgow; then their problems were really exposed by Queens Park — the Spiders were always popular visitors and the season's largest crowd assembled at Easter Road to see them. They saw little else. Allan and Sellars put Queens two up in seven minutes, and they led 6–0 at half-time. Mack did score one for Hibs in the second half, after Queens had made their tally seven. Wins against weak opposition, Leith Harp and Glasgow Thistle, did nothing to appease the supporters' discontent; moreover, they were in no doubt who was responsible for their side's demise, and so when Celtic appeared at Easter Road on October 20th, they were received by a large and threatening assembly.

'The excitement was intense, and when in ten minutes a clever centre by Connors let Coleman score, the point was received in silence.' Egged on by the crowd, Hibs replied with vigour, but Dunbar, another defector, scored a second. Offside was refused and the game restarted amid prolonged booing, then, 'when Groves looked like doing something sensational and Brown took the ball off his toes, the applause was deafening'. Dunbar scored a third before half-time and the crowd's humour was not improved by it.

In the second half, Hibs had an equal share of what play there was. Three times the crowd invaded the pitch: several hundreds swarmed on and every Celtic player was surrounded. It seemed unlikely that play would be resumed, but it was, until, with ten minutes remaining, 'the whistle ended the game, arrangements apparently having been made that full time should not be played, though Hibernians were averse to this'. It seems that these steps were taken to catch on the hop any who might have yet more hostile intent for the end of the game.

Hibs' problems were now chronic. Two more players had left, this time for Burnley — Cox, and the promising young centre Sandy McMahon, whose career had started with Darlington St. Augustine's. A superb dribbler, if ungainly, with a terrific shot, McMahon could also head the ball with as much force as anyone in the game, and like many Hibs players of the 1880s he found it easier to impress the selectors once he moved to Celtic later on.

Back at Easter Road, only a few hundred turned out for Hibs' next appearance against Leith Athletic three weeks later, and Hibs had to recruit from amongst them to field a team. To lose 5–3 was therefore not too bad, and another scratch eleven performed creditably at Tynecastle, losing 3–1, but exhibiting forward play that surprised even their own followers.

There were signs to encourage Hibs' vexed support from time to time. Their team beat Clyde 4–3 in only their third game in eight weeks. Clyde were having difficulties as well, but for Hibs to win after being 3–1 behind at half-time showed spirit at least. McMahon and Cox returned to the fold in time to take part in a 3–3 draw with St. Bernards in February and a good 4–3 win over Dumbarton in which Hibs were three times in arrears. There were also two three-goal wins against Leith Athletic.

On the other hand, when Hibs rather ambitiously tackled Third Lanark at Cathkin they lost 7–2, a score which however flattered their opponents, since Hibs had been only one down midway through the second half. Similarly, when Hibs lost 6–0 at Tynecastle, 'they were by no means outplayed' and were on top for a considerable spell. But obviously Hearts had their moments too! Hibs now included Kelly in goal, Hillon and McCallum at full-back and McCambridge at centre.

Whether from remorse or otherwise, Celtic played Hibs at Janefield on March 5th, with the entire proceeds going to the visitors. The score was quite creditable too, 5–4 to Celtic, although it took two very late goals to bring Hibs that close.

Meanwhile, Hibs' plight was the rather improbable theme when Mr. Sneddon, the President of the East of Scotland FA (as the Edinburgh FA had recently renamed itself), spoke at the Heart of Midlothian annual concert in the Oddfellows Hall. 'For various circumstances which all deplored and were familiar with', he said, 'Hibernians have been weakened this season, and from the quarter least expected. Better things might have been looked for from the club from which Hibernians received their blow, and if it was a ray of consolation, it was the universal sympathy expressed for them. (Applause) All hoped Hibernians would regain the club's loss of prestige and place it as formerly among the front rank of Scottish football clubs.'

Hibs declined to play in the Charity Cup in 1889. One of the sides who did compete, Mossend, eliminated Hearts, being two goals to the good when proceedings were brought to a close by a riot. St. Bernards qualified to meet them in the final, but only beat Leith at the third attempt, and with seven of Third Lanark's Cup-winning side as guests. Mossend won the final at Tynecastle by 4–3, and it was some consolation to Hibs that before the final took place, they had wins over both finalists, 4–3 against the winners and 3–1 against the losers. Unfortunately they followed these up with another defeat at the hands of Hearts, this time by 5–2.

Glasgow Hibernians Too!

The history of Ireland has been one of internal quarrelling, even more than that of Scotland. The Celtic club was run by a large committee of men of Irish descent if not birth, and so it is no surprise to discover that in less than a year, and despite Celtic's reaching the Cup final at their first try, dissension should have caused a split to occur. The dissatisfied parties approached Hibs to persuade them to move to Glasgow, but the Edinburgh club obviously felt they had enough trouble coping with the new competition from Celtic at a range of over forty miles and decided to stay put. So the splinter group formed their own side and called it Glasgow Hibernians with a pitch just off the London Road and not far from Celtic Park. It was more bad news for Hibs. The new club recruited more widely than had Celtic, but their opening line-up included Tobin, Clark, Smith and B. Coyle of Hibs, although the goalkeeper had not been with the Edinburgh side for a while.

By this time Hibs had beaten Glasgow Thistle 4–3 with a hat-trick from their loyal captain McGhee, but had lost at home to Linthouse (6–4) and Airdrieonians (2–1). They lost their next game too, 5–1 at Cowlairs, but put up a reasonable show in the Scottish Cup.

Armadale was the scene of Hibs' first-round tie, and, against rain, wind and slope, Duke put Hibs ahead in seven minutes. McGhee scored two more before Fleming replied for the 'Dale amid deafening cheers. Hibs held the local side fairly comfortably in the second period although they lost one goal near the close. They would also not have been unduly upset to learn that neither Celtic nor Glasgow Hibernians had reached the second round.

This round brought more West Lothian opposition, Mossend, and a chance to avenge the defeat of the year before. Despite ground advantage, Hibs had to contend with a large and loud West Calder support, but this time they had the game well in hand, after an early fright, when the ball struck their post and rolled along the line before being cleared. McMahon sent a twenty-yard header spinning through, and McGhee quickly kicked a second 'after dodging through a crowd of Swifts'. Mossend pulled one back in a scrimmage before half-time but lost two goals to Smith after it. Near the end Swifts did succeed in bringing the score back to 4–2 — or 4–3 depending on how one interprets *The Scotsman's* report.

In the third round, Hibs had things all their own way for an hour against Dunfermline Athletic and led by goals from Flannagan, McMahon, Charlie McGhee and Smith, but then they lost just as many and had to replay a week later at home. This time there was no mistake and James McGhee and Smith had hat-tricks in an 11–1 win.

Next came a trip to Dumfries to meet Queen of the South Wanderers, and after losing two goals in an initial onslaught, Hibs hit back to lead 3–2 at the interval. Then 'Wanderers ... seemed to get out of the running as they were able to add only one goal to their opponents' four'. A bye in the fifth round put Hibs in the quarter-finals, where they were balloted to meet Abercorn at Underwood Park, Paisley. Throughout, the home side's controlled football was not upset by Hibs' more vigorous stye, and they scored regularly, six times in all, against two by McMahon. Meanwhile Leith Athletic, with a difficult draw at Hampden, were doing well, losing by the only goal scored five minutes from time by Hamilton.

Leith had knocked Hibs out of the Shield the previous year by 3–2, and there was a repeat on November 2nd, despite McGhee's scoring in less than a minute. McLung headed the equaliser and an own goal by Hillon gave Leith the lead. In the second half McMahon delighted the Hibs' support with a beautiful goal followed by a period of wild shooting, which was not surprising, thought the reporter, because of the yelling the players were subjected to. Nevertheless the scoresheet tells us that Lawrie had at least one further shot on target. In the earlier rounds Hibs had beaten Bonnyrigg Rose and the Cameron Hignlanders without a lot of trouble, although 'some of the Highlanders were summoned to appear on account of their foul language to opponents and referee'.

The first half of the season was also remarkable for some high scoring friendlies, especially with St. Bernards. Hibs beat the Saints 6–5 at Easter Road, with four goals for McMahon, then lost 7–5 at the Gymnasium in a game in which they quickly led 2–0, but trailed 6–2 at the break. Against Celtic 'for fully ten minutes Hibernians played a much superior game to their opponents' and scored first, but thereafter Celtic seem to have had the edge because they won 7–1. Hibs also played Lugar Boswell, James McGhee's old side, and won 6–1.

The new year in comparison was a little flat, although the games with Hearts were beginning to catch the imagination again. When they met on 25th January, 'the huge crowd reminded one of the days when the Irishmen were invincible', but unfortunately the result did not. Baird put Hearts in front within a minute and the Tynecastle men won 5–2, but an exciting game ought to have ended closer. Hibs by now had Kelly of Glasgow Hibs in goal, and for the return at Tynecastle they had also Naughton back from a spell with Celtic. McMahon put Hibs ahead with a lovely long shot just after half-time but Hearts came back to draw 1–1. The third meeting was in the Charity Cup and excitement was even higher with the news that Groves, McLaren and McKeown were guesting for Hibs. In the event the huge crowd that packed out Logie Green was disappointed that only Groves turned up, and also that Hibs' rearrangement to accommodate him did not pay off and Hearts won 3–2.

The Final Straws

By August 1890 the decline of Hibs was just about complete. Their financial position was demonstrated when their opening two fixtures against

Linthouse and Airdrieonians were witnessed by 'only the immediate followers of the home club'. Their playing prospects were gauged by the fact that they won neither. As the city of Edinburgh expanded, Hibs were now in perpetual fear of losing their ground to the developers, and in a desperate move they offered the St. Bernards guarantors £300, a huge sum, for the transfer of the lease of Logie Green and the fittings of the ground. This venture was not successful, and the end, as they say, seemed nigh.

Elsewhere, season 1890–91 was a memorable one for a different reason. The Scottish League was formed with eleven teams; Hearts, the only representatives from east of Cambuslang, lost 5–1 to Rangers, and a week later while Hibs were losing 4–1 to Abercorn in Paisley, notched up an Old Firm double of sorts by losing 5–1 to Celtic.

Hibs' problems were more cruelly exposed in the fourth of a midweek series of games at Edinburgh's Exhibition Grounds (Meggatland). Queens Park provided the opposition and 'it was soon clear that the visitors were masters of the situation'. Hibs held out for twenty minutes, then Paul scored a hat-trick before half-time. Then 'a long series of disasters befell Hibernians … and goal followed goal' until the tally was nine, although the playing time was restricted to eighty minutes.

Another defeat followed, 3–1 at the hands of St. Bernards, before Hibs finally pulled off a win against the local Wanderers at Kirkcaldy, in the opening round of the Cup. T. McGhee, McMahon, Lafferty and J. McGhee were the scorers who gave Hibs a 4–1 lead early in the second half, but Hibs were distinctly fortunate to weather a spirited fight-back to win by one goal. Other new names in Hibs' team included Barry at centre-half and Halfpenny at inside-forward, as the search for suitable players continued. The surprise of the round came at Kilsyth where Kilsyth Wanderers put out Renton, whose season was not to be a lot happier than Hibs'.

Hibs achieved another narrow win, also by 4–3, at Mossend where success had often eluded much stronger Hibs sides, and then Hibs entertained the Fife village side Lassodie in the first round of the Shield. The crowd was small 'as it was widely anticipated the home side would have a virtual walkover and the result indicates that this fear was well founded'. Hibs won 7–1.

By now Hibs had indeed been told to quit Easter Road. Their last game at the scene of so much success was their next Cup tie, against their Cup final opponents Dumbarton.

The Cup at this stage was still 'regional', but the regions were drawn up with a curious sense of geography — Edinburgh and Dumbarton were included together presumably on the grounds that they were both outside Glasgow. Anyway the result was not long in doubt. Within a minute a slip by

James McGhee of all people presented the 'Sons' with a goal, and though Hibs had a brief spell when McMahon shot a splendid goal, Dumbarton led 3-1 at the changeover. The second half was worse. Goal followed goal and few were around when Taylor finally made it nine.

A fortnight later, after a 2-2 draw with Partick Thistle, Hibs met Hearts at Tynecastle in the Shield tie which aroused great interest, although 'it appeared to be at the mercy of the Shieldholders'. However, Hibs 'displayed astonishing form' and it took Hearts all their time to beat them. Hearts scored quickly but Halfpenny equalised near half-time 'amid scenes of unwonted excitement'. Then in the second half, 'just when the game seemed anybody's, Taylor dashed down the right and beat Kelly with a magnificent shot' to complete the scoring.

Hibs played a further four matches in the next seven weeks, all on their opponents' grounds and they lost them all, to Linthouse, Hearts, Glasgow Thistle and, finally, Leith Athletic on November 29th. Strangely, they also had three men, Kelly, Quigley and James McGhee, chosen for Edinburgh to play Cleveland; but by now these district games were of much less importance than of yore.

It was a month after the last game with Leith that Hibs fielded a side against Hearts in a 2nd XI tie. Not only did Hearts win, but some of the Hibs players were reported for having played in the Factory Competition, which the SFA considered illegal. Hibs were by now finding it impossible to carry on at all and their final appearance was on February 14th at Bank Park, where Leith Athletic 'generously ... played on behalf of their once formidable opponents'. There was general disappointment 'at the non-appearance of the cream of the Hibernians' — McMahon, Barry, Kelly and even James McGhee were missing. Those who did appear were beaten 6-1 and the last goal of the original Hibs fell to Halfpenny. The difference in fortune between Hibs and Hearts could not have been greater — seven days earlier the Tynecastle side had lifted the Scottish Cup.

Dumbarton and Rangers shared the first League Championship, and played a decider at Celtic Park which was drawn. The League had earlier been reduced to ten clubs by the expulsion of Renton. St. Bernards had been suspended for infringing what was left of the amateur code, and Renton suffered the same fate for playing them. One result was that in early 1891 the SFA called for all member clubs' accounts for auditing. Renton's were returned unread, while of the others, three clubs were found guilty of doctoring their books for the occasion. Cowlairs were suspended as a result, but the other two 'had gone defunct of their own accord'. One was Hibs, who would have taken little comfort from the fact that the other was Glasgow Hibernians.

On August 18th, the SFA secretary reported that eighteen clubs, including Hibs, had failed to pay their subscriptions, and their names were deleted from the roll. A similar scene was enacted the next week at an East of Scotland FA meeting.

However, the story of the season would not be complete without mention of another attempt to keep Hibs going. In the first week of February 1891, before the last game with Leith, a new club, Leith Hibernians, was formed with Mr Payne as president, and as many Hibs players and friends as could be persuaded. Leith Hibs made their debut in February at Logie Green against Edinburgh Northern, a scratch team of St. Bernards players who had escaped suspension. Edinburgh football had certainly seen happier days.

Leith Hibs won 2–1, and another week later, entertained Mossend Swifts at their new ground at Hawkhill: the result was 1–1. Problems arose with Hawkhill also, so this turned out to be Leith Hibs' only home game. Defeats by Leith Athletic (4–2), Broxburn (6–0) and Kirkcaldy Wanderers (3–1) preceded the new club's only other win, 3–1 at Motherwell, followed by a 4–4 draw with Northern, again at Logie Green. Only three further games were played: Leith Hibs lost 6–0 to Hearts and Broxburn, and after losing 8–1 at Mossend, it was decided to call it a day. Their last appearance was at Leith Athletic's five-a-side competition on July 18th at Bank Park.

CHAPTER 5
Reorganisation, 1892–97

The early 1890s were years of great change in Scottish football. Those who believed in the equality of a truly amateur sport could no longer resist the pressures of the bigger clubs, with bigger overheads and greater ambitions, who were finding games against the minnows unprofitable. The first decisive step on the part of the more powerful clubs was, as we have seen, the formation of the Scottish League, so that they would generally play each other only. When this was soon seen to be a success, the other clubs up and down the country organised themselves in various combinations, suddenly afraid of being excluded. The strongest of these were the Scottish Alliance with Kilmarnock, Airdrie, Morton, Partick Thistle etc. and only St. Bernards from the east, and the Scottish Federation, with Falkirk, Motherwell, Albion Rovers etc. Below these were several regional leagues, and indeed one of the last acts of the old Hibs had been to organise an Eastern Alliance, with mainly West Lothian clubs.

Another success for the bigger clubs was the introduction of a qualifying competition for the Scottish Cup; this took place in 1891–92 after a number of similar attempts had failed, and shortly afterwards the main Edinburgh clubs forced through a similar reconstruction of the East of Scotland Shield competition.

There was also the introduction of the penalty kick in 1890. This measure was introduced because of the incidence of deliberate handling to prevent a goal, which itself reflected the change in attitude to the game which was prevalent. It was now more important than hitherto to win, and another tenet of the amateur game was being sacrificed. Professionalism itself was not finally introduced to Scotland until May 1893, so before that arrived it was preceded by the so-called 'professional foul'. It was more than coincidence that it was in 1893 that Queens Park became the last amateur side to win the Cup, and also the last non-league one.

Other changes included the introduction of goalnets in 1892, and the same year *Scottish Sport* reported that 'The Bovril-at-matches idea is evidently catching on. The Rangers are granting a company larger and better accommodation under their grandstand so that next time there is not likely to be a clear-out'. The 1892 Scottish Cup went to Celtic and the League title to Dumbarton; Linthouse won the Alliance, Arthurlie the Federation and Hearts the East of Scotland Shield. The League was reduced from twelve to ten clubs when Cambuslang and Vale of Leven failed to be re-elected.

Although Hibs had not been represented at all on the field during 1891–92, not all of the friends had found watching Leith Athletic an acceptable alternative, and by March 1892 the *Leith Burghs Pilot* was able to report that 'Strenuous efforts are at present being made to resuscitate the old Hibernian FC. It is stated that £100 has already been collected to this end and that steps are being taken to secure suitable ground'. The perhaps more cosmopolitan readership of *The Scotsman* had to wait till October 22nd to read the following. It seemed that the fund-raising had slowed up a bit.

'RESUSCITATION OF THE HIBERNIAN CLUB. A meeting to consider the advisableness of resuscitating the Hibernian Football Club was held last night in St. Mary's Street Upper Hall. There was a crowded attendance and Mr. C. Sandilands was called to the chair. In his opening remarks, the CHAIRMAN said the gentlemen interested in the promotion of the club wished it to be distinctly understood that it would be promoted on somewhat different lines from the old club. They desired it should be non-sectarian. They desired also to keep clear of the old committee and up to the present time had had nothing to do with them. He then proceeded to give a statement of what they had already done towards reviving the club, mentioning that the promoters had their eye on a field which they had hopes of securing. Up to that time they had guarantees of £115 which however was nothing like sufficient to start the club. He intimated that they desired to open with a first class team and a first class ground. He concluded by inviting suggestions; and after several questions had been put and answered, MR. FLOOD moved a resolution declaring that the formation of the Hibernian Football Club had now become an urgent necessity, and empowering those willing to join to proceed to make any preliminary arrangements they might think fit. This was seconded by Mr. Mitchell and unanimously adopted. On the motion of Mr. Galwin it was agreed to accept five shillings from anyone present towards the guarantee fund, that sum afterwards to go towards their first membership ticket. The CHAIRMAN intimated before the meeting ended that the guarantee fund had risen to £130 and names were then taken of persons desirous of guaranteeing with a view to membership, a good number going forward.'

So preparations were put in hand, and it is worth while noting the names of those responsible for them. Apart from Charles Sandilands, the original group included Charles Perry, Frank Rennie, Pat Smith, T. Lang, T. Gilhooly, J. Pollock and Owen Brannigan, whose service to the club was to extend for more than another half-century. The acquisition of the desired field was entrusted to Ernie McCabe, who was in the legal profession, and the site in question, at the time part of the larger open space known as the Drum Park, is that of the present stadium. At that time it had a much greater

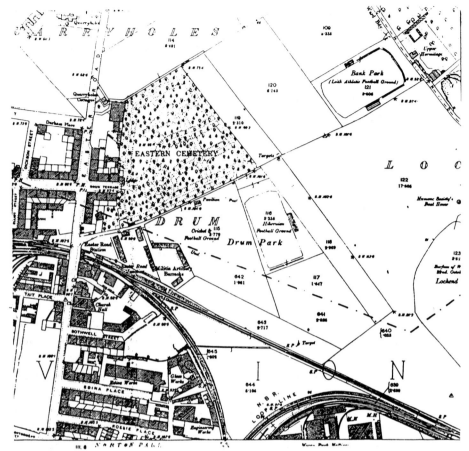

Map showing the second Easter Road Park in the 1890s, as well as the development of the previous ground and the proximity of Leith Athletic's Bank Park. The only access was by the footpath alongside the Eastern Cemetery.

slope than now, and was only a stone's throw from Leith Athletic's Bank Park. There was one uneasy moment in the negotiations, when the proprietor mentioned a group of wild Irishmen who ran a football team in the neighbourhood a year or two earlier, whose outlandish name he could not remember, but Mr. McCabe assured him that he had no idea who that could have been!

The new lease of life was planned to begin on February 4th, and when the great day arrived 'a large and ever increasing crowd lined the enclosure' to see how the new side would fare against League opposition in Clyde. The outcome was satisfactory although the Glasgow side won rather luckily by the odd goal in seven. Apparently lacking only in the teamwork that would surely come, the Hibs team which all but turned round Clyde's three-goal half-time lead was Cox (Leith Athletic), Meechan (Broxburn Shamrock), McPhee (Bathgate Rovers), Gallacher (Hearts Reserves), Adams (East Stirlingshire), Murphy (Benburb), Murray (Campsie), Cox (Burnley), Morton (Glasgow Northern), Goldie (Newton Thistle), Gibb (Rangers). It was not a bad team in the circumstances, and Meechan and Murray later played for Scotland, the former admittedly as a Celtic player.

Hibs were of course too late on the scene for any of the season's competitions, but played over twenty games by the end of May in preparation for the challenges to come. They earned a 3–3 draw in the return fixture with Clyde, again after being three goals down at the interval, and also met League opponents in Renton (2–2), St. Mirren (4–2 at home and 3–4 at Paisley), Leith (3–1 at home, 1–3 and 0–1 away), and Hearts, who beat Hibs 2–1 in May with both sides below full strength. It seemed then that already Hibs would not be disgraced in the League.

Amongst their other opponents Hibs defeated a team of Irish internationalists 2–0, although the visitors included only four of the side that had played against Scotland three days earlier, and drew 1–1 with Middlesbro Ironopolis, the quaintly named Northern League champions who achieved League status the next year. Old friends Cambuslang and Mossend Swifts, both by now well past their most formidable, were beaten 6–1 at Easter Road, and the away draw with East Stirlingshire was restricted to an hour because most of the Hibs' party took the wrong train at Polmont.

As we have seen, Queens Park took the Cup, but an achievement of equal merit was that of Broxburn Shamrock who reached the last four. Celtic took the League by a point from Rangers, while Hearts continued their monopoly in Edinburgh. They took both the Shield and Charity Cup at the expense of St. Bernards, but the latter only after a 3–3 draw in which the Saints were sufficiently upset at a goal of theirs being disallowed to refuse to have anything to do with a replay. It was just like old times.

The Second Division

It was timely that the Second Division of the Scottish League should be formed in 1893, and Hibs took full advantage to be founder members. About half of the sides involved came from the Alliance, and the number also included Clyde and Abercorn who had failed to be re-elected to the First Division. Their places went to the newly organised Dundee and St. Bernards, giving Edinburgh three sides in a League of ten clubs.

After losing to Leith at the Carnival and Floral Fete at Comely Bank, Hibs had three matches in preparation for their League games, and lost the lot, 3–5 at Celtic Park which was not too bad, a close 2–3 to Second-Division comrades Cowlairs and a horrific 10–2 to Hearts at Easter Road before a capacity crowd of 8000.

However, once the League got under way, it was soon clear that Hibs were a match for the field. Their first game brought a narrow but competent win over Glasgow Thistle at Braehead Park, but it was at home that they were unstoppable. Morton were the first visitors to find this out; the Greenock team were soon two goals ahead, but by half-time were 7–2 down and they lost two more after the changeover. Abercorn held Hibs to 2–2 in the first half but lost 7–2. There was a slight hiccup when 'Hibernians played the worst game they have done this season' to lose 4–3 to Cowlairs — who couldn't have been as good as Hearts — but they came back to form to thrash Motherwell, reckoned most likely to test Hibs in the Division, by 8–2.

Hibs won all their other home games easily, and ended them with a 10–1 rout of Port Glasgow Athletic to total fifty-seven goals in nine games, a record of over six goals a game which has not been seriously challenged. If their away form was less spectacular, they were beaten only once, at Motherwell, and they turned the tables on Cowlairs to gain an important 3–2 win in Glasgow in March — because in the end they took the League title from the Springburn side by just two points. The finale to the League season came in May when Hibs defeated a team selected from the rest of the division 5–3 in what was reckoned to be the season's high spot at Greenock.

Generally in the early days of League football, the championship was decided by about Christmas, since there were only eighteen or so games. The Second Division sides soon found that their competition went on a bit longer, because it was interrupted during the autumn by the new Qualifying Cup; 1893–94 saw Hibs' only entry in this competition. They won narrowly but deservedly at Cowdenbeath, and beat Broxburn easily 5–0 at Easter Road, before being drawn to face Vale of Leven at Alexandria. This was a bit unlucky, with teams like Polton Vale, Inveraray, Dunblane and Cronberry Eglinton there for the taking, and the only goal fell to the Vale's Gillies after twenty-five minutes. The exempted sides were the previous year's semi-finalists plus twelve others, so Hibs' League record earned them exemption for 1894–95.

If their Cup dismissal left Hibs' season a little flat, then there were still the local competitions, and it was the Shield this year that added a little spice to things. The entrants had by now been reduced to four qualifiers and four seeds, and two of them, Hibs and Hearts, met on December 9th. With fewer chances, Hibs did well to lead 2–1 at the interval, but thereafter Hearts equalised and took the lead. Hibs desperately rushed through an equaliser of their own which Hearts bitterly disputed but to no avail, and then when soon after a free kick went through Hearts' goal and seemed to touch no-one *en route* and the referee awarded Hibs another goal, a hot dispute arose and Hearts refused to play out the last ten minutes. Then 'the referee for some reason not apparent left the field'. Hearts successfully appealed about him.

A huge crowd attended the replay three weeks later. 'Used as they are to their peculiar pitch', Hibs made a good start and Martin, proving by now a redoubtable centre, put them ahead, but by early in the second half it was the Tynecastle team who had a goal advantage. Hibs were being outplayed now and it 'riled more than one of their number', but especially Rooney, it seems, who was sent off for jumping on Michael. Few believed that Hibs could hold out, but they did, and in the closing moments Howie equalised amid wild scenes.

The third game, at Tynecastle, was an anticlimax. There was severe frost and snow and it seemed unlikely that the game would take place, and when it did 'it was generally agreed Hibernians had decidedly hard lines', as they were leading when they lost goalkeeper Donelly with a broken thumb and Hearts managed to win 3–2. Nevertheless, Hibs had done well against the First-Division runners-up, and in between they had soundly beaten St. Bernards, one place below Hearts, 3–0, as a result of which they were 'entitled to be regarded as a powerful set of fellows'.

They went on to beat St. Bernards another three times, including the final of the City Cup and the semi-final of the Charity Cup, in the final of which, after much wrangling over dates, they eventually got the better of Hearts by 4–2 at Powderhall, and with a hat-trick by Allan Martin. In other games against top leaguers Hibs beat Dundee three times, Leith Athetic twice and even got a draw at Celtic Park; they nearly got a draw at Ibrox too, but lost to two late goals to Rangers.

There were two games of some interest, against Clyde under electric light at Parkhead in February, where the ground was even worse than the illumination, and against Sunderland at the same venue in April for the benefit of Glasgow Thistle, attempting to delay their slide into oblivion. Hibs beat Clyde by the only goal and lost 4–2 to the Tynesiders.

Promotion and relegation were not automatic in the Scottish League until after the First World War, and had hitherto been decided by voting, the bottom three sides in the First Division having to apply for re-election. Dundee and Leith were re-elected, but Renton, who had amassed just four points, were not, and their place went to Clyde, at the expense of Hibs and Cowlairs. There was a certain amount of antipathy towards Hibs in some quarters — at least one newspaper stated that they 'were not the type of club wanted in the First Division', and there were suspicions that Celtic had led the lobby against their promotion — so another season of the Second Division was in prospect.

Even before the League campaign started it was clear that Hibs were too good for the Second Division. They beat both Hearts and Rangers away from home and trounced Morton 9–0 at Easter Road. When the League did get under way, they scored twenty-four times in their first four games, and over the eighteen games accumulated no fewer than ninety-two goals, an average of more than five per game and a record for British football that no-one has since come close to. Hibs' top score was nine against Renton, and they scored eight against Cowlairs — twice. They also lost to Renton, and, for the second time, at Motherwell. Their exciting play attracted big crowds everywhere they went, and Dundee Wanderers even took over Dundee's East Dock Street ground because their own Clepington Park was too small. One scoring record that Hibs missed fell to Airdrie when they beat Dundee Wanderers 15–1 on December 1st.

Free from Qualifying Cup engagements and before the Cup proper, Hibs twice found time to take their skills south of the Border, where they beat Newcastle United 3–1 but lost by one goal in three to Newton Heath, a side with romantic beginnings in the goods yard of the Lancashire and Yorkshire Railway Company, and who have achieved rather more recognition under their present name of Manchester United.

When the Cup ties did come round Hibs dispatched Forfar Athletic with scant ceremony, before the second-round draw provided them with the plum they had looked for — against Celtic at Easter Road. Hibs thus 'satisfactorily brought about what they had otherwise been unable to achieve, meeting the redoubtable Glasgow combination at Easter Road'. There had been bad feeling for some time over Celtic's unwillingness to honour an agreement to play a return fixture in Edinburgh, and with Hibs' home record of six goals a game, their supporters anticipated the tie with rather more relish than Celtic's. Additional staging and banking gave the record 15,000 crowd a good view, and as the pent-up enthusiasm of the crowd communicated itself to the players, neither side could take any of their chances in a frantic first half. But the second half had hardly begun when M. Murray made a splendid run up Hibs' left wing and sent the ball into the net 'amid a scene of almost indescribable emotion'. Celtic came back, and were awarded a penalty for tripping, but McGinn tipped Madden's kick over the bar. This signalled the turning point, and Murphy scored again for Hibs in the last minute.

The euphoria of Hibs' victory soon evaporated, however, when Celtic's protest that wing-half Bobby Neill had played a game for Ashfield the previous June, four days after signing for Hibs, was upheld. A replay was ordered, and the admission raised to one shilling to prevent the troubles of the first game. But Celtic had alienated most of their support both in Edinburgh and Glasgow, and the 3000 spectators who surrounded the snowclad pitch greeted the Glasgow team with hoots and boos.

Again a stiff first half was followed by the opening goal at the start of the second, but this time it fell to Celtic. Hibs fought back, but unfortunately 'Martin invariably did the wrong thing at the crucial moment' and the deficit remained until the controversial finish. A free kick by Doyle, who had made a speciality of them since his ealier days with Hibs, went into Hibs' net without touching anybody, but the referee awarded a goal. Some Hibs players were on the point of leaving the field in disgust, but the club president, Mr. Perry, persuaded them to continue, once the crowd had retired from the pitch.

That replay was on December 29th, and the disappointment of it was shown in the faint-hearted displays that resulted in 6–1 defeats by Hearts and Rangers on the first two days in January. But better results came in the remaining friendlies, with St. Mirren, Celtic, Queens Park and Third Lanark all losing at Easter Road — Third Lanark by 8–1 — and Hibs drawing 4–4 at Cathkin and losing only 3–2 at Celtic Park.

Meanwhile the East of Scotland Shield had gone to Bo'ness, after a wrangle over its organisation had ended with Hibs, Hearts, St. Bernards and Leith Athletic resigning from the Association and so not taking part. Instead, the four formed the Edinburgh League, a competition which signally failed to catch the imagination, and in fact was often unfinished. In its first year, Hibs came out on top against Saints and Leith but lost two vital points in their opening game at Tynecastle. The most important local derby beyond any doubt was the Scottish Cup semi-final between Hearts and St. Bernards, which the latter won by the only goal in 180 minutes of play. St. Bernards went on to beat Renton in the final at Ibrox to become the third Edinburgh side in nine years to lift the trophy.

There was trouble too in the Charity Cup; Hibs and Leith Athletic drew 1–1 at Logie Green but Hibs refused to play extra time and so the tie was given to Leith, who went on to lose to Hearts.

Second Time Lucky

This time Hibs' claim for promotion was irresistible, and they achieved it at the first ballot. The votes were Dundee 14, Hibs 11, Dumbarton 10, Motherwell 4 and Leith 3, so that Hibs replaced Leith Athletic. Leith were

THE LEAGUE RACE.

The above Illustration gives the positions of the First Division League Clubs up to, but not including, to-day.

Edinburgh sides dominated the 1895–1896 League Championship race, as this illustration from the 'Evening Times' shows.

sufficiently upset by this to propose at the following year's meeting that promotion should be decided by Test Matches, as was the case in England, but they found little support.

In their opening First Division fixture at Cathkin, 'Hibernians forwards combined like clockwork, and the Volunteers famous half-back line was fairly outclassed' as the Edinburgh side scored seven times. This was followed by a convincing win over Celtic. Oddly, Celtic had at this time three players from the different eras of Hibs — Sandy McMahon of the old Hibs, Martin recently transferred, and the winger Blessington who had played for Leith Hibernians, although he was better known in the capital as a Leith Athletic man. If Hibs were unable to keep this form up, they did top the League with eleven points from their first six games, and were serious challengers for the title until three successive defeats around the end of November ended these aspirations, and they finished third, behind Celtic and Rangers.

Martin, as we have seen, had gone to Celtic, but his replacement was another promising young goalscorer, John Kennedy, who formed a lethal wing with Pat Murray, while another addition to the staff was the prodigal Willie Groves after spells with Celtic, West Bromwich Albion and Aston Villa, during which he had played for the English League against the Scottish League.

Kennedy scored hat-tricks in consecutive League games against

FIRST GOAL FOR HIBS. — BELL FOOZLES AN
EASY SHOT.

RANGERS' SECOND PENALTY KICK — M'COLL, THE HIBS'
CUSTODIAN, CLEVERLY CATCHES THE BALL.

THE REFEREE CAUTIONS "NICK" SMITH.

BOBBIE O'NEIL OUTSTRIPS AND FAIRLY BOXES OSWALD.

One of Hibs' most notable cup successes was the victory at Ibrox in February 1896. These illustrations indicate how the main incidents were seen by the 'Evening Times' artist, who had them all ready in time for the 8 o'clock sports edition.

Dumbarton and Hearts. Although Martin and Murphy had played in international trial matches the previous season, Bobby Neil became the first of the current Hibs to be capped, against Wales in March 1896, and he was followed a week later against Ireland by right-winger Murray. Inside-forward W. Smith, another regular marksman, made the international reserve side.

If the League campaign had gone smoothly if a little quietly, the Cup provided the drama. It was not noticeable in the early rounds where East Stirling put up a sterner fight in the first than Raith did in the second, but the third round tie at Ibrox was a memorable one. A crowd of 15,000 was present, and 'the display of football was considerably above that expected in a Scottish Cup-tie'. Hibs scored first when goalkeeper Bell unaccountably let in a long shot from Smith, and a second came in a melee occasioned by a well-placed free kick by Breslin. Smith of Rangers then headed a goal but Oswald lost the chance of equalising by sending a penalty high over the bar. When the second half started, Rangers had a goal disallowed, but from the free kick they got instead, McCreadie scored easily. No sooner was the ball centred than Groves put Hibs ahead again with a fine effort, and as the excitement mounted, Rangers were given a second penalty, but McCall stopped McPherson's shot in brilliant fashion to give Hibs the win their play had earned. After the game, the Rangers' goalkeeper Bell, taking the defeat personally, put on his clothes in silence and left the ground. He was never seen there again, so it is not known what he thought of Oswald and McPherson.

The Logie Green Final

The semi-finals brought Renton to Easter Road, where Hibs appeared nervous and conceded a quick goal to Campbell, but they got going eventually and Murray ran the ball in when for once goalkeeper Dickie was unable to clear cleanly. Renton were not the same force in the second half, but it took a shot by Neil through a crowd of players with just five minutes to go to beat them. Renton in fact did not think they were beaten yet, and they protested that Hibs' back Robertson 'had committed' himself during the close season. The judgment went against them on the grounds that admission to the game in question at Larkhall had been free, but Renton still would not accept the position, and sought an interdict to prevent the final taking place. Lord Low turned this down and so Hibs were able to turn out in the final — against Hearts at Logie Green, where the game had been moved despite the doubts of some. 'It was accepted that the 22001st man who entered the ground was in no hurry to die at 1/- admission and the attendance numbered 16034' (Reid).

Those who did turn up did not have long to wait for a goal; in three minutes Robertson handled, and Baird's penalty for Hearts went in off McCall's legs. Groves' dribbling was conspicuous early on but he tired later, Murphy in particular was off colour, and Hearts were generally on top. There was no more scoring in the first half, but early in the second King rattled the ball along the goalline and though McCall got a hand to it, it fell into the net. This took a lot out of Hibs and Michael soon headed a third. O'Neill did get a goal but it was too late to matter. The Hibs side at Logie Green for the only Scottish Cup final outside Glasgow was: McCall, Robertson, McFarlane, Breslin, Neil, Murphy, Murray, Kennedy, Groves, Smith, O'Neill.

The East of Scotland competitions provided little attraction after the Cup defeat. Hibs made little show in the Edinburgh League, losing twice to Hearts and failing to beat Leith Athletic. The title went to Tynecastle, and Hibs also lost to the maroons in the Rosebery Cup, though on this occasion they were most unfortunate to do so. Hearts won that too, beating Leith 8–2 in the final.

The only worthwhile result that Hibs achieved after the Cup final was the beating of English league champions Aston Villa 2–1 at Perry Barr, even if the Midlanders got their own back with a sparkling 5–2 win at Easter Road a fortnight later. There were several friendlies between Scottish and English sides, and Everton supporters might like to know that their team lost 5–2 to East Stirlingshire and 4–1 to Wishaw Swifts. So might Liverpool supporters.

If the Scottish Cup provided the memories for 1895–96, the following season provided the most exciting scrap for the League title to date, with Hearts, Hibs, Celtic and Rangers all in at the death.

Hibs got off to the best possible start with two points at the expense of Celtic; a huge crowd of 10,000 welcomed the new season, an excellent win and the return of Martin in a Hibs' jersey. Although there was an early slip-up at Dundee, the results continued to be good, and by November 21st Hibs had played all but four of their eighteen League matches, and had collected 23 points. They had beaten Hearts 2–0 before an even bigger crowd, and shared the points in two exciting games with Rangers, in each case the home side coming from behind to win 4–3. Hibs were three points ahead of Hearts, four of Celtic and six of Rangers, but both Glasgow sides had two more games to play.

Hibs' next two games were crucial. The first of them took them to Parkhead where 18,000 spectators saw Hibs rescue a point with a late equaliser by Martin. Celtic, however, had not been able to field a full-strength team, as Meechan, Battles and Divers refused to turn out unless the press were excluded, because there had been newspaper criticism of their performances in a Glasgow cup tie the previous week. A week later Hibs lost both points at Tynecastle, where McColl failed to hold a shot from Robertson in the opening minute in the muddy conditions. Hibs indeed were fortunate to be behind by only that goal at the interval, and later the experienced Baird went back and successfully reinforced his defence to thwart Hibs' second-half rally.

This left Hibs' possible total 28 points, with two games to go, both against St. Mirren, Hearts had the same maximum with three to go, Rangers 27 with four to go and Celtic, now favourites, 30 with four games to go.

Rangers lost at Logie Green on Boxing Day and that effectively ended their aspirations, but a week earlier they had beaten Celtic, which reduced their possible score to 28 too. Hearts beat Third Lanark at Cathkin.

The deciding games were not played out till February. Hibs had to play St. Mirren twice because their game earlier in the season at Easter Road had been abandoned, goalless, after half an hour, and their match at Paisley had been declared a friendly on account of ground conditions and Hibs had won that 3–2. It proved unfortunate because after beating St. Mirren 3–0 at Easter Road, Hibs lost the return 2–0, both games again taking place in dreadful conditions. Hibs' title hopes floundered as much as the players did in the Love Street mud, because Hearts were beating Clyde 5–1 in Glasgow, with the prospect of a home game to come against the same opposition.

Hearts duly scored another five against Clyde a week later, and could hardly have believed their ears to hear that Dundee had scored the only goal at Celtic Park to give them the title.

So Hibs finished second, and they did achieve a 100% home record, the only time they have achieved this. Of course, with only nine home games it was not altogether a unique feat, and in fact Rangers managed it as well the same season.

After the excitement of the League, the season fell a bit flat in Edinburgh. Hibs' cup run extended to a 10–1 win in Perth against Duncrub Park, although 'not apparently eager to score', and then a 3–0 defeat at Ibrox where they never looked like saving the tie, and the goals came from McPherson and Low (2).

The Edinburgh League had been altered, without greatly enhancing its appeal, by calling it the East of Scotland League and including Dundee and East Stirling. Hibs beat Hearts 5–1 with some rare inspiration and a hat-trick by Dougal, but lost the return as well as one match to each of the other sides except Leith, and thus the title went again to Hearts. Hibs, however, took the Charity Cup, beating Hearts 3–0 with goals from Martin (2) and Murray, after thrashing Leith 7–0 in the semi-final.

One pleasing feature of the season was the inclusion of three Hibs' men in the national team against Wales, the right-wing triangle of the consistent Pat Breslin, Kennedy and Murray. Internally there would also have been satisfaction at the performances of the two new forwards, Price and Dougal, and the half-back play of Raisbeck.

The next season fell a bit flat a bit earlier. Hibs' opening League engagements took them to Parkhead and Ibrox, and they returned pointless. This made their third game with Hearts an important one, because Hearts were only one point better off, and both were keen to keep in touch with the Old Firm.

The outcome was a rough game. First, McCartney, the Tynecastle back, rushed at Kennedy with the ball yards away, but Martin's penalty attempt was saved. Hibs were having the better of things, and 'Murphy's clean and timeous kicking' was noted, but 'often Hibernians' good work was thrown to the wind by the uselessness of Smith'. Still, when Murray passed McCartney with apparent ease and centred, Martin scored from close in. Robertson soon equalised from twenty yards, and until half-time 'play was really class'.

It seemed that Michael had been singled out by Hibs as a likely source of trouble, and they had shown an awareness of this throughout the first period. Hearts therefore reorganised their formation on resumption for his benefit, 'but the referee continued to fail to notice how he was occasionally knocked about'. And 'once away on a likely run a couple of Hibernians sandwiched him and threw him in a manner sufficient to have killed any ordinary mortal'. Michael, it seems, was a character; according to Reid, 'he was known to his friends as the india-rubber man, to other people as the battering ram. He would have charged a stone wall and risen up, rubbing his cranium. Then, spying the ball at a distance he would have gone for it as a terrier goes for a rat'.

On the present occasion, however, even Michael's remarkable qualities were unable to break the deadlock, and the points were shared. Then a defeat from St. Bernards after being two up meant Hibs had lost seven out of eight points.

Eight straight wins did put them back near the top, but Celtic and Rangers, who had dropped only five points between them, had three games each in hand. With Hearts dropping points quite regularly, when Hibs lost again to Celtic and Rangers, the latter by a decisive 5–0, at Easter Road, it was truly a two-horse race which Celtic finally won, unbeaten. So when a week after the Rangers game Hibs met Hearts again, 'the onlookers were slow in finding material to get excited over'. Nevertheless, Hibs finished third, with 22 points, and Hearts fourth.

Underwood Park, Paisley was a quagmire when Hibs started their Cup campaign on it, and with Abercorn scoring in the first three minutes, Hibs were relieved that a second-half goal from Murray meant that the tie could be decided at Easter Road. In due course it was, by 7–1, then East Stirling put up a stiff fight before a late goal by Atherton gave Hibs the comfort of a two-goal lead. Atherton, the only newcomer to establish a regular place during the season, was a Welshman, and the only Hibs player to date to have been capped by that country.

Hibs' Cup run ended one game later at Cathkin, where Beveridge scored the only first-half goal, and Gillespie the second after Hibs had spent most of the afternoon deep in defence.

The four main Edinburgh clubs were now back in the East of Scotland FA, having agreed that Hibs and Hearts should get byes to the Shield semi-finals, with Leith and St. Bernards meeting the qualifying competition finalists to reach the last four. Hibs made a rather ignominious start to the new arrangements by losing to Leith, who lost in turn to Hearts.

The other local tournaments did not go too well either. Hibs took eleven points from their eight League games, but that was not enough to prevent the McCrae Cup going to Tynecastle again. The Charity Cup ended up beside it. Hibs beat St. Bernards 4–1 after a draw, but were drubbed 6–1 in the final. The only creditable result that the Easter Road side achieved after their Cup exit was a 4–2 win over English league runners-up Sunderland on the Spring holiday.

CHAPTER 6

The Cup Again and the League, 1897–1903

A tendency to nomadism characterised the entire histories of the Edinburgh clubs, but especially in the five years spanning the turn of the century, this wanderlust became an epidemic.

It was not always voluntary. It was the Property and Finance Committee of the Heriot Trust who evicted St. Bernards from Logie Green in 1899, and they spent a while with rather unsatisfactory facilities at Powderhall — there were always long delays while the ball was recovered from the Water of Leith — before moving on to the Gymnasium. Leith had left Bank Park for Beechwood Park, and in 1899 moved again, to their former home at Hawkhill. They even became defunct in September 1901, but a new club was immediately formed and fulfilled the club's fixtures from the same week, and by November Leith were installed at Logie Green, no less, albeit at a pitch rather nearer Powderhall than had been the one used by St. Bernards.

Even Hearts and Hibs were not satisfied where they were. Hearts tried to acquire Meggetland from the Caledonian Railway Co. in 1897, but their bid was turned down, while at the end of 1902 it was reported that the proposed amalgamation of three local clubs to form the present Aberdeen FC was agreed to counter a move by Hibs to the Granite City to get away from both the competition and their unsatisfactory sloping pitch in Edinburgh.

If the five years under consideration produced uncertainty in Edinburgh football, they also produced a swing in fortune towards the capital. It certainly did not start there, because season 1898–99 saw Rangers' notable record of full points from their eighteen games. At the start it looked as if the main challenge would come from Easter Road, as Hibs dropped only one point from their first six games, which included their first of not too many doubles over Celtic.

However, at this point Hibs ran into Hearts at Tynecastle, and the keen struggle anticipated failed to take place as Hearts won easily by 4–0. Three weeks later there was a repeat, Hearts winning 5–1, and Hibs' title chances seemed to have gone, but they won their next two games before they first met Rangers.

It was anticipated that Rangers would find it as hard to maintain their run at Easter Road as anywhere, and it certainly turned out that way. No side could have such a run as the Ibrox side were having without some luck, and it will surprise few that they owed their win against Hibs to a disputed last-minute penalty, claimed by their captain, Hamilton, for a foul by Robertson near the corner flag. To make matters worse the referee was the former Hearts full-back Jimmy Adams, whose popularity had vanished by the time he ended the game, and hustled and assaulted on his way to the pavilion, he was fortunate to leave Easter Road unharmed. Rangers were in fact lucky enough to be on level terms when the game reached that stage, as they had only equalised Hibs winger Gemmell's third goal a little earlier while Hibs' other winger was off injured.

Five weeks later the sides met in the return fixture, and the script came from a different pen. On a dreadfully heavy pitch Hibs crossed midway only once in the opening fifteen minutes and were lucky to be level. In the next fifteen minutes Rangers scored five, though it is recorded that before the interval Martin did have a shot at goal. In the second half it was soon seven, and as 'feeling was imported into the play of Hibernians', they conceded two penalties. Fortunately, one was missed, but Smith soon scored the ninth: 'the Hibernians were now all over a beaten team,' concluded the reporter rather unnecessarily and went home, missing yet another goal. That, on Christmas Eve, was Hibs' last League game; they took only four points from the last six games and finished fourth.

It wasn't Hibs' year in the Cup either. In the first round they beat Royal Albert 2-1, but did not get much praise, since Hearts reserves had beaten the same opponents 6-0 a week earlier. Queens Park beat them 5-1 in the second round, being four up at the interval.

The rest of the season was hardly more encouraging. West Calder's kick and rush tactics nearly paid off in a mudbath in the first Shield tie, and with Porter, Atherton and Breslin all disabled in a rough match, Hibs were glad enough to win 3-2. They defeated Leith easily enough in the semi-final, by 10-1, but lost the final by the only goal to a Hearts side weakened by sickness.

In the East of Scotland League, Raith made the numbers up to six, and beat Hibs at Kirkcaldy. Hibs in fact only managed about a point a game and were not in contention for the title. They were not in contention for the Rosebery Cup either after another defeat by Hearts in the semi-final.

Building for Success

While there had undoubtedly been some disappointment at the way Hibs had failed to maintain their early challenge in 1898–99, it must also be said that that and the following season were a period of transition, and their record in the years immediately following shows that the changes which took place were in general for the better. Martin had spent much of the season just

The Hibs' team of 1902, apparently photographed through a telescope. Unfortunately the identities of the players are unknown.

ended on the sidelines through injury, and more than one new centre was tried before the job of leading the attack fell to Hamilton Handling, who had already shown an aptitude for scoring from his previous position of centre-half. Inside left Callaghan from Jordanhill had made his debut in February 1899, and was to stay for almost two decades, filling many roles including goalkeeper on a number of occasions. William McCartney, a big robust tearaway sort of player, had made the right-wing berth his own, while Bobby Atherton had established himself on the left. And James Main, later to be capped as a full-back, made his first appearance in October 1899, at centre. The full-back duties were currently the responsibility of Hogg and Bob Glen, who had captained Renton's Cup final team of 1895 and had come to Hibs via Rangers, while McCall in goal and the experienced Breslin played in the international trial matches during the season.

If success was not immediate, then at least Hibs were only pipped by a point by Celtic for the runners-up spot in the League, with Hearts a further point adrift. Hibs even got their first League win over their Tynecastle rivals since 1896–97, with Handling rushing through the only goal when goalkeeper Rennie could only partially clear. Hearts had been almost invincible around Edinburgh for some time, so 'such an unusual occurrence as an Edinburgh side defeating the Heart of Midlothian naturally aroused much enthusiasm, the Hibernians players being congratulated on all sides'.

Handling was also the marksman when Hibs completed the double four weeks later. Hibs were masters throughout, but McLaren put Hearts ahead with a lucky goal. Hibs' centre equalised from a defensive slip, then scored the winner from a second-half penalty. Over the League campaign, while it is true that Hibs managed only one point from the Old Firm, they did not lose to anybody else, and so third place was a fair reflection of their performance.

The Cup brought more excitement for Edinburgh fans when Hibs and Hearts met again, in the second round. Goals from half-back Robertson and Handling (2) had given Hibs a narrow first-round win at Hamilton, and their supporters were more confident of success at Tynecastle than for some time.

The crowd was 13,000 and the home element were soon cheering as Michael bustled Hogg so much that he shot through his own goal. Hibs responded, and Handling set up the chance for Atherton to equalise 'while the centre and Callaghan were attending to the goalkeeper'. In the second half, play was rougher and poorer 'and it was apparent that a draw was inevitable'.

The replay was 'one of the most exciting football matches played in Edinburgh for many days'. The start was even, then a long shot from Buick 'apparently found the goalkeeper unprepared', and before half-time a mistake by Glen gave Hearts a second goal. After the changeover, 'seldom could Hearts get out of their own half', but by the close Hibs had only one scrambled goal from Reid to show for their desperate attacking, and it was Hearts who made the third-round ballot.

The two Edinburgh sides saw a lot of each other in 1899–1900. Apart from the East of Scotland League games, they also met in the new Inter-City League, which they formed with the four main Glasgow sides. As they also both reached the finals of the East of Scotland Shield and the Charity Cup — the latter went to a replay — that meant eleven meetings in all, with each side winning three.

In the Shield, Hibs beat Mossend Swifts quite comfortably by 3–0, then St. Bernards 2–0 after a 2–2 draw, before the final with Hearts. Hibs ultimately won easily enough, 3–0, but McWattie had to save a penalty before the first goal came. The Charity Cup was the reverse. Hibs had a late goal by Murray to thank for squeezing past Leith Athletic by 3–2, but put up little resistance in the final after Bobby Walker had scored two early goals and went down 3–0.

Hibs' interest in the East of Scotland League lasted even less time than hitherto, with defeats from Hearts and Dundee before the end of August. They lost only one more, but on that occasion were 4–0 down at half-time to Raith Rovers — it ended 4–3 — and Hearts clinched the title with a 0–0 draw at Easter Road in May.

The Inter-City predictably went west. Hibs drew twice with Hearts, but took only six points from eight games with Glasgow opponents, four from Queens Park.

It was in August 1900 that Hibs made their biggest scoop in the transfer market for years. Harry Rennie, Hearts' international goalkeeper, was transferred to Celtic, but there was some mix-up over terms, as a result of which the player 'was cast back on the Hearts', and before the Tynecastle side could sort things out, Hibs had nipped in and signed him. Hearts were a bit upset about this, and charged Hibs with paying a bonus greater than the permitted £10, but Hibs claimed that the money was close-season wages since May. 'Since it was the first case of its kind, Hibs were exonerated, and the facts referred to the International League Board for a definite ruling.'

The extrovert goalkeeper had indeed an unusual style of discharging his duties. He often kept goal on the half-way line — goalkeepers were allowed to handle anywhere in their own half until 1912 — and his play would resemble in some degree that of a modern sweeper, who can be found far from his own penalty box when his team is in possession, but whose main job is to be on hand when danger threatens. Rennie's anticipation and speed seem to have enabled him to play his strange game generally with great success, but reports of the odd goal lost with Mr. Rennie out of his goal conjure up pictures of the custodian stranded somewhere in midfield, rather than caught two feet off his line by an ultra-accurate lob.

While it could not by any means be said that Hearts had been a one-man team — after all they still had Bobby Walker and others — they certainly missed Rennie, and finished the League programme in second-bottom place, having to apply for re-election. Then came a complete reversal in the second half of the season, as the Tynecastle men went on to win the Cup.

Hibs meanwhile had another quite successful season, finishing third in the League behind Rangers and Celtic. The highlight of this performance was the superb win on the September holiday over Rangers, 'their most crushing defeat for a long time and their first this season'. Raisbeck and Atherton each scored twice as 'Hibernians held their redoubtable opponents at all points' and won 4–1. A month later they made up for this by losing at Easter Road to give Queens Park only their second League win.

There were eleven teams in the League in 1900–01; Partick Thistle and Morton had been elected to the positions held by St. Bernards and Clyde, and Queens Park, who had long realised their mistake in not joining the League, had now publicly admitted it by applying for admission. The amateurs still had enough friends to ensure success at the first attempt, and an extra place was made available. Of the new sides, Morton were easily the most impressive, finishing fourth and taking three points from Hibs on the way.

Another feature of the autumn was the bad weather, and Hibs had three games abandoned in the space of nine weeks. The League game at Cappielow was stopped without trouble in October, an East of Scotland League game with Leith was cut short in November without many noticing, then in December, when a League game at Ibrox was abandoned with Rangers leading Hibs 2–0, the police had to check an attempt to storm the pavilion, and numerous window panes were broken.

When the Cup ties came round, they provided one of Edinburgh's most successful days ever, with the four sides scoring twenty-four goals in total without reply. Hibs' contribution was seven against Dumbarton, and Hearts matched this against Mossend. St. Bernards beat Partick 5–0, and Leith scored four at Forfar. Hibs found the second round harder, and were thankful that an early score by Atherton got them a draw with Royal Albert on a tight and very soft pitch at Larkhall. Two second-half goals from Handling and Robertson against Morton then gave Hibs a semi-final tie at Tynecastle.

It was a repeat of the previous year. In the first game, Bell gave Hearts a rather fortunate first-half lead. Hibs fought back persistently in the second period, and 'away the Hearts could not drive their opponents' who nevertheless could do no more than equalise through Murray. In the replay, Porteous gave Hearts a lead at half-time again, and Walker increased it before Handling converted a penalty for 'an infringement by Allan within the dreaded line'.

There were still the numerous lesser competitions. In the Inter-City League, Hibs beat both Rangers and Celtic at Easter Road and took four points from Hearts, but their tally of fourteen points from ten games did not bring the title. In the East of Scotland League, with Hearts not their usual dominant selves, Hibs' final match at Dens Park was the decider. Hibs had to win, but lost 2–1, so Dundee were the champions.

Only in the Shield did Hearts get the better of Hibs, by the only goal after a draw in the first round, only to find that Leith Athletic had selected 1901 as the year for their only win in the competition. Leith beat Hearts 3–2 in the final. Hibs were back in form for the Charity Cup, though; an Atherton hat-trick eliminated Leith, and Hibs did even better to rout Hearts 4–0 in the final.

The strange thing about Hibs' next season was how it mirrored Hearts' previous one. Hibs managed to finish sixth in the League but had only six wins to their name and were level on points with Queens Park who were third bottom. Early on it did not seem likely that Hibs would do even that well, with only three points from the first six games. Their best performances in the championship were reserved for the games with Rangers and an 8–1 hammering of Queens Park in September.

Hibs' victory at Ibrox was based on a curious goal, when McCulloch of Hibs, not even meaning to shoot, put the ball too far ahead of himself but goalkeeper Dickie, coming out to collect it, took his eye off the ball completely and it rolled slowly into the net. The win was deserved largely on the performance of the defence, which did not need the cushion of Handling's 'safety' goal ten minutes from time. In the return, Hibs were not far off a rare double, as they led with only five minutes remaining, but Rangers equalised from a penalty and stole both points with a further goal in the last minute. Hibs had a new grandstand under construction, and it provided seating for the first time for the game with Rangers.

Two more changes were needed during the season. Murray retired and was rewarded with a benefit against Celtic, while later in the year Handling had to call it a day after a serious injury, and his benefit later on was against Hearts. Hibs at this time ran quite a small pool for an ambitious club, with only about fifteen players, Rennie, Hogg, Glen, Breslin, Harrower, Robertson, McCartney, McGeechie, Divers, Callaghan, Atherton, McCall, Gray and McCulloch, regularly involved, and Paddy Canon trained them.

Once re-election had been avoided, attention switched as usual to the Cup, and Hibs swept through their ties with a panache which had not characterised all of their campaigns. McCartney and Divers scored the goals in a rather low-key victory over Clyde, then McGeachie had two as Hibs won easily at Port Glasgow. Despite the big League score earlier in the season, Queens Park were expected to be a stern test for Hibs in the third round, and despite Hearts' playing at Parkhead and Kilmarnock at Ibrox, a crowd of 12,000 turned out to see if they were. The game started amid great excitement, and Queens delighted their friends by scoring first, but by half-time McGeachan had scored three and Divers another, and thereafter 'what had seemed to be a great and keen struggle ended in a comparative farce' and a score of 7–1.

The semi-final took Hibs and 30,000 spectators to Ibrox, and for the third round in succession Hibs won far more easily than expected. Divers opened the scoring when Smith miskicked, though Rangers thought him offside. Dickie was so sure of it that he made no attempt to save. Then Hibs were awarded a penalty but Divers blasted it high over. Hibs were even more on top in the second half, but goals would not come, and the fear arose that Rangers might just be let off the hook and snatch a goal. McCartney allayed these fears when he scored the second, but later had the misfortune to break his leg.

A Neutral Venue

The final was also arranged for Ibrox, but two weeks after the semi-final came the first Ibrox disaster, when wooden terracing collapsed during the game between Scotland and England, causing many deaths. With Hampden under reconstruction, the final was switched to Parkhead. It was just too bad that Hibs were to meet Celtic.

Hibs' preparations for the 1902 final provide a distinct contrast to the modern 'away-from-it-all' build-up at a several-starred hotel with saunas, golf, steaks etc. After the day's training, the players had to report back to the ground, where they were penned in the spartan room below the stand to play dominoes and the new game of table tennis until ten o'clock, presumably to keep them away from the temptations of the city. They were sustained through this nightly incarceration by potted head sandwiches of the doorstep variety and huge mugs of cocoa to make sure that they were in the best physical shape when the important day eventually dawned.

For the final, McCartney was replaced by the youthful McCall, while Celtic still included McMahon, the last playing member of the 'old' Hibs. McMahon was much involved in the first half, as the gale which blew the length of the park ensured that Celtic would monopolise the attacking. The feature of this period was the play of Harrower and Glen in protecting Rennie, who was obliged to remain in the conventional position between his goalposts. Half-time arrived with the goalkeeper still unbeaten, and when play resumed the wind was stronger than ever. Several Celtic clearances were blown for corners, yet on one occasion Livingstone got far enough upfield to rattle Rennie's posts. Against that, Atherton had what seemed a good goal disallowed.

Then with just fifteen minutes remaining, Hibs scored, from yet another corner. Callaghan took it, and when the ball reached Andy McGeechan, he, never one afraid to try something different, wheeled round and backheeled the ball past McArthur. The story was prevalent after the game that McGeechan had only got the ball because, in a fair imitation of McArthur's West of Scotland accent he had told Barney Battles, the Parkhead full-back, to leave it alone. In any case the goal stood, and with such support from the elements one was enough and Hibs took the Scottish Cup for the second time. The line-up at Celtic Park was Rennie, Gray, Glen, Breslin, Harrower, Robertson, McCall, McGeechan, Divers, Callaghan and Atherton.

The trophy was presented to Mr. Phil Farmer, the club president, in the Alexandra Hotel, before the team boarded their train. 'It was strange,' reported the *Scottish Referee*, 'that the Hibernians' victory was so universally popular', and 'there were high jinks in Edinburgh when the Hibernians' special arrived. The rejoicings after Hearts' victory last year were not in it.' A band was waiting to greet them at Haymarket, secretary Dan McMichael carried the cup onto the four in hand, and captain Bobby Atherton held it aloft as the party was conveyed along Princes Street.

At the east end, the assembly numbered about ten thousand, and traffic in Princes Street and Leith Street had to be stopped. It was Edinburgh's sixth Cupwinning team in sixteen years, 'and no previous one had received a warmer or more enthusiastic welcome'. So enthusiastic in fact that the majority were unable to hear Bobby Atherton's musical rendition from the balcony, apparently a clever parody on the popular ditty 'Dolly Grey'. The trophy itself was quietly taken to the president's shop in Leith Walk, to frustrate the more serious souvenir hunters.

With the popularity of their success, Hibs took part in more competitions this year. They had started the season by losing by the only goal to Celtic in the Glasgow Exhibition Cup, but ended it by thrashing the same opponents in the Glasgow Charity Cup, one of the most handsome pieces of silverware up for competition. They had beaten Rangers and St. Mirren, the latter at Tynecastle, strangely for a Glasgow tie, to reach the final, and at Hampden turned on a superb exhibition to beat Celtic 6-2, with a hat-trick for McGeechan. This was the only occasion that the Glasgow Charity Cup left its native city, and the Hibs' line-up on that particular occasion was Rennie, Gray, Glen, Breslin, Hogg, Robertson, Stewart, McGeechan, Callaghan, Atherton and Buchan.

Back in Edinburgh, McGeechan was also on the mark to score the only goal against Hearts to take the Rosebery Cup, but the Tynecastle men took the Shield by the odd goal in three. A further move to restrict this competition to the four senior sides was defeated by nineteen votes to seven. There was a better than usual performance in the minor leagues — Hibs won the local one and therefore the McCrae Cup, but in the Inter-City one, two

THE LEAGUE CHAMPIONSHIP.

WHAT WILL THE CARD BE?

The League Championship of 1902–03 was for a time a three horse race, and the 'Scottish Referee' was disinclined to forecast a winner. This cartoon suggests that Hibs' victory was just magic!

defeats in a week by Hearts took the title instead to Tynecastle. Both leagues were by now starting to suffer from fixtures not being fulfilled, which continued for a year or two until they were abandoned because of a lack of suitable dates.

1902 preceded by some considerable time what we know as the welfare state, and many problems such as old age, sickness, unemployment and accident were the more severe for the lack of government assistance. The Ibrox disaster immediately brought penury to scores of the relatives of its victims, and several matches were arranged during the following months to assist them. Amongst these games in the autumn of 1902, Hearts beat a Rest of Edinburgh select including Rennie, Stewart and Callaghan of Hibs by 3–2, and Rennie, Glen and Breslin were in a Scottish XI which, in unusual black and white stripes, defeated Ireland 3–0 at the North East Agricultural Association in Belfast. There was also a knock-out tournament for the Rangers' Benefit Trophy in which Hibs beat Third Lanark but lost to Morton.

When the League got under way, Hibs started with a draw with Celtic, a good result in the absence of Divers and Breslin, and then came a festive day in Port Glasgow. The local side had been newly elected to the First Division and had extended their Clune Park for the occasion at the enormous cost of £750. The visit of the Cupholders for the opening was heralded in fine style — 'Welcome to Hibernians' and 'Success to the Port' read the banners and bunting, and Col. Denny, the local MP, unfurled the Second Division flag. Port Glasgow has not seen many days of celebration for its footballing sons, and its citizens were not to know that the debt they had incurred was to be so onerous as to be instrumental in losing the club their top-flight status before many more years. The festivities did not see out that first afternoon, as Hibs, kept on the defensive by their hosts' rather unscientific approach, defended resolutely and stole away in the second half to score the only goal. This fell to George Stewart, small and speedy, on the right wing for McCartney, who, like his unlucky predecessor, gained international recognition in that position.

Wins against Queens Park and Kilmarnock followed, and a raging if goalless draw with Hearts, but still Hibs were two points behind Dundee who had won all their games so far. So it was vital for both Hibs and Rangers to win when they met on the Edinburgh holiday. Rennie in goal was outstanding, and again after defending most of the time, it was a late goal by Stewart that took the points for Hibs. Hibs next slipped up at Cathkin, in what proved to be their only defeat, but it was enough to make a win over Dundee at Easter Road the next week another must.

A huge crowd of 18,000 included 4,000 in special trains from Dundee, and a better game had seldom been seen. McCartney was back for Hibs and it was he who got possession from a free kick by Breslin, dodged two defenders and sent a tremendous twenty-yarder into the far corner of the net. With the breakthrough Hibs gradually got on top and were able to preserve their lead, and catch their opponents' points total, albeit with a game more played.

In the following month, Hibs effectively ran away with the title. They

It is not often that Hibs have held both the Scottish Cup and the League Championship. Early in 1903 they did, along with the Glasgow Charity Cup, the Rosebery Cup and the Macrae Cup, and the successful committee and playing staff as pictured above were:

Back (l to r) — P. Cannon, C. Carolan, P. Smith, A. McPhee, O. Brannigan, D. McMichael, F. Rennie, B. Lester, J. Pollock and Mr. Brandon.
Second back — J. Buchan, J. Hogg, A. Gray, R. Glen, H. Handling and J. Divers.
Second front — J. Stewart, B. Breslin, J. Harrower, R. Atherton, A. Robertson, J. McColl and H. G. Rennie
Front — P. Callaghan and W. McCartney.

started on the Glasgow holiday by scoring five goals at Ibrox, the only time so far they have achieved this. Half-time was 1–1, then McCartney, Atherton, Reid and McCartney again gave Hibs a four-goal lead which they lost a quarter of just on time. While Hibs kept winning, Dundee lost to St. Mirren and Hearts so that when Hibs won comprehensively by three goals at Dens Park late in October, they had twenty-one points, with Rangers, Celtic, Hearts and Dundee all on thirteen. Hibs' run continued, included their biggest win at Parkhead on January 2nd, and gave the team a six-point advantage in the final table, despite Dundee losing only twelve goals in the whole campaign.

Dundee had their revenge in the Cup. Callaghan had scored three as Hibs beat Morton 7–0 in the first round, and all four against Leith in the second, before Hibs and Dundee met in the third round. Fifteen thousand watched at Easter Road, 25,000 at Dens, then 30,000 at Ibrox before the wind took a

Bobby Atherton, capped nine times for Wales. A versatile player, he appeared for Hibs at wing-half, inside forward and on the wing. A captain of Hibs, he also captained Middlesbrough after leaving Easter Road. He was one of the first players to make football a full-time career. He was drowned during the 1914-18 war.

cross from Bell to deceive Rennie and bring the first chink in either of two sterling defences.

Dundee also won the East of Scotland League and beat Hibs twice in so doing. The Dens Park club had joined the Inter-City League too, with Partick Thistle and St. Mirren, so that that League was the same as the First Division except for Port Glasgow. Fortunately the teams were to play each other only once, and the title went again to Hearts with twelve points from eight games. Hibs and St. Mirren had eleven each.

But both local cups came to Easter Road with little difficulty. In the Charity Cup, Hibs beat St. Bernards 2-1 and Leith 3-1, while in the Shield there were wins over Cowdenbeath 2-0, Broxburn 5-1 and Leith 4-3. Leith had eliminated Hearts from both. There was also a further modification of the Shield competition, with Hibs and Hearts to be given byes to the semi-finals and Leith and St. Bernards to meet the finalists of the qualifying competition.

Sadly, 1902-03 marked the end of an era, and it was to be some time before Hibs were to taste such success again. The story was no different from that of many successful sides in Scotland outwith Rangers and Celtic. Among those playing south of the Border shortly afterwards were Atherton at Middlesbrough, McGeechan at Bradford, and Robertson with the newly formed Manchester United.

CHAPTER 7

The League Expands, 1903–09

After labouring long and hard to reach the top, it took Hibs very little time to lose their new status, no longer in fact than their opening match of August 1903 at Clune Park, Port Glasgow. Gone were the banners and bunting of a year earlier, and in contrast to their previous spirited victory, 'Hibernians could do nothing right' and were beaten for the only time in the League by the Port. Even then Gray missed a penalty and Reid scored a good goal to make it 2-1, but the overall impression was only to be confirmed by the experience of the following years, that the days of greatness had gone.

During the next six seasons, Hibs were an average side — almost exactly. They lost two more games than they won, and scored one goal fewer than they conceded. Of these years, the first was the worst, and Hibs finished fifth from last, only one point clear of Airdrieonians who had to apply for re-election. Apart from the results, a feature of that season was the weather — it was terrible. Hibs' home game with Hearts was declared a friendly because the pitch was frozen, and the replay took place in a downpour. Both games with Queens Park went on at the refurbished Hampden, with tiny crowds because of the inclemency of the conditions. Of the four Saturdays in November, the first was foggy, on the second it poured, 'boisterous conditions' spoiled the third, and weather 'of the worst description' the last. As late as April, a local game between Hibs and Leith took place in snow and sleet.

The League itself was in a state of expansion, and Airdrie and Motherwell made the numbers up to fourteen. The title went to Third Lanark, and that was significant in that only once more before 1948 did it go outside the Old Firm. Two years later, Falkirk and Aberdeen increased the number of teams to sixteen, and a year later Clyde and Hamilton were also included, despite the Second Division title going to Leith Athletic. The increased success of Rangers and Celtic was not entirely unconnected with the increased numbers, as the championship was increasingly a matter of stamina and consistency and so favoured the clubs with the greater resources. During the same period to 1948, the Cup eluded the Old Firm only thirteen times.

1904–05 was a bit better, and Hibs finished fifth, though with only a point a game, but after a poor start. By the middle of October they had had only narrow wins over St Mirren and Partick and were sufficiently unimpressive to make more people watch Leith v. Cowdenbeath in the Qualifying Cup than Hibs' league game with Motherwell. Still, a 3-0 win against Hearts a fortnight later, and an unbeaten home League record from then on helped to woo back their friends. New Year's Day 1905 brought the first Ne'erday in Edinburgh's League encounters, and it is sad to relate that Hearts won by the only goal, scored by Thompson from a late penalty.

The unsatisfactory eleventh place the next year could likewise be ascribed to a bad beginning — a very bad one in fact as Hibs lost nine of their opening ten championship matches. Goalscoring was the main problem, and although Hibs made a spirited fight and finished with twenty-five points, they scored fewer goals than anyone else in the League. The season 1906–07 was not very different — Hibs won four of their first five League games, but none of the next nine, and again finished eleventh, with roughly the same scoring rate, although this year Port Glasgow who finished bottom managed to score even less.

At length a goalscorer was found, in the former Crystal Palace player Harker, and Hibs' fortunes showed a big improvement, finishing fifth in 1907–08 and scoring fifty-five goals including twenty from the ex-Anglo, who made a speciality of scoring spectacular goals, but whose clever play also set up many chances for others. In the last of the seasons under consideration, Hibs finished sixth, but more because of a good defensive record than because of another meagre tally of 41 goals scored in 34 League games.

This change in fortune occurred largely because of a large change in personnel in 1908–09. For most of the period, the defence had been fairly settled in front of the unusual talents of Rennie. The full-back duties had been performed by Gray, Glen and Hogg, until the last-named had retired with knee trouble. Now not only had the goalkeeper moved on to pastures new, to be replaced by W. Allan, transferred from Falkirk, but both backs were new too, Main and S. Allan. The former was such a success that he was capped in a short career which ended tragically, late in 1909.

The experienced wing-halves Breslin and Harrower had both finished their careers, although the latter made one or two later appearances to help out, and in 1908–09 these positions were filled by Grieve and Duguid, who had arrived from Albion Rovers as a striker — and under a false name that caused Hibs to forfeit his debut appearance against Hearts. McConnachie had taken over the centre-half role from Buchan, but had himself been transferred to Everton in 1907. Judging by the reports, McConnachie seems to have had a panache for missing penalties, but perhaps the Liverpool side already had a spot-kick expert. It was in August 1908 that Mattha Paterson made his debut for Hibs at centre-half, the start of a long and successful stint that included not a few goals as a stand-in centre-forward.

That day in August really was an auspicious one, because another

James Main, Hibs' brilliant right back, who was capped before his tragic death at 23 years of age.

debutant was Willie Smith on the left wing, and he was to be another faithful servant noted for accurate crosses and some strikingly individualistic goals.

It was among the forwards that the problems lay, and many were the names that appeared briefly in the team lines in attempts to find a successful blend. Throughout it all was Paddy Callaghan, who was still playing occasionally during the First World War. Divers was the centre at the start of the period, but his was a short-term signing in view of his age, and he was missed. Centre-half Buchan was tried, and a string of trialists. Peggie was signed from East Fife and Duguid from Albion Rovers and each made a little impact, though the latter more as a utility player than as a striker. Harker was the only real success, though Morton seemed to benefit from his presence. Unfortunately, Harker was soon to move across the city to Tynecastle. McGeachan went to Bradford City in December 1904 and the inside-right berth went first to Donaghy, formerly of Belfast Celtic and Derry Celtic, whose arrival brought a flurry of goals before he soon faded from the scene. The next incumbent was also Irish, the internationalist Hagan, who with Findlay spent some time with Port Glasgow.

The wingers had been John Campbell, the ex-Ranger on the right, for whom Stewart had moved to the left. Stewart had gone to Manchester City for £650, a large sum when the first-ever £1000 transfer in England had not long since been concluded for Alf Common, and his place was not adequately filled until Smith came along. Campbell had still not been satisfactorily replaced, although Burnett was beginning to establish himself in the team.

Little Joy in the Cup

While for the professional game the League championship has to be the most important tournament, it was still relatively newly established as such, and it was the Cup which brought out the biggest crowds. But whereas in the recent past the League had been finished by the turn of the year, with more teams it went on into the spring, and it was not so important for clubs to survive in the Cup to prevent the second half of the season being meaningless. This was just as well, because in the six Cup competitions of 1904–09, Hibs only once made the semi-finals.

It took a late goal by Campbell to pull Hibs through their first tie of 1903–04 against League newcomers and strugglers Airdrie, and two soft goals gifted early to Rangers before a large crowd of 17,000 in the second round were a handicap too big to overcome. A year later Hibs went out to Partick Thistle, whom they had beaten twice in the League, and after a replay in which Hibs had forced the pace all through, but had nevertheless found themselves four down at one point.

Twelve months later they got their own back. Hagan managed to equalise in both the first match at Easter Road and the replay at Meadowside, and the third game went to Ibrox. Partick again scored first, but McConnachie scored with a penalty and McNeill headed a second before half-time. Hibs held out, but only just, because Partick missed two penalties. The second round brought the Cupholders, Third Lanark, to Easter Road, and the game, fought at a desperate pace, went to the Cathkin side as always seemed likely. Thirds had scored right at the start, and try as they might, Hibs never quite caught up.

In 1906–07, Hibs beat Forfar easily in the first round, Johnstone after a replay in the second, then St. Mirren in extra time of a second replay at Tynecastle in the third round. Celtic were running away with the League, and Hibs were drawn to meet them at Parkhead, where a splendid defensive display before 27,000 spectators earned them a second game with ground advantage. Unfortunately, Hibs were not able to capitalise on their good result, because a second draw took the tie back to Parkhead for some reason, and this time Celtic won quite easily by 3–0.

One year later Hibs beat Abercorn and Morton at home with the minimum of difficulty, but then surprisingly lost by the only goal on a stormy afternoon to Kilmarnock, after having ninety per cent of the game. Their shortest Cup run for a while came in 1909, with a tight 2–1 win over Ayr seen by only 2,000 people, and a defeat at Shawfield, where Clyde, who finished third in the League and were no easy touch, scored the only goal in the first minute.

Although Hibs' part in the 1909 Scottish Cup was rather undistinguished, it was a memorable competition for two reasons. The first was the first-round tie between Broxburn and Beith. After two draws, this tie moved to Ibrox, where two further replays with extra time took place on the 3rd and 4th of February without settling the issue. Beith finally won at Love Street on 5th February, and had to return to the same venue only forty-eight hours later to be eliminated by St. Mirren.

The second reason was that nobody won it. Rangers and Celtic reached the final, and drew twice. A section of the crowd, in ignorance of the rules, thought that extra time was to be played, and when it was not a full-scale riot ensued, involving the burning down of the pay-boxes, and the Cup was withheld.

In the early years of the century, Cup semi-finals were still not played on neutral ground, and some may find it yet stranger that Celtic and Rangers sometimes met at this stage. In fact in the decade ending in 1909, the Old Firm met on eight occasions, not counting replays, including two semi-finals and only two finals.

With the expansion of the Scottish League, there was even less time to play off the local leagues, and these failed to survive. In the East of Scotland League, a big effort was made in 1905–06 to complete the fixtures, and in addition the Hearts v. Dundee game was counted as a championship decider for the previous year. Hibs had never put up a very good show in that competition, and excelled themselves by getting only one goal in their five matches. They were probably not too sad when the Committee failed to find available dates for the following season and the League lapsed.

Much the same befell the Inter-City League. It too was first restricted to teams playing each other once, and by 1905–06 was defunct. But despite the problems that were being encountered in playing off the games to which they were already committed, Hibs, Hearts and Dundee joined with Newcastle, Sunderland and Middlesbrough to form the North British League at a meeting in the Imperial Hotel in Leith Street in September 1904. Approval was won from both the SFA and the FA, but this league failed ever to get started.

The local cup competitions continued unabated, and indeed two more sprouted. For a few years it had been a source of discontent with the

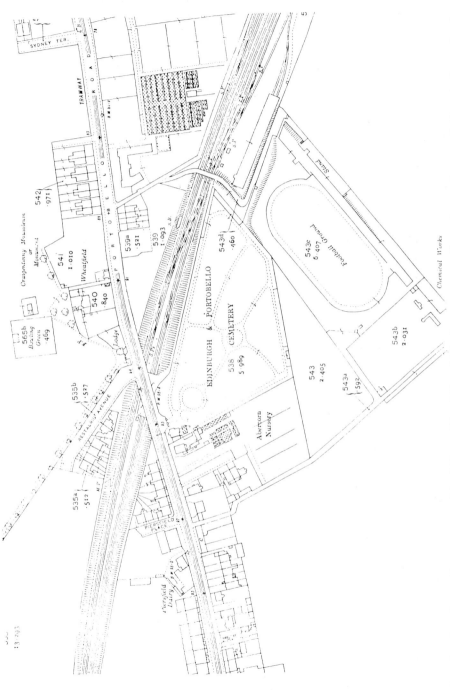

Map showing the stadium proposed by Hibs at Piershill, which they were not allowed to make use of. Portobello at the time was not part of Edinburgh.

Edinburgh clubs that the Glasgow Cup took precedence over League games but the East of Scotland Shield did not. In 1908–09, the North-Eastern Cup was inaugurated, a knock-out competition for Hibs, Hearts and the other First Division sides in the north and east. The first round was played on the same Saturday as the Glasgow Cup ties, and Dundee were the first winners of the new trophy.

The other innovation was the Wilson New Year Day Cup, presented by Robert Wilson, a director of Hearts, and competed for by Hearts and Hibs. The first match for this new trophy was at Tynecastle on 1st January 1906 and was won by Hibs, by a late goal from Miller. More often than not, however, it was squeezed into the many outstanding games played off at the end of the season.

The Shield matches were not without incident. Hibs were scratched at the semi-final stage in 1903–04 for refusing to play St. Bernards a second time at the Gymnasium. A year later the same sides met again, and Saints won 2–1, but had sinned in playing an ineligible player, so Hibs were given a second chance. They drew 0–0 and 1–1 before Hibs got through, and it took another three games to defeat Hearts in the final.

Much the same thing happened in 1905–06. Hibs beat Hearts in the semi-final but were caught playing the unregistered Duguid under the clever alias of 'Smith'. Hearts won the right to a replay, and after a goalless draw beat Hibs 2–1 in the third game. Leith put Hibs out rather ignominiously in September 1906, but Hibs won the next two competitions, albeit after replays both times.

Finally there was the Charity Cup, and a lean spell for Hibs, since they reached only two finals out of six, even if they did win both – in 1906 and 1909.

Overall there was no doubt that the period following their League and Cup successes was a sore disappointment to Hibs, and they were no more successful off the field. It was still their objective to find better accommodation than their pitch at Easter Road, where in any case they lived uneasily under threat of eviction from their landlord, the Trinity Trust, and so they took over a new site on Northfield Broadway, next to the cemetery and almost opposite the present Royal High Prep School. Hibs' plans were well advanced, on the most up-to-date lines, to build a stadium to accommodate 50,000 spectators, when the North British Railway Company suddenly required the land to join two lines together, and obtained Parliamentary approval to ensure that Hibs had to abandon their ambitious project. In fact nothing much seemed to happen to the ground, and a football pitch remained at the site for years, being used for minor finals and the like.

CHAPTER 8

Another Final, 1909-14

When the new season opened in August 1909, there was yet another new trophy to play for. This one was presented by Mr William Sharp of Leith, and was intended as an early season tournament for the four Edinburgh sides, Falkirk and Raith. Mr Sharp was clearly a more modest man than Mr Wilson, because his trophy was called the Dunedin Cup. Leith and St Bernards later dropped out of the competition, and the games were often relegated to April, but in its first year Hibs met St. Bernards on August 16th.

An undistinguished game was drawn, and Hibs led 2-0 in the replay when lack of light brought about its early conclusion. Hibs were held responsible, for turning up late, and a replay was ordered, which Saints won 1-0, and they went on to take the trophy.

Curiously, the same thing happened in the Shield later in the season, with Hibs leading by eight corners to two, and five minutes to go. There were four votes for Hibs, since St. Bernards had left the field, and seven for a replay because Hibs were late again, and so a second game was ordered. Hibs scratched, obviously having had enough of being told what to do by the organisers, and it was perhaps no surprise that Owen Brannigan of Hibs was replaced as President of the East of Scotland FA after a marathon stint.

It was also in August 1909 that Hibs went to Dundee, where 'the new senior Irish club' which had been formed in that city opened its doors for the first time. They were called Dundee Hibernians, played in Hibs' colours of green shirts, and Hibs were their first opponents. Lord Provost Urquhart kicked off, and the new side did splendidly to hold Hibs till half-time, but shortly after, O'Hara, the Hibs' half-back, burst through and scored a brilliant goal. This won him 'the handsome bicycle presented by Mr. P. Reilly', the home side's manager, to the scorer of the first goal. The game ended 1-1.

The fact that that game took place at Tannadice may be a clue to the Dundee side's present identity, and at the time of writing, with Celtic, Aberdeen and Dundee United the three top sides in Scotland, it is interesting to note Hibs' involvement in the formation of all three.

However, once the League got under way, it was not long before it was clear that it was largely a case of the mixture as before. In the five years before war came, Hibs took 166 points from 174 League games, which was slightly down on the previous few seasons, but against that, they did reach one Cup Final. In League matches Hibs fared particularly badly at Shawfield, where

One of a series of football club shields published around 1911 by J. Baines, Oak Lane, Bradford, who seems to have discovered something about Hibs' origins which has eluded the author. The players are Willie Smith (left) and Willie Harper.

they lost all five games, and against Hearts, who scored nine wins in the ten matches between the clubs.

Hibs started their 1909–10 League campaign with five successive wins, including a notable autumn double of Rangers and Celtic, but a solitary success over Queens Park in their next nine brought them back to mid-table. Then in December came a devastating blow at Firhill; playing with four reserves on a frostbound pitch, Hibs were already up against it before right-back Main was carried off badly injured. The internationalist was brought back to Edinburgh by his colleagues, but a few days later died of his internal injuries in the Royal Infirmary, after appearing to have made a slight improvement. He was 23. The season continued, and it took seven points from the last four games to give Hibs eighth place, with exactly a point a game. With the departure of Harker, there was once again a desperate need of a goalscorer. The job had mainly fallen to Peggie, and defenders Paterson and O'Hara as stopgaps, and the outcome was only 33 scores in 34 games.

A year later Hibs managed two more points, and eleven more goals, but they finished ninth. Paterson spent more of his time up front and scored seventeen goals, including some penalties, benefiting from the inside-forward play of the brothers Anderson. Rae was on the right with Smith on the left, and Callaghan, as usual, was available to fit in anywhere when needed. There was another autumn double — Hibs lost 4–0 to each of Rangers and Celtic.

The Shield semi-finals had been arranged for the autumn holiday, but

Hibs had opted for the more remunerative League game with Celtic. So at the East of Scotland FA meeting that followed there were moves to disqualify Hibs from the Shield, until it was noticed that under the rules this could not be done without expelling Hibs from the Association. This was further than the majority were prepared to go, and Hibs were reluctantly given another chance, but is was generally felt that the 4–0 drubbing from Celtic was no more than the deserved.

Season 1911–12 started with a Dunedin tie between Hibs and Hearts 'ending in a draw much in favour of Hibernians' but the replay ended in a 2–0 win even more in favour of Hearts. The feature of their League campaign was their away form. After Hibs' fourth successive away defeat on September 16th, there was sympathy about the ill luck that had dogged their efforts that far. By the time Christmas had come but the first away point had not, it had largely evaporated.

In particular, the defeat at Ibrox would not be easily forgotton by centre-half Paterson. First he handled, and Bennett converted the penalty. Then he had his face smashed in a collision with Chapman and retired hurt. He came back, but was not fully into the swing of things when he and Chapman bumped heads again, and Paterson made his final exit, semi-conscious, after only fifteen minutes.

By the time the return game came round in January, Hibs had made some team improvements. First, Jimmy Hendren was signed from Cowdenbeath and proved quite an acquisition, although he took the rest of the current season to find his feet. Then Sam Fleming, a right-winger or inside-forward, and Bobby Templeton, junior internationalist left-back of Neilston Victoria, went straight into the team in December.

Against Rangers, a new young centre was played, by the name of Bell, and 'in one of the greatest surprises known to Scottish football, the apparently weakened Hibernians fairly routed' the prospective champions. Rangers finally won the title by six points, a margin they had already established in January. In just a few minutes Rae beat his man and shot for the far corner, and Campbell, trying to clear, helped the ball in. A few minutes later, after a similar move, Rae scored a second off the crossbar, and when Anderson banged in the third, the crowd were beginning to believe it. In the second half, Bell got the fourth from a pass from Anderson, and then when Fleming and Bell got mixed up and seemed to have passed up a chance created by Rae, the young centre coolly made amends by backheeling the ball home. That completed the rout, and unfortunately also the noteworthy achievements of young Bell.

In 1912–13 it was a case of a good recovery from a bad start. When Hibs lost at Ibrox in October, they were second bottom, with six points from nine games, but they finished a creditable sixth. Had points been gathered all

D

season at the same rate as in the last twenty-five games, Hibs would have been third. The goal tally this year was 63, with 18 from Hendren, and with Fleming too in double figures. Yet despite this, against the five sides that finished above them, Hibs had only one victory, at Brockville in April.

It was in October 1912 that yet another league came into being. This was the Inter-City Midweek League, to cater for those, like shopkeepers, who were deprived of weekend football. But either the numbers of these frustrated enthusiasts were greatly overestimated, or else early closing day was Tuesday in a lot of cases, because these Wednesday games were played before mere handfuls of spectators. Fewer than 500 watched Rangers and Hibs at Ibrox, and the six teams involved decided to abandon the competition after only four weeks. For the record, at home Hibs lost 3–2 to Celtic and beat Hearts 2–0, while they lost 2–1 at Ibrox and won 2–0 at Pittodrie. Dundee were the other side involved.

In 1913–14, Hibs were back in the lower half of the table, in a League now extended to twenty clubs. Ayr United were newly formed from Second Division sides Ayr and Ayr Parkhouse, and defeated Hibs 5–0 on their first visit to Easter Road, mainly because a chap called Ramsay scored four goals, though Hibs had had to field a very weak side, and even then the margin greatly flattered their guests. The other new side were old friends Dumbarton, and the first meeting of these old adversaries at Boghead aroused considerable interest. It was apparently not maintained, however, because the return was played before only 1000 spectators, though admittedly between the two instalments of the Cup Final.

The goalscoring of 1913–14 was very similar to the previous year, with Hendren matching his previous tally, and Fleming likewise. Hendren also scored five in one game against Leith in the Charity Cup. The difference this season was more in the goals conceded, where the reason lay in the number of changes in personnel in the defence.

Allan remained in goal, and Templeton at left-back, and Paterson confirmed that his place was really at centre-half. Peter Kerr was signed to replace Main, but he developed into a first-class right-half, and Neil Girdwood came in behind him. The left-half berth by 1914 had been taken over by Sandy Grosart, who moved to Aberdeen after the war. Among the forwards, Hendren, Fleming and Smith were automatic choices, with the other places going variously to Williamson, primarily a winger, Wood, an inside man, Reid, a centre, and Wilson, another inside man, while Callaghan continued to make appearances now and then.

If Hibs had a dreadful time against Hearts in the League around 1910, then at least they did a bit better in the Cup. The two main capital sides met in the third round of the 1909–10 competition, after Hibs had eliminated Hamilton and Ayr, but not without difficulty because of their goalscoring

Sam Fleming was the 'character' of Hibs' team in the days before the First World War. He is seen here in a tussle with Hoare (Queens Park) in a cup tie in 1914.

problems at the time. A huge crowd of 27,000 packed into Easter Road for the tie with Hearts, and the ground was bursting at the seams. This was no exaggeration, because at half-time it burst. Hundreds poured onto the playing area, and when play was resumed, it was constantly interrupted before being finally abandoned with twenty-five minutes to go. It had been a poor game and Hearts were leading by a first-half goal. However, the pitch invasion was a comparatively good-humoured one, caused only by the crush of people, and a pale imitation of the Old Firm's fans' wrecking of Hampden a year earlier. Hearts and Hibs agreed, subject to the SFA doing likewise, to count the game a draw, and so a replay went on at Tynecastle the following week. Surprisingly, Hibs were the better side more or less all through, and the only goal was an opportunist one by Peggie soon after the interval.

This took Hibs to a semi-final with Dundee. It was a bit reminiscent of the tie of seven years earlier: 18,000 watched at Easter Road, 30,000 at Dens, then 17,000 at Celtic Park, where Hunter headed Dundee in front just into the second half, and one was too high a tally for Hibs to equal. In fact, Hibs' eight games in the Cup yielded only six goals. Dundee also accounted for Hibs the next year in the first round, and a year after that there was another classic from Hearts and Hibs.

Just Like Old Times

This time it was a first-round tie at Tynecastle. 'The game's finer points were missing' but the game was keen enough, and Hibs had rather the better of a goalless draw. The replay was the following Saturday at Easter Road, and the crowd saw a 'wonderfully fast and good game' considering the dreadful conditions. Heavy snow obliterated the lines, and it was declared a friendly, although this fact was only communicated to the crowd and the press reluctantly after the game. Rae put Hibs in front, but Abrams equalised when 'W. Allan fumbled a passback and let it roll over the line but had it out again before the referee noticed'.

The SFA were not too happy about these arrangements, especially as they broke the rules of the competition. The referee reported that he had instructed the teams to clear the lines but this had not been done. Hibs and Hearts were each fined £25 for their part in the proceedings, and Hearts, who considered it none of their business to clear the lines at an away game, and whose indignation had some justification, only finally paid up several weeks later under threat of suspension. The referee was also fined, one guinea, for failing to abandon the match when it was clear that the teams were ignoring him.

When the next instalment came off at Easter Road a week later, the result was the same. Fleming headed in a perfect cross by Smith in the first half, and Mercer equalised in the last ten minutes. It was another good game, but only a few hundred Edinburgh enthusiasts saw the tie decided, because that was done conveniently at Ibrox. Hearts were better all through on this occasion, and Dawson (2) and Abrams gave them a three-goal lead before Rae scored for Hibs in a late burst.

But Hibs looked well on the way to a good run in the 1912–13 competition, when they defeated Motherwell in a second replay at Ibrox and then held Raith to a draw in Kirkcaldy. Unfortunately they then hit a bad day and lost to the Fifers at Easter Road in a poor game before 23,000 spectators. They did have a good run a year later.

Hibs played well to draw at Greenock, and finished the job with more to spare than the 2–1 score against Morton would suggest, and then the next round brought Rangers and 30,000 fans to Easter Road. It must have been quite tight, considering the experience of the earlier Hearts tie. Reid put the Glasgow side in front, but marvellous saves by Allan and good defending generally restricted them to that one at half-time. As Hibs' confidence grew, they were able to attack into the wind, and Hendren scored a capital goal. Hemmed in and against the wind, Rangers were forced into kicking-out tactics in the second half, and as the pressure and excitement rose, Wilson forced a corner and Smith scored from it.

That was enough, and it earned Hibs a third-round tie at Hampden, where they were far better than Queens Park. Paterson scored in ten minutes, and Wilson added two more. The semi-final with St. Mirren was similar, which was no surprise because the Paisley side had finished bottom

Bobby Templeton is seen stopping Owers, Celtic's English centre-forward, in the cup final at Ibrox in 1914.

of the League by five points. Wilson opened the scoring with a long shot in fifteen minutes, and he and Williamson scored the later goals in another 3–1 win.

The final was at Ibrox and the opposition Celtic. The game did not lack thrills, and both teams had frights, but the nearest to a goal was when Wilson, who was having a good run, beat goalkeeper Shaw only for McNair to knee the ball off the line. When the replay took place the next Thursday, Hibs were caught cold. Twice in the opening eleven minutes, defensive indecision let Celtic score, and both goals fell to the young centre Jimmy McColl, brought in for this game, and in his time to score many goals in Hibs colours. Brownlee was fouled by Girdwood but allowed to go on, and he made it 3–0 at half-time. Brownlee scored again to make the position hopeless, though Smith did score a consolation goal. It was a big disappointment to bow out so tamely, and the general attitude of the fans can be gauged from the attendance in Hibs' next home League game against Motherwell — 500.

The period up to 1914 was a good one for Falkirk — the best that that club has had, and they were certainly the best side outside Clydeside, and regularly League challengers. In addition, Hearts, Dundee and Aberdeen all finished above Hibs more often than below them during this time, so that Hibs' tally of one North-Eastern Cup and one losing Dunedin Cup final appearance is no worse than one would have expected. Their only success came in 1910–11, when Hibs beat Falkirk, although it took an own goal by

Agnew to give them even this win. Their Dunedin Cup final was also against Falkirk, in 1913–14, and the Bairns won this one quite easily by 4–1. It was lucky that Hibs had only St. Bernards to play to reach the final, because Hearts had beaten them in the semi-finals for the previous three years.

In the Shield, Hibs followed their withdrawal of 1909–10 with three wins, and strangely their opponents in the finals were St. Bernards twice and Leith. In 1912–13, Hibs and Hearts drew in the semi-final but Hearts withdrew because of pressure of fixtures. Hibs, who had more games outstanding than Hearts, carried on and beat St. Bernards in an evening game — after beating Hamilton Accies in a League match the same afternoon. Hearts won the 1913–14 competition in a hectic end to the season which saw them beat Hibs in the Shield, Wilson Cup and Charity Cup all in little over a fortnight.

In the Wilson Cup, where games were often played as double headers with League points at stake, Hearts had three wins in the five years to Hibs' two, while in the Charity Cup Hibs won four in a row, all with different opponents. This came about because in 1912–13 Hibs were due to meet Hearts in the final, but the Tynecastle side were away on tour, so Hibs met the Rest of Edinburgh, i.e. Leith, St. Bernards and Hearts reserves, and won by seven corners to four in a game which attracted all of 200 spectators.

A. Gray, P. Boyle, R. Glen, J. Hogg, D. McMichael (Secretary), P. Smith (Treasurer), F. Docherty (Vice-President), R. Atheron, P. Callaghan, J. Harrower, H. Rennie, H. Handling, Wm. McCartney, A. Robertson (Captain). The Hibs team around the turn of the Century.

CHAPTER 9

Struggling Through the War, 1914–19

Trouble had threatened in Europe for some years, and in the summer of 1914 the Great War at last got under way. It was not expected to be a long war. It was obvious to the military experts that a modern war could not be sustained over a protracted period, and victory was confidently expected by Christmas. The theme of the recruitment advertising was exhortation to get a bit of the action before it was all over, and *The Times* launched a series of weekly 'History of the War' magazines so that those left behind could read of the glorious deeds done.

In the circumstances, Scottish football got under way as usual, and slightly in advance of the war, although the excitement of the latter meant that there was comparatively little football coverage in the press. Hibs started off with their usual defeat at Shawfield, but after eight games had managed a point a game. At this stage they hit such a bad run that nineteen goals were conceded in six consecutive defeats, and a home draw with Dumbarton was considered a great improvement. Hendren was having a lean spell with only one League goal to date, but both he and Robert Lennie claimed five as Hibs lost only one of the remaining seven games — to Hearts — to the end of the year.

During the latter part of the year, it was becoming clear that the optimism about a quick win in the war was misplaced, and there was concern that football should not interfere with the recruitment drive. There was also some rancour within the game that football should be the only sport to be considered. In early December the Scottish representative to the International Congress gave an undertaking to the Under-Secretary of the War Office that there would be no Cup ties that season. This caused a row because, apart from its being ridiculous to claim that Cup ties but not League games affected the numbers enlisting, it was not clear that the representative had any authority to give such an undertaking. Many clubs badly needed the extra cash generated by the Cup ties. Nevertheless, at an SFA meeting just before Christmas, the lobby that believed that the SFA should bow to the War Office's request regardless triumphed by a single vote, and there was no Scottish Cup competition in 1914–15. It was too bad for the sides who had battled successfully through the qualifying tournament, but they were all included in the main competition when it was next held.

A million men were in uniform by the end of 1914, but apart from the

Cup, the football season ran to its close as normal. Hibs were never in contention for the League title and finished eleventh, but they did have a say in where it went. At the halfway point of the season, Hearts had only dropped three points, and even after losing to Rangers on February 20th were two points clear of Celtic, when they visited Easter Road. Hibs chose the day for one of their most inspired displays, and although a goal behind and getting very much the worse of things, managed to get a late equaliser through Robertson, a recruit from Broxburn, and deprive Hearts of a point. It was a different story at Parkhead a week later. Dodds scored an early penalty, then after Fleming had equalised for Hibs, it was Robertson again who turned the game, this time with an own goal. Hibs didn't get back, and Celtic scored three more. Celtic went on to win the League by four points, but only because Hearts lost their last two games once they had lost the title.

Hearts did beat Hibs in the Dunedin Cup Final (6–0) and the Wilson Cup (2–1 on January 1st). The other finals provided an unusual double for young defender Connell McColl of Hibs. In the Shield, the only feature of the game was the number of chances missed by both Hearts and Hibs, and it was decided by an own goal by McColl midway through the second half. In the Charity Cup, Hibs met St. Bernards, who had eliminated Hearts, and an exciting game was poised at 3–3 after ninety minutes. Then in extra time McColl again provided the vital breakthrough with another own goal, and for good measure Lennie was sent off as feelings ran high.

By the start of season 1915–16 it was obvious to even more people that the war was far from won, and newspaper editors and readers' letters raged about the immorality of professional football when those so engaged could be fighting the Germans. Not many of these letters seemed to have Flanders postmarks.

The football authorities were anxious in any case not to hinder the rush to enlist. The rate of payment allowed for playing was cut back, and only those in steady employment outside the game were permitted to take part. It was true that the League in England had been regionalised, but the Scottish League did not require more travelling than an English region anyway. The Scottish Second Division was regionalised inasmuch as the official competition was discontinued, and was replaced by an Eastern and a Western League each with twelve clubs.

During 1915 a further two million joined the forces, and the effect was seen in the team lines for the new season. Hearts were as hard hit as any, with only three of the previous year's successful side available, and when Hibs kicked off against Queens Park, they had to parade three new men, Alexander, Taylor and Newton. No less a celebrity than Sergeant Ripley V.C. was present on recruiting duty, and he saw all three make a reasonable

Willie Miller, who came to prominence as Hibs' leading scorer in 1917–18, before developing into a fine centre-half.

impression in a 3–0 win. Hibs followed this up with an excellent win at Ayr, and then immediately ran out of steam. Although a series of draws kept them unbeaten away from Easter Road until their trip to Cathkin in mid-November, their only further win before the turn of the year was a narrow success against St. Mirren a week later. Even then Hibs were a goal behind until very late on, but the points were rescued by two goals from Henry Hutchison, recently signed from Falkirk to fill the troublesome vacancy caused by Hendren's departure. It was unfortunate that this rare sight took place on a day so dark and foggy that the spectators were in ignorance of most of it. Hibs were by now second bottom, but although they did touch bottom briefly in March, they finished two points above Raith. Two more goals from Hutchison unexpectedly brought Hibs the Wilson Cup, but Hearts had their revenge with a 4–0 thrashing in the Charity Cup, the only other one played for.

By the start of 1916 it had occurred to H.M. Government that the war was taking longer than intended, and conscription was introduced in January, which made it harder still to raise a team, and was especially unfavourable to the eastern teams. This came about because it was on the heavy industries of Clydeside that the supplies for war depended, and in which therefore were to be found most of the reserved occupations, which meant exemption from conscription.

It was around this time that Wm. Allan had to be replaced, and Hibs' new goalkeeper was Henry McManus, from Parkhead Juniors, and by the following season most of the regulars, including Girdwood, Paterson, Kerr, Grosart, Williamson, Wood and Hutchison, were always or usually unavailable. Moreover, in November 1916 right-winger Alexander injured an arm at work and an amputation was necessary. Over the season Hibs had to field twenty-five players, but two of their youngsters in particular, Willie Miller and Willie Dornan, were to prove valuable servants.

1916–17 was not a bad year for Hibs — compared with those round about — although they finished in fourth bottom place. Their best result was a point from runners-up Morton at Greenock, and they scored fifty-seven goals, shared largely between Tommy Kilpatrick, Charlie Campbell, John Meaney, Lennie and Alexander until his mishap. Celtic won the League without losing a game, then lost their second last one to Kilmarnock. No eastern side finished in the top ten, with Dundee, Hibs, Raith and Aberdeen all in the bottom five.

All Quiet on the Eastern Front

The situation of the east clubs continued to deteriorate. The Eastern League of 1916–17 was reduced to ten teams because Leith and Kirkcaldy United could not carry on. In 1917 Aberdeen, Dundee and Raith withdrew from the Scottish League, although there was no guarantee of readmission. The latter two joined the Eastern League, but even then that league had only seven members. St. Bernards had closed down, and the only side south of the Forth was Armadale.

Then in 1917, instead of the war finally being over, it reached crisis point. Lloyd George's coalition had taken power in December 1916, and one of its measures was to replace men by women in certain jobs, so that more men still could go to France.

In the circumstances the thoughts of few were on football in the autumn of 1917, and Hibs' early results did not bear thinking about. They lost their first five games and failed to score a goal, including a home defeat by newcomers Clydebank, who had been only too willing to even up the numbers after the withdrawal of Aberdeen, Dundee and Raith.

Hibs' first goals came in the Shield. With no tournament for the last two years, the East of Scotland FA were in just as bad a state as the clubs, and were glad to accept an offer by Hibs and Hearts to play home and home games for the trophy. St. Bernards objected, but as they had had to close down, nobody listened to them. Hibs won the first game surprisingly easily

4–0 on the autumn holiday, and the second was drawn 1–1 on the spring holiday.

The League results had to improve, and they did — rather more than might have been hoped for. Hibs finished above Clyde and Ayr, and only four points behind St. Mirren who were eleventh. Much of this comparative success was due to Miller, who found some success as a marksman with fifteen goals, while Moir and Meaney contributed about the same number between them. A year earlier Hibs had had their first win at Shawfield for seventeen years, but it still came as a shock that they scored five times there in October in what was their only away win. Apart from the Shield, Hibs also took the Wilson Cup (3–1) and lost 5–3 after extra time to Falkirk in the revived Dunedin Cup.

By August 1918, with *The Times* weekly magazines into their third hundred, the football scene did not reflect the national optimism that, with the Americans in Europe, the end of the problems was in sight. Earl Haig, in charge in the field, had been told that the 1918 offensive had to be successful because there were no more men left to send. The state of those who fulfilled the Scottish League fixtures later in the year can therefore be imagined, especially the group of them who played for Hibs, in view of their record during the season. The Eastern League had by now stopped altogether, so that only Hearts and Hibs remained of seventeen eastern clubs who had been operating three years earlier.

Hibs used thirty-five players in 1918–19, and even then were not able in all cases to put eleven on to the field. At times it appears that anyone walking down Easter Road before kick-off time thereby demonstrated the availability, fitness and skill that Hibs could demand. Full-back Templeton often turned out in goal, a spare winger was borrowed from Hearts for a while, and men from the other Edinburgh clubs helped out. Hearts were not a lot better, and had to recruit a goalkeeper from the crowd before the Wilson Cup game on January 1st.

Hibs finished bottom of the League, with seven points to spare, and only five wins and thirty goals in thirty-four games. Of the thirteen players who shared in this bonanza, nine were new men, and of them, only two, Willie McGinnigle and Hugh Shaw, were to make their mark in Hibs' post-war side — and neither as forwards. Others, however, were useful in forming the nucleus of the reserve side that Hibs started a year or so later. Big defeats were suffered at Kilmarnock (7–1), Ayr (5–0) and especially Greenock, where Hibs' lightweight and inexperienced forwards were simply swamped in the mud, and an overworked defence conceded nine goals.

But with winter came the armistice, and players long gone began to trickle back. Williamson and Wood were among the first to return to Easter Road, and they made a welcome improvement to the attack. A Victory Cup was organised and twenty-six teams were able to compete, all the remaining League clubs with eight others, of which the furthest east was Albion Rovers. Hibs had a first-round bye, then a home tie with Ayr, which they won by a single goal from Kilpatrick and a fine display by the current goalkeeper Stevenson. Next came another home tie, with Motherwell. Hibs had not beaten the Fir Park side in the five years of the war, but Williamson and Wood, now back, each scored to give Hibs a 2–0 win.

The semi-final was also at Easter Road, against St. Mirren. Williamson headed Hibs into a half-time lead, but Saints were superior in the second period and Thomson equalised in a scramble. So extra time was required, but at the start of it, Hibs' top scorer Bobby Gilmour broke his collarbone, and Thomson and Clark gave the Paisley side the result. By coincidence, St. Mirren also won the final 3–1 after extra time, against Hearts.

The record books show the war years as pretty dismal ones for Hibs, but the results were of secondary importance to the success of carrying on through a very difficult period. Hibs did not record a win against Aberdeen, Celtic, Clydebank, Morton, Motherwell or Rangers during the period, and their crowds, like everyone else's, were down, so that the financial position was a serious one. The one set of green jerseys that the club possessed were streaked yellow with the sweat of years past, and the goalkeeper's one was dark grey instead of its original white. It was only the good run in the Victory Cup which enabled the club to buy a new set, which attracted some comment in the Glasgow press.

The ground was banked on three sides but yet unterraced, so that spectators gradually slid down during a game until they reached the wooden fence that separated them from the playing area, and proved a hazard to the players from time to time. The only seating or cover was provided by the pathetic little stand, known disparagingly as the 'Eggbox', which was separate from the spartan stripping box level with the eighteen-yard line.

That Hibs had carried on at all was largely due to the energy and pride of one man, Dan McMichael. McMichael had been one of the men who had helped revive the club in 1892, and after it became a limited liability company soon after the turn of the century so that it was no longer run by a committee, he became the first manager, while during the war he had combined that role with that of groundsman and just about everything else. McMichael had been a noted sprinter in his youth, but latterly was more famous for his moustache, which Jimmy Edwards would have been proud of. Unfortunately he died in the flu epidemic of 1919.

Hibs were well off for athletes, because the club trainer, Paddy Cannon, was a top-class middle-distance runner and almost unbeatable over three or

four miles, and in fact when he moved on, Hibs' next trainer, Di
Christopher, was also a runner of some note.

On Dan McMichael's death, Davy Gordon took over as manager. He
was already at Easter Road, having joined the club a year or two before from
Hull City as a half-back.

(Players) — Dornan, Shaw, Harper, Miller, Ritchie, McColl, Kerr, Walker,
McGinnigle, Halligan and Dunn. (This is the famous Hibs' team that reached the
Scottish Cup final in 1923 and 1924 and lost on each occasion.)

CHAPTER 10

Harper, McGinnigle, Dornan..., 1919–25

By the time that the new season kicked off on August 16th 1919, those who could had returned from the war, Europe was patching itself together and things were returning to normal. Admission charges had doubled to one shilling — the war had brought about the first experiences of serious inflation — but sizeable crowds turned out to see the opening engagements. Hibs' home gates during the autumn averaged about 15,000, which was more than three times the level of the previous year.

There had been little opportunity to go talent-spotting since hostilities ceased, as little minor football had taken place, so it was not surprising that new faces were few. Hibs still had the services of William Stage the Bury inside-forward, and like most sides their line-up was a mixture of their pre-war players who were still available and the youngsters who had filled in during their long absences. A typical Hibs' team from the autumn of 1919 was Stevenson; McGinnigle and Dornan; Kerr, Paterson and Smith; Kilpatrick, Stage, Williamson, Gilmour and Ritchie. The others in greatest contention for places were deputy goalkeeper Scott, Templeton, the long-serving back, wing-half Grosart who was soon to go to Aberdeen, inside-forward Wood, later of St. Mirren, and youngsters Shaw and Miller who were yet to establish themselves.

Since Hibs had not had a top-rate team either during the war or before it, it was not to be expected that the present combination were now to become worldbeaters. Nevertheless, as early as their fourth game — a defeat at Motherwell — *The Scotsman* noted that they were 'developing into a capital team'. That was, admittedly, before they visited Parkhead in October, where the *Evening News* still took the optimistic line that Hibs had done exceedingly well to pierce the redoubted Celtic defence and score on three occasions, and only grudgingly admitted that Celtic had not exactly been overawed by this performance, and had scored seven themselves. Still, goals were what the customers wanted, and there were plenty a week later too as Hibs beat Partick Thistle 6–2, with four goals for Williamson, after being two in arrears.

The League was bigger than it had ever been, although there was only the one division, with Western, Central and Eastern leagues in addition. Aberdeen, Dundee and Raith had all been taken back into the fold, and so that left an odd number again. The ballot to fill this twenty-second place resulted in a tie and the casting vote fell to the chairman, a Mr. Thomas

Hugh Shaw as a young player shortly
after the First World War.

Willie Harper

Hart, who showed just how little he thought of Cowdenbeath, the last
champions of Division Two, by voting for Albion Rovers. The bigger league
meant that League games predominated right through the season till April,
and the local competitions, in which interest was continuing to wane
anyway, were squeezed into the last few evenings of the season.

For most of this extended League programme Hibs cruised along quite
nicely in the top half of the table, though with no pretensions to honours.
There was just the occasional hiccup, if one forgets the 7-0 trouncing at
Ibrox, much as those involved tried to do. There was also a curious win on
New Year's Day, when Hearts men scored three of the four goals scored. It
was the Cup ties that seemed to make things go wrong.

Hibs were due to play at Galston, the Ayrshire village recently bypassed
by the road to Kilmarnock. The pitch was tight, and the local partisans very
close to it. It was also sodden, notwithstanding the drying effects of the gale
that was blowing. Conditions were not improved by recent subsidence that
had hastily been filled in, and it was not hard to believe that it was only three
miles to Moscow. The local team's direct approach contrasted with Hibs'
more studied style, and so suited the conditions that it seemed that they were
well used to them. Hibs' ambition stretched to no more than survival, which
they achieved after a particularly fraught second half in which they defended
the deep end with a determination matched only by their desperation. The
replay was also a grim affair. Stage put Hibs ahead after half an hour, only
for Scott to misfield a long shot into his net in a Galston breakaway, and there
were only six minutes left when Ritchie restored Hibs' lead.

The Cup competition was remarkable for the feat of Albion Rovers, who were bottom of the League but reached the final after beating Rangers in three games in the semi-final. That of Armadale was of no less note, however, as three First Division sides in succession went under at Volunteer Park. Clyde were first, Ayr third, and there are no prizes for guessing who came in between. Armadale took less than a minute to score against Hibs, and despite a lot of effort on the part of the Easter Road men, the longer it went, the likelier it seemed that if there was to be further scoring, it would not be done by Hibs.

The effect on Hibs' League performance was dramatic. They won only one of their remaining seventeen games, and that by a late and disputed penalty against Queens Park following two orderings off. The final table showed that Hibs had slumped to eighteenth place.

They did get some revenge over Armadale in the Charity Cup, but of a very hollow nature. Hibs were much under strength but took an early lead when the 'Dale goalkeeper banged the ball in off one of his defenders. Armadale fought back and scored twice by half-time but shortly afterwards had a player sent off. Then McGinnigle missed a penalty, and there were only five minutes to go when Williamson headed an equaliser. The tie went into extra time, and Armadale soon lost their goalkeeper too, so there were only nine opponents when Thomson eventually scored the winner, which was just as well because the nine were leading by two corners at the time. Hibs maintained their form and lost 2–0 to Hearts in the final.

But despite their inauspicious start, it was for their Cup exploits that the Hibs side of the early '20s is remembered, and several of them were already established in the team. Willie McGinnigle was right-back, a stocky player who was skilled at placing the ball at a time when full-backs generally were judged on the distance they could hoist it upfield. The stocky full-back earned a League cap for his endeavours and formed a fine understanding with his partner on the left, Willie Dornan. As left-half the massive Hugh Shaw had seen off all opposition. Shaw was well able to look after himself in the event of any rough play, and was only too willing to help out less well-endowed colleagues who might have been seen by opponents as a softer touch. Apart from his physical attributes, Shaw was also a skilful player with the ability to switch play, and he was seldom flustered under pressure. At right-half, Peter Kerr was an automatic choice, and was to form a formidable triangle in years to come with the right wing of Ritchie and Dunn. Harry Ritchie played on either wing at this time, and with his left foot even stronger than his right, liked to cut in from the right and drive across goal with his left. Ritchie was a big man for a winger, scaling thirteen stones, and was not one of those whom Hugh Shaw often felt required his services as a minder. Like Arthur Duncan later, Ritchie was such a favourite that the Easter Road crowd let him away with just about anything.

The autumn of 1920 was not one of Hibs' best and they were fifth bottom in November, but a more satisfying aspect was the further new players brought into the side. The most significant date was September 1st, despite a home defeat by Airdrie. One debutant was Willie Harper, a big strong goalkeeper from local juniors Edinburgh Emmet. He had also been the Scots Guards heavyweight boxing champion, and is remembered by those who saw him as the best last line of defence that Hibs ever had. From the start Harper seldom failed to impress, and by 1922–23 he had also established himself in Scotland's goal, where he played four times against England without defeat. Not many Scottish goalkeepers can claim that.

A second debutant against Airdrie was Jimmy Dunn, a junior cap from St. Anthony's who gained full honours later on. Like most Hibs players, Dunn did not collect a Scottish Cupwinners medal, but both he and his son later won FA Cupwinners badges. It was not long after Dunn came in that Ritchie finally settled on the right wing, partly because of the arrival of John 'Darkie' Walker, a left-winger from Kirkintilloch Rob Roy, in November. Johnny Halligan from Shawfield Juniors had consolidated his position at inside-left, so with the tireless Mattha Paterson still turning out at centre-half, Hibs had a fairly settled line-up. It was just centre-forward that posed a problem.

Williamson had been the man in possession first and had scored over twenty goals when Hibs went to Galston. He seemed to suffer more than most and quickly disappeared from the scene. The main aspirants for his place were Davy Anderson from Newton Stewart, who was top scorer in 1920–21 with fifteen goals, and Archie Young who was Hibs' leading scorer the following year, although he only just reached double figures in a season in which Duncan Walker hit 45 for St. Mirren. Walker and Paterson were tried and in November 1921 Davy Duncan was signed from Musselburgh Bruntonians without making a noticeable improvement.

Jimmy McColl

It was in October 1922 that the problem was solved by the signing of Jimmy McColl. McColl had played against Hibs in the 1914 Cup final and his signing was seen as a short-term measure. McColl had left Celtic to go to Stoke, but his wife had failed to settle in the Potteries and so he had returned to Partick Thistle, from whom he moved to Hibs. When Paterson at length

Jimmy McColl   · Harry Ritchie

retired to become a chauffeur, the duties of pivot fell to Miller, and the team which was to contest successive Cup finals had come together — Harper; McGinnigle and Dornan; Kerr, Miller and Shaw; Ritchie, Dunn, McColl, Halligan and Walker.

Before that, Hibs were to reach only the second round of the 1921 and 1922 competitions. In the former they had six ties, the first three against Third Lanark before a Halligan goal saw them through, and a further three against Partick Thistle. The first of these three was 'one of the dullest ties imaginable' but the second had more excitement, if still lacking subtlety and goals. The third was another poor affair at a wet and stormy Parkhead, and 'scoring did not seem a probable thing to happen at either end' until McFarlane headed in a free kick midway through the second half to avoid further tedium. Over 150,000 spectators watched Hibs' six ties. Partick must have been capable of better things, because they went on to beat Hearts, Motherwell and Rangers to take the trophy.

A year later, Hibs met Armadale again, and this time won 3–0, although it was only in the last quarter that they seemed sure to win. West Lothian sides were all riding high — there were four of them in the Second Division and they all finished in the top seven. In the Cup, Bathgate put Falkirk out, and Broxburn, who had won at Tannadice in the first round, took Hearts to three games in the second. Hibs went out at Motherwell, in a game that was always going away from them, and goals from Young and Dunn still left them one behind at the close.

THE CUP FINAL: "GREENS" GET "THE BLUES" AT IBROX.

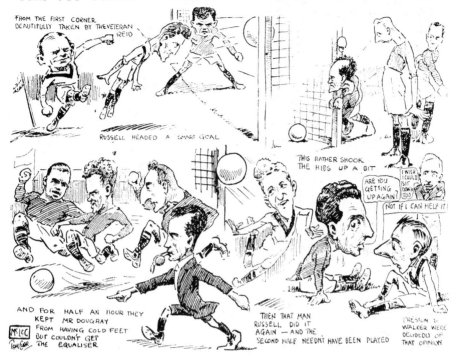

How 'Evening News' cartoonist Tom Curr saw Hibs' defeat by Airdrie in the 1924 cup final.

The Cup of 1923 also had its moments — mostly on January 27th — in the second round. Hibs struggled against Peebles Rovers and had to concede the honours to the Tweedsiders' defence that earned a draw. Hibs took this second chance all right, and were probably thankful not to have been in the shoes of Hearts, who lost at Bo'ness, or Rangers, who went down at Ayr. Nithsdale Wanderers won at Tannadice, and Dundee could only draw with St. Bernards.

Having beaten Clackmannan in the first round, Hibs took full advantage of their situation all the way to the final, and kept their goal intact in doing so. They beat Queens Park in a tie that was keenly anticipated and quickly forgotten, then likewise beat Aberdeen by two goals. Dunn scored within a minute, after the goalkeeper had turned his first effort on to the bar; and after Shaw had been magnificent in thwarting Aberdeen's comeback, a cross from Ritchie in the second half went in through a crowd of players.

The semi-final was against Third Lanark at Tynecastle. Hibs were on top for twenty minutes, and Dunn forced Muir to drop the ball and let him score.

Hibs had Harper to thank this time when the backlash came, but Thirds always seemed to be struggling against the collar, and Hibs held on to win.

With McColl having recently moved ahead of Dunn as Hibs' top scorer, it was fitting that Hibs' opponents in the final were again Celtic. This one was at Ibrox, and so were 80,000 spectators. Unfortunately they were not very well entertained, as both defences held such sway over their opponents that thrills were few. It took a mistake to break the deadlock, and when it came midway through the second half, it was a tragedy for, of all people, Harper, who came out for a cross from McFarlane but missed it to let Cassidy head home. With all the forwards continuing to be subdued, one was enough, and another Cup final chance had gone.

But the next year came another, although Hibs hardly reached the 1924 final in style. Ritchie scored the only goal against Dundee United in a disappointing tie, then Hibs struggled to draw with Alloa at Easter Road, although they did break loose and score five in the replay at Recreation Park. The third round brought Hibs' only memorable performance of the competition, at Ibrox.

The Scotsman thought Hibs' win against the League champions 'a sensational achievement', especially after Meiklejohn had scored from the corner of the penalty box as Rangers, with the wind, gave a clever exhibition. McGinnigle and Shaw excelled to restrict the Light Blues to the one goal, and soon after the restart Ritchie beat McCandless and crossed for Walker to touch in the equaliser. Corners and scrimmages in front of goal were common at Harper's end, but Hibs survived it all, and in the closing stages Murray, Hibs' makeshift centre, scored a winner for Hibs. The attendance was 52,885.

Hibs' next opponents were Partick Thistle, and they made things hard for themselves by gifting the Maryhill side two quick goals midway through the first half, so that it took all Hibs' best efforts, and goals from Murray and Dunn, to earn a replay. Still without McColl, Hibs took an early lead through Walker and looked like winning by it till Harper inadvertently fisted the ball to an opponent with just six minutes to go. The third game was at Parkhead; Dunn scored two good goals in the first half, and though McGinnigle kept up the level of hospitality with an own goal, Hibs held on to win.

Aberdeen were the semi-final opponents, and it was Walker who opened the scoring against them — Dunn hit the post, Ritchie was so taken by surprise that he totally missed the rebound, but in the melee that followed, Walker got a fortuitous touch to divert the ball between the goalkeeper's legs. It had taken just a minute short of five hours, and came as a relief to everyone, as scarcely a chance had been created during that time. This second replay took place at convenient Ibrox, despite a request from both clubs to play it at Tynecastle.

More Blues at Ibrox

The final was also at Ibrox, against Airdrie, which at this distance in time seems surprising, but the Waysiders in the early '20s had their best ever side, a statement which is unlikely to go out of date in the foreseeable future, and they were in the middle of a run of being League runners-up in succession.

The game itself, like many Cup finals — and especially the ones that Hibs have played in — was a disappointment. There were long listless spells and the impression at half-time was that Airdrie had already won it. They had. Hibs never recovered from Russell's headed goal in the opening two minutes, and even his second before half-time was superfluous. Hibs were far below their best — and the team selection of an unfit Dunn, on the sentimental grounds of fielding the same side as the previous year, cost them dear, as he soon had to change places with Ritchie, thus lessening the winger's impact too. Miller always seemed to have more on his plate than he could cope with, though as this came in the shape of Hughie Gallacher, the Hibs' centre-half can hardly be criticised.

The last Cup run considered in this chapter, that of 1925, was a short one. Hibs met Aberdeen for the third year in succession but failed to make it three wins. 1924–25 was more notable for Hibs' League performances than their Cup exploits, and they finished third in the table, the only time they made the top three between their championship-winning years of 1903 and 1948.

All through the period Hibs did better than for a long time, although they were seldom in contention. Season 1919–20 was the poorest, with Hibs finishing thirteenth out of twenty-two after a poor start in which the team was chopped and changed as a suitable blend was sought. It was in 1921 that a Second Division was restarted. The Central League had applied *en bloc*, as easily the strongest of the regional organisations, but although they were turned down, most of their member clubs were admitted individually, with a few Western League clubs such as Vale of Leven and Johnstone.

This made 1921–22 a more entertaining season, as automatic promotion and relegation had also been introduced, and so there was the novelty of avoiding the latter. It didn't concern Hibs that year, but it did Hearts, who avoided the first big drop only by winning at Pittodrie on the final day of the season. Hibs had quite a successful time, finishing seventh, but to their supporters a better yardstick of their success would have been their five wins out of five against their Tynecastle rivals. This dominance paved the way for a clean sweep in the local competitions, although the most meritorious was probably the Dunedin Cup in which Hibs beat Raith and Falkirk, third and fourth in the League respectively.

Season 1922–23 was another reasonable one for Hibs; they finished eighth in the championship, but only a point adrift of Aberdeen who were fifth. They got off to a good start with full points in August, at the end of which they were top, and were especially hard to beat at home — all five top teams lost at Easter Road. McColl missed the first quarter of the League programme, but still ended up Hibs' top scorer. Of their local trophies, Hibs retained only the East of Scotland Shield, but the crowd of 22,000 for the final against Hearts showed that these two at least could still pull out the fans for local ties.

The New Easter Road

It was also in 1922–23 that Hibs seem to have decided to stop looking for new premises, and make the best of what they had. They didn't have very much, in fact, because their lease was just about up, but they negotiated a new one for twenty-five years from Whitsunday 1925 at £250 per annum. A previous attempt to purchase the site had been turned down because it came into the Corporation's plans for their town-planning project for Craigentinny.

With their future thus secured, Hibs next set about improving their ground. This was a major task, and involved moving the pitch sideways about forty yards in order to build the new (i.e. present) grandstand on the other side of the pitch, on ground at the time occupied by old buildings. The pitch was also greatly levelled — so there must have been some slope before — and a new road and new entrances were planned for what is now known as the Dunbar end. The cost was to be an enormous £20,000, and the new capacity 45,000 with 4,200 seated under cover.

Meanwhile, Hibs were seventh in the following season, and McColl again had a big say with twenty League goals. They had been fourth as late as February, and in fact ended two points behind Raith who finished in that position. 1923 saw the start of a Third Division, of which only East Stirling, Queen of the South, Montrose and Brechin are present-day League members. Brechin started their campaign in August and scored their first League goal as early as November 10th, and the title went to Arthurlie. Leith Athletic were not in this League, but were still in the Western League for some reason.

Work had not progressed as fast as intended on Hibs' ground improvements, and in particular a builders' strike meant that it was not in

TENNYSON'S BROOK TOUCH AT EASTER ROAD.

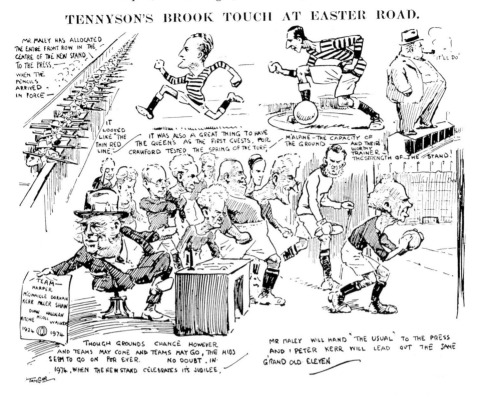

An 'Evening News' cartoon of September 1924 on the occasion of the opening of the stand at Easter Road. Peter Kerr led out a settled home team which gave one of its best performances to beat Queens Park 2–0.

order for the opening of season 1924–25. Hibs managed to get the use of Tynecastle until they were able to play at Easter Road again, but they had to do so on Friday evenings because St. Bernards were also playing at Tynecastle while their Gymnasium ground was being refurbished after several years as an army training ground, and they had asked first. As it turned out, Hibs played only two home games on Hearts' ground, with full points from their meetings with Partick Thistle and Motherwell, before Queens Park hanselled the new Easter Road on September 13th and Hibs won a good game 2–0, largely because Ritchie was at his very best.

As we saw earlier, Hibs had their best year for a long time in 1924–25, and finished third, and indeed they were top in October, and again briefly at the end of March, though in the latter case only because Rangers and Airdrie had had more success than Hibs in the Cup and so had played fewer League games. Hibs' best performance was the thrashing of the champions at Easter

Road, where they were four up before Rangers got a consolation goal near the end. Dunn was top scorer this year with 23 goals to McColl's 22.

Hibs also won the Shield, and the Wilson and Charity Cups, beating Hearts 1–0 in each of the three finals. It was Dunn who scored in the Charity Cup, beating several opponents and leaving the goalkeeper helpless with a terrific shot from thirty yards. It was of course the final match of the season, and therefore a fitting way to complete Hibs' first fifty years.

Things had come a long way since the early scenes of chaos in the East Meadows and elsewhere, yet the official programme for the 1924 Cup final still noted that 'for a present-day Football Club it [the Hibs club] is a very close and private concern'.

(Back row l to r) — Di Christopher, Buchanan, Duncan, Paterson, Harper, Shaw, Miller, Strong, T. Cannon and P. Cannon. (Seated) — Young, Halligan, Dunn, Director Owen Brannigan, Director John Farm, Director Alex Maley, Dornan, McGinnigle and Walker. The trophies — East of Scotland Shield, Dunedin Cup and Rosebery Bowl. The picture was taken in front of the old pavilion at Easter Road in May, 1922.

CHAPTER 11

The Great Slump, 1925–31

One of the main features of Hibs' comparative success in the first half of the 1920s was their ability to field an unchanged team in so many matches, but the seeds of their subsequent fall from grace had been sown at the same time, because in 1923 it was decided to do without a reserve side, and that decision arguably cost Hibs the League title in 1925. A second string was restarted about two years later, but with the latter part of the decade marred by a dispute between the Glasgow junior sides (amongst whom Hibs had always recruited heavily) and the senior clubs, it was a long time before Hibs made up the lost ground.

It was under Alex Maley's managership, of which more later in the chapter, that the reserve team was scrapped. Maley had taken over from Davy Gordon, and was given much of the credit for the achievements of the team that his predecessor had built. His appointment in the first place had not been without opposition, since he was related to the Tom Maley who had played for the old Hibs, and who along with his relatives Coleman and Dunbar was widely blamed for the mass poaching by Celtic in 1888. Maley's tenure ended in 1925, and it was hoped that Paddy Travers of Clyde might be persuaded to follow him, but he wasn't, and the job was given to the veteran full-back Bobby Templeton, apparently to the disappointment of Peter Kerr, a servant of even longer standing.

In the game itself, a major change in 1925 was in the offside rule, which was altered so that two rather than three defenders had to be between a forward and his opponents' goal line. The effects of this were very noticeable, and topical in view of more recent attempts to alter it further. The number of goals per game in the First Division in the four years following this change was one third higher than that in the four years before it, although there had been something of a rising trend in the earlier period anyway. But it was no coincidence that so many of the game's scoring records were established in the late '20s — Jimmy McGrory's eight for Celtic against Dunfermline, Jimmy Smith's 66 league goals in a season for Ayr and Dixie Dean's 60 for Everton both in the same season, and Hughie Gallacher's five for Scotland in Belfast, to name a few.

Hibs' first game under the new conditions was at Parkhead, and a shambles it was. No-one seemed to know who was offside and who was not, including the referee who was seen at half-time studying his directive on the new law from the authorities. There was not much doubt which way the

John 'Darkie' Walker.

breaks went, because Celtic won 5–0 in 'a rout as complete as it was unexpected', while some in the Hibs' party were adamant that not one of the five should have stood.

With this orgy of goalscoring, it was a measure of Hibs' problems that they played six consecutive games without scoring once in the autumn of 1925. McColl at centre was having a lean spell, as the press were not slow to point out, but the main trouble lay further back, and related again to Hibs' lack of back-up. A succession of injuries affected the rear half of the side, and reached a peak in October when only Miller of the recognised back six was fit to play at Pittodrie, when Hibs crashed 5–0. A month later, after a defeat at Hamilton, they reached bottom position of the League, so it was with some relief that the Easter Road faithful watched their team beat Hamilton in the return in December by 8 goals to 4, with three of the visitors' scores coming from former Hibs Williamson and Miller.

It was during this lean spell that Hibs lost the irreplaceable services of Harper. The big goalkeeper had spent most of the early season injured, although he did turn out on occasion though lame, and it was clear in his absence that there was no suitable stand-in on the books: the manager himself had stood in on occasion. When he was fit again, it took only one game to show that he was as good as ever, after which he was transferred to Arsenal. Scotland's national side had been having a run of success against England for a few years, and as usual the Scottish League was pillaged by clubs from the south trying to buy their success. Of the team which had won only in April, Harper was the fourth to cross the Border.

Harper's stay with Arsenal did not prove to be too happy. He lost his place for both club and country, and was ever at loggerheads with the former. For a while his future seemed to lie in North America; later he went there on a temporary basis and was suspended *sine die* on his return. Eventually he put down roots at Plymouth, where he remained long after he stopped playing.

Back at Easter Road the second half of the season brought some improvement, though not a lot more than the minimum needed. There was a gruelling Ne'erday win at Tynecastle, where two goals in a minute just after half-time by Ritchie put Hibs three up and safe, but later feelings ran high and White of Hearts was sent off. Two weeks later Hibs led League leaders Celtic three times but had to settle for a 4–4 draw, and Ritchie scored a second-half hat-trick as Hibs won 5–2 at Cappielow. But there were moderate performances too, and it took a fortunate goal from a drooping free kick by Shaw to earn the points at Clydeholm Park, Clydebank and banish fear of relegation. Hibs had not done themselves any favours a week earlier by losing at home to Cowdenbeath and missing three penalties in doing so.

Moreover, Hibs had won only the East of Scotland Shield locally, had taken two games at Easter Road to put Broxburn out of the Scottish Cup before losing at home to Airdrie, and had been slammed 4–1 by Leith in the Charity Cup.

Leith were Third Division champions and in line for promotion, but as usual fortune had no difficulty in avoiding them. Nine games were outstanding in the Division when the season closed, so promotion and relegation were scrapped. This was hard on Leith, who had played all their games in time, and their Cup-tie attitude, all too rarely seen in the Charity Cup, was an attempt to gain support for their election to the Second Division. This ambition foundered when Hearts beat them in the final by 9–0, and Leith had to be content to join the new Alliance set-up. This consisted of former Third Division sides and First Division reserve sides, and was split regionally. With the curious sense of geography peculiar to Scottish football through the years, Leith were placed with Hibs 'A' and, among others, Peebles Rovers — in the North Section.

Back at Easter Road, it had been obvious that Hibs' reserve strength was not all it might be. In particular, neither Sharp nor Millsop had filled Harper's place satisfactorily, and so Hibs were delighted to acquire the services of Willie Robb, the experienced Rangers' keeper who had two League caps and had played against Wales just the previous autumn. Hugh Shaw went to Ibrox, and as Peter Kerr had also gone, on a free transfer, to Hearts, two new half-backs were needed too. Willie Dick and Eddie Gilfeather were signed from Airdrie and Celtic, and shortly Finlay from

Willie Robb, noted for his taste in caps and long shorts, seen making one of many saves which earned Hibs a draw at Tynecastle in October 1928.

Dundee United joined them. Finally, Walker had been slow to re-sign, and by the time he did, he had lost his place to Jackie Bradley from St. Rochs.

St. Johnstone were Hibs' first opponents, and they too had been round the summer sales, with five men signed from English clubs. Once it was all sorted out who was playing for whom, it was Munro of Saints who caught the eye, mainly on account of his scoring four goals and making another. Aberdeen were the next visitors to Easter Road, and when they won too, it was neither obvious that the season would after all be better than the previous one, nor that that would be because of a fine home record.

Hibs however were not beaten on their ground between late August and late March, and rose to the occasions with stirring displays against the top sides. Their 2–2 draw with the champions Rangers was earned primarily by their determined defence, while their win over Airdrie was due more to dashing forward play as well as to two early goals by Dunn. On the September holiday Hibs came back twice from being behind to beat Celtic 3–2, and likewise came back twice to draw 2–2 with Hearts on Ne'erday. These last two results were good, but Hibs did even better to get the same scores at Parkhead and Tynecastle, the former stemming from a display of 'electrifying footcraft' from Dunn. Of course there were much less memorable performances too, and Hibs lost to four of the bottom five teams.

Nevertheless Hibs finished ninth, and none of the front five failed to take

A Hibs' programme from 1928: this one is Hibs v. Airdrie, which is not obvious from the front cover.

his goal tally into double figures; Dunn played against Ireland, Ritchie against the English League. But in local competitions Hibs took only the Wilson Cup, and in the Scottish Cup went out by three first-half goals at Cowdenbeath, although in fairness that score was out of all proportion to the balance of play.

Season 1927–28 was not unlike its predecessor, with Hibs finishing in mid-table, 12th with 35 points. Only Clyde and Airdrie beat them at Easter Road, but Hibs again showed they could lose almost anywhere else, and of the teams at the foot, only Dunfermline failed to beat them.

At least in 1928 there was a lengthy Cup run, starting with a walkover against Dykehead. Their second-round tie was at Cathkin; Third Lanark, the pacesetters in the Second Division, were more dangerous in the first half, but Hibs stayed the pace better, and Ritchie and Dunn scored the second-half goals that won the tie.

Falkirk visited Easter Road in the next round, and the game was exciting and strenuous, though for Hibs a disappointing result, 0–0, emerged. The replay was even harder fought. Falkirk had slightly the better of play, but it was McColl who broke the deadlock with a fifteen-yard drive in extra time. In the fourth round Hibs visited Dunfermline, who were building a reputation for Cup surprises, but fortunately the Fifers were unable to live up to their supporters' expectations, and goals by Halligan, Bradley and Dunn (2) gave Hibs an easy win.

Hibs' prize was a semi-final match with Rangers, and it brought about one of their most remarkable Cup successes. The number of times that Rangers have played matches on 'neutral' ground in Scotland outside Glasgow is neither large nor expected to grow much, but the semi-final with Hibs was fixed for Tynecastle. That in fact was the last time the Ibrox side have moved outside Glasgow at that stage of the competition, despite their apparent penchant for avoiding their main local rivals.

Spice was added to the tie when Hibs beat Rangers in the League a week before it, and after the Light Blues had scored in the first minute, but the match at Tynecastle was a big let-down for the 44,000 crowd. A mistake by Robb let Archibald score in two minutes, and Rangers took a grip of the game from which Hibs found no escape. McPhail netted from close range after half an hour and Simpson headed a third in the second half. Rangers went on to beat Celtic 4–0 for their first Cup win for twenty-five years.

A Wembley Wizard

Three Hibs men were honoured during the season. Robb played against Wales, Ritchie and Dunn against Ireland, and Dunn was one of only three home Scots who played against England and became Wembley Wizards — the others were Jack Harkness and Alan Morton. For Jimmy McColl there was the distinction of becoming the first man to score a hundred League and Cup goals for Hibs, although it is worth mentioning that of Hibs' two earlier more successful teams, that at the turn of the century only played about half as many League games and the first Cup-winning side played none at all. McColl did not win the race by much because Dunn passed the same figure shortly before the season ended.

Dunn did not make the ton with a lot to spare, because when the next season started, he and Ritchie were in Everton's colours. Their immediate replacements were Finlay and Geordie Murray, the veteran utility player. Harry Brown soon took over the inside position and was likened by some to Dunn, but Ritchie proved a harder act to follow, and a succession of candidates failed to measure up.

In addition, Dornan had stepped down and knee trouble was soon to force McGinnigle to do likewise, so that Bertie Stark, who had deputised for both, formed a new full-back partnership with Hector Wilkinson, soon reckoned to be the best uncapped back around. At centre-half, Dick had taken over

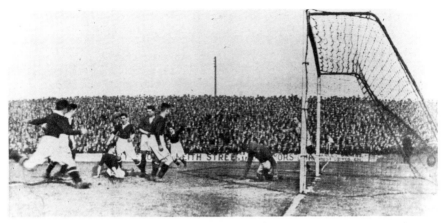

Barney Battles scores for Hearts in the 1930 cup tie at Easter Road. The terracing can be seen to be at its present height.

from Miller. McColl was by now a veteran too, but there was no-one to displace him.

It was a somewhat transitional Hibs team, then, that slipped a further two places down the table, and their goal tally of nineteen fewer indicated the reason for it. It would have been worse but for the generosity of John Thompson, the Celtic goalkeeper, of all people. Jimmy McGrory claimed that Thompson only had one bad game for Celtic, and that was Celtic's 'home' game with Hibs at Easter Road in April while Celtic Park was under repair. Thompson gave away the first two goals, an unheard-of occurrence, and as McStay kept up the good work by spooning a pass-back over him for an own goal, Hibs had to do little to win.

That was an unusual ending to what had been a fairly uneventful season, apart from Edinburgh's worst day in the Scottish Cup. Hibs, Hearts, St. Bernards, Leith Athletic and Edinburgh City — in their first season — all lost in the first round, leaving only Murrayfield Amateurs to represent the capital in the second. Hibs went down at home to a St. Johnstone side keyed up to a high pitch to do well, and who scored twice shortly before half-time. Bradley got one back as Hibs fought hard, but there could be no quibbling with the result. The final weeks of the season brought Hibs and Hearts together in three local finals — and Hibs lost eighteen goals.

The decline continued in 1929–30. After four games Hibs had just one win, were fourth bottom and got worse. At times there was only St. Johnstone below them, and by the turn of the year they were engaged in a hectic relegation battle. Hibs had fourteen points, the same as Dundee United and Airdrie and one more than the Perth side.

GOALS, AND MORE GOALS AT EASTER ROAD.

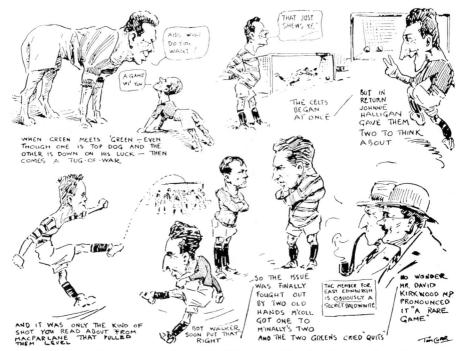

Another Tom Curr cartoon from the 'Evening News', this one from January 1926, and an exciting encounter in which eight goals were shared equally between Hibs and Celtic.

Airdrie were the first to ease clear of the bottom three, and then in February a run of two wins and two draws, their best of the season, let Hibs establish a five-point advantage over Dundee United. The Tannadice men went down with St. Johnstone, while Hibs eventually finished ahead of Morton too.

Hibs' team problems seemed no nearer a solution. Bob Sclater, Jimmy Dobson and Archie Connell were three young centres tried, and none fitted the bill. McColl was used as a stopgap right-winger where another problem existed, but at least he was on hand to move back to centre to try to save matches that were going badly. McColl's ability more than made up for the greater dash and energy of younger men, and the same could be said of Halligan, now also past his prime at inside-left. No-one was comparing Brown to Dunn anymore either, so it was not surprising that Hibs' forty-five League goals were the lowest tally in Division One. Meanwhile, Harry Ritchie was not hitting the high spots on Merseyside, but when he left Everton in February 1930, it was Dundee who brought him back to Scotland.

Hibs on the attack at Tyncastle — goalkeeper Crossley foils a Hibs' forward, probably Andy Main, during the League clash in September 1930.

With the wing-halves no more than adequate, Hibs' defence was the strongest part of the team. It was held together by Dick, while at full-back Wilkinson had been joined by Duncan Urquhart, a tough tackler from Newton Stewart: Stark went to Leith Athletic. In goal, Robb continued until January when he dislocated a finger. This was unlucky for him, because not only was it sore, but by the time it wasn't he had lost his place to George Blyth and did not regain it.

The rest of the season brought no greater cheer. Hibs beat Leith Amateurs in the Cup, but only by 2–0, then won at Ayr, which was a bit of a turn-up as they had yet to put an away League win to their credit. The third-round draw produced a derby with Hearts, and 28,000 spectators crowded into Easter Road. The deciding factor was at centre, where Hibs had Sclater, who was totally subdued although he did score in a scramble, while Hearts had Battles whose two goals and general leadership showed how weak Hibs were in that department. There was some hollow revenge as Hibs beat Hearts to win the East of Scotland Shield and the Wilson and Dunedin Cups, two of them admittedly on corners, but then Leith Athletic beat them in the Charity Cup.

Nevertheless in April *The Scotsman* had been sufficiently optimistic to comment that Hibs were 'a team of distinct possibilities', despite the occasion being a defeat at Kilmarnock. Unfortunately the possibility that was realised was that a year later Hibs were relegated.

They won only one of their opening nine games, though an important one, at Ayr, whose team were Hibs' main rivals all season to accompany East Fife down to Division Two. The defeats included a six-goal thrashing at Parkhead and a home defeat from Leith Athletic, who scored in their only serious attack owing to a slip by Wilkinson. Neither of these results was exactly morale-boosting, but a win over Airdrie in October did put Hibs above Ayr.

The New Deal

There had been dissatisfaction with the affairs of the club for some time, especially from the debenture holders, most of whom had financed the ground improvements and had seen the status of the club along with their prospects of repayment diminish ever since. With the recession, many clubs in both Scotland and England survived only with difficulty, and a few failed in the effort, so there was cause for concern. Matters came to a head with the debenture holders holding out for, and getting, representation on the board by the transfer of shares from the by now elderly Pat Smith to the representatives of the new class of creditor. Owen Brannigan, although very elderly by this time, became chairman and Alex Maley joined the board, but the more significant change came when Harry Swan, a master baker from Leith, and Tom Hartland took their seats.

This shift in power was considered so significant that one previous history of the club considered the third Hibernian club to start from this date; although Hibs had been a non-sectarian club in the playing sense, control of it had always been kept within the small group who resuscitated the club in 1892, and all share transfers had to be approved by them. Swan was the first non-Catholic to hold shares.

It was of course not long before Harry Swan became chairman and started to fashion the club to suit his ambitions for it, although Hibs' traditional support did not find him entirely to their liking, and felt somewhat alienated by a number of measures during his chairmanship — the requirement that priests apply for tickets to ensure their traditional free entry to Easter Road, and the unpublicised removal of the harp from above the main entrance to the ground, as well as the rumoured intention to change the name and colours of the club to widen its appeal.

Swan was not overtly anti-Catholic, even in the '30s when many were, and the Protestant Action Society, who specialised in terrorising Catholics and were especially strong around Leith, won over thirty per cent of the votes in local elections. He was however a freemason, a fact not lost on the visiting Celtic supporters in particular, and evidence of uncontrollable grief on his part when the previously powerful Lester family had no longer any representation on the board is difficult to establish.

The new administration immediately went into the transfer market and acquired the services of Joe Miller, the Middlesbrough right-half who had recently won three Irish caps. Miller went straight into the side at Pittodrie, where, with internationalist Yorston unable to turn out for the Dons, Hibs were hopeful, and outplayed their hosts for half an hour. Then came a complete collapse and Aberdeen scored seven, all but one claimed by Merrie, Yorston's deputy. Miller in fact, far from adding a great deal to the team, was out of it as much as he was in it, and the same was true of the ex-Clyde forward Wallace in the second half of the season, after Hibs had paid a substantial sum to Burnley to bring him back to Scotland.

Far from finding a forward blend, Hibs were thus further away than ever from it, because veterans McColl and Halligan were now appearing only intermittently, and so there were no automatic choices in the front rank, although it would not have taken a world-class player to be one. A further centre, Andy Main from St. Johnstone, was probably the pick with fifteen goals, while Harry Brown, Taylor, Bradley, Clelland, Ross, Dobson, Lauder and others vied for places. Even Dick was tried at centre, being able to be spared from his defensive duties by the emergence of 'Ginger' Watson from Stoneyburn Juniors at centre-half, easily the most promising of the younger brigade.

Meanwhile Hibs managed to stay above Ayr United and East Fife, if no-one else, and successive draws against Hearts and Celtic at New Year gave them a five-point advantage over Ayr who had played two games less. The match three weeks later against Ayr was crucial, especially as Ayr had meanwhile beaten East Fife, but Hibs won that one because of a good first-half display which included goals from Main and Brown. Hibs led Ayr by four points with two more games played when the Cup got under way.

The first round of the 1931 Cup competition brought a spate of scoring as never before. Partick Thistle led it with sixteen, three others made double figures and fifteen teams altogether scored six or more. With a home draw against St. Cuthberts Wanderers, Hibs might have been expected to participate in the orgy of goals, but the most that can be said of their 3–1 win was that Saints' goal was scored by Pagan. In the second round Hibs earned a hard-fought draw at Hamilton which depended on Hamilton's Watson missing a last-minute penalty, then in the replay McColl celebrated a temporary recall to centre by scoring four times in a 5–2 win.

This success encouraged a crowd of 33,300, a ground record, to attend the next tie with Motherwell, but what they were disappointed to discover was that McColl was not fit to play. Motherwell scored after half an hour, and while it never seemed likely that Hibs would win, the Lanarkshire team were able to relax only after they had scored a further two goals in a minute in the last ten minutes of play.

Attention was thus once again fixed on the League. Hibs' home win against Cowdenbeath was a scrambled affair but widened the gap with Ayr to six points, but then they dropped a home point to Morton and were completely outplayed at Methil, which was especially disappointing as hopes of a double over the doomed Fifers had been high. The disappointment was only partially offset by the news that Hearts had beaten Ayr by 9–0.

So with five games to go, Hibs had 22 points and a much better goal average than Ayr, who had 16 points and eight games to go. But while Hibs won only one more game, by a last-minute goal against Hamilton, Ayr lost only two, at Parkhead and Ibrox, and nearly became the first team all season to win at Motherwell. Four wins meant that after the last Saturday of the season, when Hibs had drawn at Falkirk, Hibs and Ayr were level on points, with Hibs having the better goal average, but with Ayr having an outstanding home game with Kilmarnock. Tolland scored the only goal for Ayr with fifteen minutes to go and Ayr left the field to a standing ovation from their 14,000 supporters. Hibs were relegated.

(Back row l to r) — Gilfeather, Stark, Robb, Finlay, McGinnigle, Murray. (Front row) — Frew, Halligan, Dick, McColl and Preston. The Hibs' team of 1928.

CHAPTER 12

The Second Division, 1931–33

This is a short chapter, which is a good thing because it describes Hibs' stay in Division Two.

As is still the case, the lower reaches of the Scottish League were the home of the clubs from the smaller outposts of football civilisation in the north and east, while the bigger clubs tended to operate from the cities and larger towns, especially in industrial Strathclyde. For the aesthetic travelling supporter there were pleasant outings to rural Dumfriesshire, Angus and Fife's East Neuk, and admittedly Coatbridge. For the gourmets there were visits to the homes of Forfar bridies and Arbroath smokies, not to mention Dumbarton rock! However, the cheques earned from these places did not compare with those brought home from Parkhead and Ibrox, and this would have been more in the minds of those whose concern it was to make Hibs' time in the lower League as brief as possible.

It was soon clear that promotion was not just a case of completing the fixtures. It took 'an immense struggle' and a goal by new left-half Burke to beat Alloa in the opening game, and within a week Hibs had lost by 3–0 to St. Bernards in the Shield, and by the only goal at Forfar in the League. A 3–1 win over Arbroath still did not satisfy the 4,000 who were now the regular support, but in the next two home games Hibs scored six against both St. Johnstone, who finished up easy winners of promotion, and Dunfermline Athletic. Things took a turn for the worse at that point, and Hibs won only one of the next eight matches; St. Bernards beat them again in a game in which goalkeeper Blyth broke his leg, and Edinburgh City did the same to record their first-ever League win.

With another swing in fortune, Hibs only lost one more game before the end of the year, a curious game with Queen of the South in which the visitors were seldom on the attack but found four easy second-half goals coming their way and were grateful to leave with the points. Hibs did well at Arbroath where they salvaged one point after being three goals down.

This left Hibs with 29 points from 22 games at the turn of the year, to which they managed to add just under a point a game for the rest of the season, and they finished seventh. East Stirlingshire won the division on goal average from St. Johnstone, now helped by ex-Hib Ritchie, and eleven points ahead of Hibs. St. Bernards were fifth, so with Hearts and Leith in Division One, Hibs were only fourth of the Edinburgh sides, and they also came in behind Forfar Athletic and Stenhousemuir.

Johnny Halligan, the sole survivor of the fine team of the twenties in the team that took Hibs back to the First Division in 1933.

'Ginger' Watson, whose rugged displays earned a League 'cap'.

Hibs also failed to win a single Cup tie, losing at the first hurdle to Dundee United (Scottish Cup), Hearts (Wilson Cup), Falkirk (Dunedin Cup) and, despite a guest appearance in their colours by Patsy Gallagher, to Leith Athletic (Charity Cup).

If things were at a low point at Easter Road, they had gone through the floor at Marine Gardens. Leith Athletic finished bottom of Division One and conceded a top division record of 137 League goals, while Edinburgh City, who shared the Portobello enclosure with them, were last in the Second Division and conceded a Scottish League record of 146 League goals. In addition, following rumours in January that a First Division side would be defunct within the week, Leith felt it necessary to anounce that most of their players were being freed and they would try to fulfil their remaining fixtures with trialists and amateurs. They were not alone in trouble: Clyde introduced dog racing when it seemed they would go to the wall, while in England no less a club than Manchester United were rescued from the receiver at the eleventh hour.

Twenty-seventh in the table was rather lower than Hibs felt they should be, and when they kicked off in their second season in Division Two, there

The Second Division champions of 1933. Back row (l to r) Langton, Watson, Wilkinson, Blyth, Urquhart and McFarlane. Front — Walls, Wallace, Halligan, Flucker and Hutchison.

were four new faces in the side that made a good start by defeating Dundee United. Peter Flucker and Rab Walls were the two who were to make the greater impact, McPherson (Dalkeith) and Hart (East Stirling) the others. They were all forwards, and there was certainly a big improvement in that department — Hibs won fifteen of their opening eighteen games and scored sixty goals in doing so. Flucker with fifteen had the biggest share.

It was at this point, at the end of November, that the Second Division was upset by the expulsion of first Bo'ness then Armadale for failing to meet guarantees, thus ending West Lothian's interest in League football.

The first game between Hibs and St. Bernards, in November, had produced two points for Hibs and a ground record of 15,000 for the Gymnasium. The return at the end of March brought Hibs two more points and the Second Division title. They had yet to lose a League game in 1933, but that changed a week later when Stenhousemuir beat them, giving the Larbert side their third win in four League games with Hibs, proportionately better than anyone else. It was at this point that the League decided to expunge the records of Bo'ness and Armadale, and as Hibs thereby lost six points, they were no longer certain of winning the Division. So when Hibs beat Dumbarton on April 15th, they had won the title for the second time in three weeks.

It was as well that Hibs had no worries on that score when they met Queen of the South on April 22nd. Queens were making a late run for promotion, and a large support came from Dumfries by special train, an unusual enough event in itself. Not much went right for Hibs. Watson was unfit so Clark deputised, then he was hurt and Flucker played the second half at centre-half. Then Walls dislocated a wrist and the nine remaining quite explicably lost 2—1. Queens then had to wait and hope that Dunfermline would fail to beat King's Park, which Dunfermline duly did.

Playing with the confidence that came from their League successes, Hibs also did well in the Cup. There was a slight hiccup at the first hurdle when Forfar earned a draw at Easter Road, but ample amends were made when Hibs won 7–3 at Station Park after leading 4–0 at the interval. Hibs then travelled to Aberdeen and fully deserved the half-time lead that a free kick by Walls gave them. The second half was different, and Aberdeen were just as deserving of Beattie's equaliser. The replay brought scenes of great excitement. Aberdeen set a cracking pace, but Hibs held out and made a late fightback in which, with six minutes to go, Halligan took careful aim and fired an accurate shot into the top corner of the net for a notable win.

Hibs' reward was a bye followed by a home draw with Hearts — and a draw it was. A crowd of 33,759 packed Easter Road and was the biggest of the day, and though on the terracing 'some hotheads in red and green hats came to blows', the game was fast and free from fouls. It was also free from goals, but the replay was not. Johnstone and Murray put Hearts two ahead in half an hour, and the Tynecastle team, content to hold on to this lead, did so with something to spare. The crowd at the replay exceeded 41,000. It was clear that life in the Capital was found wanting without the League matches between the two, despite Hibs' six local derbies in the Second Division.

1933 was the fiftieth anniversary of the Rosebery Charity Cup, and to celebrate the event Motherwell, the First Division runners-up and Cup finalists, were invited to make a guest appearance. In fact they made two appearances, beating Hibs by a Stevenson goal in their first tie, and losing 3–1 to Hearts in the final.

CHAPTER 13

Light in the Tunnel, 1933–39

The 1930s were a pretty grim decade; it started with the world in depression and finished with it at war. The social and economic problems of the early '30s were much more severe than those of the recession half a century later, and likewise the war with Hitler had somewhat more desperate moments than those captured by its Hollywood heroes.

In a similar way, the impression that the '30s were a boom time for Scottish football, with huge crowds ready to roll up for every game, is based on fact and great exaggeration. This is partly because of the disproportionate amount of coverage, from the newsreels of the time to the videotaped excerpts of the present day, allotted to the big games in Glasgow. Scotland has too many League football clubs at present to make economic sense, and there were just as many fifty years ago. While it is true that more than

Centre-half Watson involved with Massie, Hearts, in the first Edinburgh derby following Hibs' return to the First Division.

Jerry Dawson is beaten by Willie Black's header which gave Hibs a draw with Rangers in September 1935.

149,000 watched the Scotland v. England game of 1937, and even more incredibly, over 118,000 packed into Ibrox for an Old Firm game two years later, most First Division games were played before four-figure attendances, many Second Division games failed to attract that many, and several clubs lived on the breadline.

In the six seasons of First Division football to 1939, the attendances at Easter Road did not increase more than marginally. Only Hearts and Rangers were able to attract 30,000 to the stadium on occasion, Celtic somewhat less and Aberdeen and Motherwell a bit above average. A typical crowd for the other games was 7,000, giving an overall average of about 10,000. The ground record set against Hearts in the 1933 Cup tie was not broken although the capacity continually increased. Moreover in most cases Hibs' away fixtures produced smaller crowds than their home ones, with the exception of derbies at Tynecastle, and it was not unknown for Hibs to play at Parkhead or Ibrox before fewer than 10,000 spectators.

When Hibs kicked off in the First Division at Hampden in August 1933, they had assembled a team in which ten men had top League experience.

Hibs started the campaign creditably. Eight points were taken from the first eight games, including well-fought draws with Hearts and Rangers.

Hibs' centre Willie Black beats Hearts' goalkeeper Waugh to the ball in the September derby of 1936, but fails to score. Waugh also had a short but dramatic spell with Hibs, while on loan from the Tynecastle club.

Watson was particularly conspicuous in subduing the dangerous Jimmy Smith, the Ibrox centre, and at times he kept the Hearts' attack at bay almost single-handed. His reward came with a League cap against Ireland, and soon afterwards Urquhart won a full cap for Scotland in Cardiff. The problems as before seemed to congregate in the forward line, but one was thought solved with the signing of Willie Moffat, the Motherwell inside man who made a quick impact.

Defeats began to become more commonplace, and by January Hibs had drifted down to the fringe of trouble, although they had certainly held their own at home. More attempts were made to improve the striking force — an outside-left, Nicholson, was signed from St. Johnstone, and another, Celtic's veteran Peter Kavanagh, came too. Flucker was excluded for the purpose of giving a run to Malloy, a centre from Arthurlie, but Hibs' major acquisition at this time was John Smith of Hearts, noted more for his ball-work and creation of goals than actually scoring them.

Smith and Kavanagh arrived just in time for Hibs' Scottish Cup tie with Clyde, and it turned out to be a game to remember. Merrie gave Clyde an early lead, but Walls matched it with a cheeky back heeler, then in the eight

Bobby Nutley, Hibs' busy little outside left at the outbreak of war.

L'il Arthur Milne, who scored a century of goals for Hibs before and during the Second World War.

minutes before half-time the roof fell in and Clyde scored three more. Over the years Hibs have made a number of notable fightbacks down their slope, but surely none better than what followed. Walls scored within three minutes of restarting, Smith got two from close range when the pressure was high, and then Mallow rounded off a combined attack with what proved to be the winner with fifteen minutes still to go.

This spirit stood Hibs in good stead a week later when they took two important points from Aberdeen after twice trailing, and then Malloy scored four in a six-goal spree against Alloa in the Cup. However, a 4–0 defeat from Hearts in the East of Scotland Shield brought them back to earth, and when they met Aberdeen again in the Cup, the Dons needed only one goal because Hibs were not able to pull it back in the remaining 86 minutes. The Cup exit was followed by a run of seven defeats in eight League games, which brought the late fear that Hibs might not after all have done enough to ensure their survival.

Fortunately their second-last game was against the struggling Third Lanark and an easy win gave relief; all that need be said about the one that followed at Dens Park is that only about a hundred people watched it — because Dundee United were playing Albion Rovers at Tannadice. It was clear that Hibs' problems were far from banished, and Wallace, Kavanagh and Malloy were among those freed to make way for the next influx of talent.

By the start of the season the only newcomer in Hibs' line-up was Borland, a winger from Shawfield, but he was soon joined by Arthurlie's centre Willie Black, a player who required all his liveliness to atone for his lack of inches. It was indeed a common criticism of Hibs throughout the '30s that their forwards were too small, and at a disadvantage against physically stronger defences or on heavy grounds — and there were plenty of both.

Another signing was made before August was out, and a major one — Peter Wilson, Celtic's international wing-half and a classy player noted for his long swinging passes to the far post as well for his unusually large ears, which the good-humoured Wilson claimed cost him a yard of pace.

The changes seemed to be for the better, and for once Hibs had something like a settled team. They beat Celtic in December which confirmed the improvement and at that time had 23 points from two games fewer. Had it not been for a very poor finish, when points for once were not vital, Hibs would have finished comfortably in the top half of the table, but as it was, they took only three points from the last seven games, lost seven goals at Airdrie and were eleventh.

In the Cup, Hibs had big wins against Vale of Atholl from Pitlochry and Clachnacuddin before the going got tougher and they were drawn to play at Aberdeen again. Hibs' strong half-back line of Wilson, Watson and Egan dominated the game, and had not captain Urquhart been injured, they might well have won. They thought they had won the replay when Anderson put the ball in the Aberdeen net in the last minute, but the left-winger was ruled offside. The third game was also at Easter Road. Flucker and Black twice gave Hibs a lead, but each time goalkeeper Hill gifted the Dons an equaliser. Aberdeen did not look back, and Armstrong scored a clean-cut goal with nine minutes to go to take the tie.

Season 1935–36 was a most dramatic one. Hibs started where they had left off in April, with only one win in eight League games and eleven in all. The only change was Tommy Brady for Moffat, and as the former turned out to be a capable footballer, one had to look further for the causes of a run that included a six-goal thrashing by Queens Park and home defeats by Arbroath and St Johnstone.

Worse was at hand when Hibs visited Tynecastle. Twice in the opening five minutes Walker scored with well-placed drives and Black, whose speed was causing Hibs a lot of trouble, added two more by half-time. Shortly afterwards the two young wingers Wipfler and Munro made it six, but then Hearts relaxed a bit and Walls, Brady and Black scored for Hibs in quick succession. Then Wipfler and McCulloch completed the highest score in the League between Hibs and Hearts.

Moreover, rumours abounded that some Hibs men had taken the field in no condition to play, especially amongst those in the 28,000 crowd who had witnessed Watson's stomach upset by the goalpost before the kick-off. The talk seemed to be confirmed when manager Templeton announced a few days later that Watson and Urquhart were being given free transfers immediately. Hibs supporters who realised that not all clubs maintained the high moral standards that prevailed at Easter Road were not surprised when the pair were fixed up with Ayr and Aberdeen within forty-eight hours.

In practical terms it was a risky move to expel the two internationalists, but virtue brought a quick reward as Hibs beat Kilmarnock, Hamilton, Albion Rovers and Dundee in succession before the bubble burst. The longer-term effect was more predictable, and with just one more win in the meantime, Hibs finished the year with a 7–4 defeat at Shawfield and in second-bottom place.

The situation was thus becoming serious when Hibs' manager and chairman travelled to Belfast in December to sign Jack Jones, the Irish international centre-half, from Linfield for an Irish record fee apparently financed by an Edinburgh bookmaker. They were also sufficiently impressed by his team-mate William Gowdy to buy him too, for a substantial fee and more than Dundee had been willing to pay a week earlier for him. Gowdy was also in the national side although not always picked for Linfield, and likewise at Easter Road he spent rather more time in the Alliance team than might have been expected.

But by February Hibs had mustered just one more win, and that a hard-earned one against the amateurs of Vale Ocoba at Alexandria in the Cup: two of the goals came from yet another Irishman, Paddy Farrell. When this was followed by a second-round defeat by Clyde, Bobby Templeton resigned as manager, apparently not under pressure to do so, and within sight of his 25th anniversary with Hibs.

A Narrow Escape

Johnny Halligan was appointed caretaker until the relegation issue was settled, and as seems to happen extraordinarily often, had instant short-term success with narrow wins over Hamilton and Albion Rovers. Defeat at

Dundee put Hibs bottom again and more signings were made — Hearts loaned Hibs their young goalkeeper Waugh who later played for Scotland, and left-back Munro until the end of the season, and St. Johnstone's winger Alex. Ferguson was bought to add height and punch to the attack. Two valuable points were won from Partick Thistle with two goals by Black, apparently aware that the signing of yet another centre, James Clark of Margate, indicated intent of replacing him too.

Hibs had taken a number of blows this season, but the worst so far was the defeat at home by Ayr United, also deep in trouble. What was worse was that Hibs were on top from start to finish, and had three goals disallowed before Farrell hit a post near the end and Walls missed the rebound from seven yards. At the other end Waugh had misjudged a high lob and given Ayr both points.

Time was running out, but Hibs finally got a break, and it was all down to the young Hearts keeper, in the fourth last match, at Kilmarnock. Brady had scored for Hibs from an early penalty, and when Kilmarnock were given a similar award, Waugh saved Robertson's kick and the rebound too. Then in the closing minutes Kilmarnock were given another penalty but Waugh saved this one too, from Beattie.

Keyed up by this final chance, Hibs had too much determination for a Third Lanark side with nothing to play for, and were only denied a rare win at Motherwell by an equaliser seven minutes from the end. This left Hibs to win at Dunfermline to stay up, and a large support crowded the ferries to Fife, without a thought about a road bridge.

It turned out to be a poor game, but Black, although generally well held, chased one long punt forward, and with a prodigious leap for one so small, got his head to the ball to divert it into the top corner of the net. There was a scare when it seemed that a shot from ex-Hib Dobson, working hard to frustrate his former colleagues, might have crossed the line, but Hibs held on and watched Airdrie and Ayr United go down. The big Hibs following celebrated the moment but worried about the future.

Willie McCartney

They had little to fear. A few days later Mr Willie McCartney was appointed manager, a big man with an enormous presence who loved to be in the centre of the stage, where he had not been since leaving a similar position at Tynecastle a year earlier. Perhaps Mr McCartney had not the figure to be one of today's tracksuit managers, but who of them could have done such justice to the bowler hat and buttonhole without which he felt positively underdressed? The buttonhole, a red rose, posed a problem, of course, because no-one had invented a green one. His first act at Easter Road was to issue a retained list that did not include Walls, Borland or goalkeeper Hill. The new broom continued to sweep clean — Hugh Shaw replaced Christie Henderson as trainer, and Johnny Halligan left Hibs to become Sunderland's man in Scotland.

McCartney's problems were both short-term and long. To help with the former, he brought goalkeeper Alex Gourlay and right-back Alex Prior from Partick Thistle, Alex Ritchie, later manager of Third Lanark came in at outside right, and the veteran Johnny McKay, whose only cap had been won as long before as 1924, played for a season too. McCartney was generally believed to be able to convince a Chinaman he had jaundice, but even he was unable to coax Barney Battles out of his comparatively early retirement.

The excitement which surrounded the new manager's arrival was reflected by a crowd of 25,000 for his first match in charge. Not surprisingly Hibs lost it, to the settled Aberdeen team, and in fact when they tackled Hearts in September again they were second bottom of the League, exactly where they had been a year earlier.

At least this time Hibs tackled Hearts with the determination expected in a derby match, and even after Munro put Hearts ahead with only ten minutes to go, they fought back and Black headed an equaliser. Still, results would not come, as McCartney tried to find a suitable blend. Black, although 'not usually regarded as of any great account', nevertheless saw off another rival, Dallas, from Strathaven, and apart from anything else, no bigger than Black. Kelso of Dalry Thistle and Davy Anderson, as opposed to Alfie Anderson, the regular left-winger, were given a chance, but it was the re-introduction of Wilson, discarded in favour of youth, that brought immediate victories over Motherwell, Dunfermline and Arbroath before he was sent off against Falkirk and the run came to an end.

By Christmas Hibs were fifth bottom, though about six points clear of the bottom two. Things did not improve very much, but at least Hibs kept the differential with Dunfermline and Albion Rovers, and also finished above Queen of the South. They had won just seven games all season, including a Cup tie at Alloa, and just two of these were at Easter Road.

Things were however much better than the first-team results had suggested and by the end of 1938 the Hibs team contained the best crop of youngsters for a long time. Tommy McIntyre (Portobello Renton), Willie Finnegan (Bo'ness Cadora) and Sammy Kean (Rob Roy) contended for forward places, while at wing-half Charlie Birse from Broughty forced Egan to compete for an inside-forward place, and Rice came in to the exclusion of Wilson. This did not amuse the former Celt, and he had a transfer refused, but it was not long before he took over as manager at Dunfermline.

And there were more changes besides. Brady had refused terms and Hibs had reluctantly sold him to Aberdeen, and Jones too had not re-signed, but nobody knew where he was. On the credit side there was one major scoop when manager McCartney was quick to notice that Arthur Milne, who had gone from Dundee United to Liverpool on trial, was not on the retained list of either, and in no time he was a Hib.

With so many new players, Hibs' results were a bit haphazard, but every now and then they clicked to give high promise of things to come. The first time came after drastic changes had followed a desperate performance at Ibrox. Hibs beat Clyde 6–3 after being behind at half-time, with hat-tricks for both Milne and Egan, and a most impressive debut for yet another junior, Bobby Nutley from Blantyre Vics.

Milne and McIntyre each scored twice when Hibs demolished Morton in half an hour, before the captain Miller was hurt and they eased up, and the same two shared the goals when Hibs slammed their next visitors, Arbroath, by 5–0. Sometimes too Hibs' youthful exuberance was successfully countered by teams with greater experience, and Hibs suffered badly at Hamilton, Aberdeen and Firhill. Halfway through the season they were in a bunch of teams above Kilmarnock and Morton who seemed to be stranded at the foot.

Then the first four months of 1938 became the setting for as intense a relegation battle as Scottish football has seen, with Kilmarnock making a splendid recovery and more than half the teams in the Division involved. At the top, Hearts and Celtic fought out a two-horse race, with Celtic's win at Tynecastle before a 50,000 crowd the decisive result.

After losing to Celtic in mid-December, Hibs were unbeaten in League games until Falkirk beat them at the end of March. Despite this they were only two points ahead of Hamilton, Queen of the South and Clyde, joint second bottom. So it was just as well that they then beat Dundee, Partick Thistle and St. Mirren in succession, because when the dust settled after the final round of matches, Dundee were relegated with 32 points, with Ayr United, Queen of the South, Clyde, Kilmarnock, St. Mirren and Hamilton all on 33 and Hibs, although in the top half of the League, on 35 with Third Lanark. Dundee had even beaten Rangers 6–1 in their effort to stay clear, but apart from Morton who were seventeen points adrift, were the only side to lose twice to Hibs.

A Donnybrook

A heavy Cup commitment was not a factor in Hibs' long spell without defeat; in a competition that produced a fair crop of surprises, not least that

History of a sort — but so was Flodden. Kelso of Hibs beats Edinburgh City goalkeeper J. R. Johnston to score his side's first goal, but the amateurs provided one of the Scottish Cup's biggest upsets by winning 3–2, in January 1938.

of East Fife winning it, Hibs had a run that has since been rivalled only by Rangers' trip to Berwick in 1967. They were drawn to play at Pilton, against Edinburgh City, but with the support of the Chief Constable and the City Engineer — not to mention Hibs — the game was moved to Easter Road.

The first blow to Hibs' complacency came in five minutes when R. Walker scored, but all was well when Kelso drove home an equaliser after Hibs had pounded the amateurs' goal. There was some surprise at the coolness and stability of the City defence, not always their strongest department, and some more when Gourlay had to bring down Walker and former Hib Carruthers scored from the penalty spot. Early in the second half Carruthers scored again, and panic set in as Hibs, and particularly Milne, missed a hundred chances. Milne even missed a penalty in the last few minutes, after Miller had cut the deficit with a header.

It is some measure of that result that in their entire and rather inglorious Cup history, Edinburgh City recorded just three other wins, against Brechin City, Stranraer and Murrayfield Amateurs, and they followed the win over

Goalkeeper Gourlay has his own way of dealing with this cross ball, but fortunately full-back Logan is covering Queen of the South centre Hay. A scene from a league match in August 1938, one of the first featuring Hibs' new strip with white sleeves.

Hibs with a 9–2 defeat by Raith Rovers in the second round. Hibs meanwhile did what they could to prevent a recurrence — they signed R. Walker.

There was a little solace for Hibs in beating Hearts 4–0 to win the East of Scotland Shield, and some more when they repeated the score in the League in September. It was Hibs' biggest championship win to date over their rivals, and it was a field day for McIntyre who had a hat-trick. Through the autumn Hibs had their best run for many a day; they thrashed Aberdeen 5–0 with three for Milne and another two for McIntyre, and St. Mirren were glad enough to contain Hibs to 6–1. Hibs reached third in the table in November, when their exciting young team started to attract the vultures from the south. West Ham and Leeds were credited with an interest in McIntyre and Finnegan in October, Liverpool and Blackpool in the Glenafton half-back Fraser and Jimmy Kerr, the brilliant young goalkeeper from Ormiston Primrose in November, and at Christmas Hibs turned down a £10,000 bid for Kean and McIntyre from Manchester United.

In the New Year game with Hearts, Milne scored the only goal on the one occasion he gave Dykes the slip, to give Hibs their first League double over Hearts for many years, but they lost a lot of games they might have won, through inexperience, and came to grief in a quagmire at Pittodrie, where Patillo scored four goals and Aberdeen reversed the five-goal margin they had lost by at Easter Road.

With a favourable series of draws, Hibs did reasonably well in the Cup, although after the previous year, nothing could be taken for granted. Forfar put up a good show against them in the first round, holding out until they were down to ten men midway through the second half. Hibs won 3-0. Their best performance was the second-round tie with Kilmarnock, who led at half-time, where Nutley got a quick equaliser, and he and Milne scored further goals from McIntyre's crosses.

That left twelve sides in the competition and Hibs could scarcely have had a more satisfactory ballot than a bye then a home game with Alloa. Again they did not have things all their own way, and Alloa even scored first, but goals from McIntyre (2) and Nutley brought success.

The semi-final was with Clyde at Tynecastle. Both had promising young teams, but on the day Clyde were the smoother and more confident, while Hibs' play was somewhat haphazard. Nevertheless when the only goal came, it did so in a spell when Hibs were clearly on top. A weak corner by Nutley was booted clear, the ball bounced well for Martin and not for Miller, and the Clyde centre left the Hibs captain and Prior in his wake as he ran on to beat Kerr. Clyde went on to hammer Motherwell 4-0 in the final.

As a postscript to 1938-39, it was the first season that Hibs turned out with the now familiar white sleeves on their green shirts.

CHAPTER 14

Hitler's War, 1939-46

By September 1939 the lights had gone out all over Europe and it was clear that 'peace in our time' was not to be for the millions who were about to die to achieve it. It would not be long before the few would be owed so much by so many and we would be getting ready to fight them on the beaches. We would not be moved.

However, all through the summer sport continued as if it would never happen, and the new football season kicked off as usual. England arranged to play the Netherlands in November and Rumania in December, and in the middle of August British golfers were among those contesting the German Open Championship.

With the abundance of young talent at Easter Road, *The Scotsman* foresaw a good season for Hibs, and expected McLeod, Cuthbertson, Gilmartin, Shaw and Ross, who scored five goals in the first public trial, to be competing for places. For such a young team, Hibs had been lucky so far in that only Ross had been called up, but nevertheless it was a surprise that the captain Miller had been released to Albion Rovers.

Hibs had won two and lost three of their five League games by the time war was declared on September 3rd, and the League Management Committee abandoned the competition with a directness that gave the momentary impression that they had a plan. They hadn't, and so at first only friendlies were allowed, and outside the 'danger areas', defined as Edinburgh, Glasgow, Dundee, Clydebank and Dunfermline. It was assumed that city sides would use peripheral junior grounds.

The restrictions were soon relaxed, with Home Office approval, to allow crowds of 5000 and then 8000 at all games, and up to 15,000 with special permission, and subject to a spread of kick-off times. Presumably permission was forthcoming if everyone promised not to tell the Germans there was a game on. Hibs and Hearts had already disbanded, but regrouped to play a friendly at Tynecastle which Hibs won 4-2.

The League then decided that the interrupted League programme might as well go ahead, and gave out a card for the following week — Hibs were apparently due at Alloa — when Sir Louis Gumley unleashed his plan for three regional competitions. So the League thought about that and came up with the idea for eastern and western divisions of sixteen teams, with six unlucky sides left out. The Edinburgh clubs were not over-enthusiastic, because while they still had their longest trips, to Aberdeen and Arbroath, their most lucrative ones to Glasgow had been replaced by games with Kings Park, Stenhousemuir, Alloa etc.

When the new competitions got under way in late October, the erratic availability of regular players and guests made it a topsy-turvy league, but in the east at least there was no lack of goals. With one quarter of the games played, Falkirk led from Dunfermline and Cowdenbeath while in the west Rangers ground unspectacularly over all opposition. Rangers' goal tally at that point was 21 for 2, while Falkirk's was 42 for 19. Falkirk won the eastern division from Hearts, with each scoring over a hundred goals from twenty-nine games. Hibs were eighth.

Hibs' young team missed Milne, who was allowed to go home to Angus and play when available for Dundee United, and they averaged exactly a point per game. They had also lost McIntyre who was assisting Hamilton, but in turn had the services of Alec Hall, the tough Sunderland full-back who stayed with Hibs throughout the war, and for a while also those of centre-half Bob Kane from Leeds United. They had big wins over Kings Park, for whom Bill Shankly was a very welcome guest, and Dundee United, despite Milne's presence, but their best performance was a 3–3 draw at Brockville.

A 25,000 crowd was specially sanctioned for the New Year derby, which was an odd affair. Hibs were leading 3–2 when the referee blew for half-time, but the official realised that he had been premature, and he restarted play for two minutes, during which Hearts scored twice. Play did not let up, and Hibs fought back to be level at 5–5, but Hearts had the last word with a goal from Walker. It was so foggy that at the close the teams left the field without the Hearts goalkeeper who did not know the game was over.

Hearts won the return easily, so it was a turn-up when Hibs routed them in the Charity Cup in June. The turning point came with Hibs leading 2–1 in the second half when Kerr had a brilliant save from a Walker penalty, and Milne had a hat-trick as the Easter Road team took their total to five. Over the season as a whole, Cuthbertson was Hibs' top marksman with 22 League goals, and Nutley was next with 15.

Permission had also been obtained to hold a national cup competition, and Hibs faced a formidable task at Brockville. They had been the only side to that time to take a League point from Brockville, but on this occasion they did not survive an early onslaught, and Falkirk went on to win 5–0. But while there is life there is hope, and Hibs fought back in the return leg. Goals from Finnegan, Nutley (2) and Cuthbertson brought them close early in the second half, but the pace could not be maintained and Falkirk went through gratefully. Rangers beat Dundee United in the final by the only goal.

The regional arrangements had not been a success. Hibs lost £2196 supporting them, and most of the other clubs also showed a loss.

Willie McCartney: a sketch by Tom Curr of the unmistakable Hibs' manager.

Cowdenbeath had pulled out halfway through, and Arbroath were not going to carry on. So the bigger clubs formed their own select company, the Scottish Southern League, which in effect meant expelling Ayr, Kilmarnock and Queen of the South from the western division and giving their places to Hibs, Hearts and Falkirk. The remaining clubs met to try to form their own competition but decided that they could not afford to.

Hibs had signed Eddie McLeod of Manchester City, and so were able to field a right wing of Adams and McLeod, as East Fife had done to win the 1938 Cup Final, but their major coup was in bringing Bobby Baxter to Easter Road. Baxter, Middlesbrough and Scotland half-back, had previously been with Hearts, and his influence in the middle of an often youthful Hibs side was immense.

Hibs finished third in the new League, and just as importantly made a profit of £488 on the year. Falkirk had been considered the pick of the eastern sides, but their reputation was 'utterly smashed' when they visited Easter Road in November. The Brockville team made their usual dashing and confident start, and Hibs were happy enough to survive it, but a sudden hat-trick in five minutes by Cuthbertson changed the picture, and Hibs won 7–1. Cuthbertson got four, and he repeated the feat a fortnight later at Hampden, consolidating his position as the country's leading goalscorer.

Gordon Smith

The second half of the season lacked the sparkle of the first, from Hibs' point of view, and gave no indication of the summer ahead. Hibs failed to qualify in their section of the Southern League Cup, largely because of an indifferent performance at Tynecastle and their inability to beat Queens Park. This cup was the same one as had seen service as the Emergency War Cup the previous year, and it had the same winners, Rangers.

Following the League Cup, only a few League games were outstanding, but one of these was the postponed New Year derby, which took place on April 28th, the spring holiday. The Hibs' attack read Weir, Combe, Smith, Finnegan and Adams, and raised a few eyebrows as only that afternoon it had been given in the press as 'from Adams, Finnegan, Yorston, Mayes, Gallagher and Cook'.

The fielding of Gordon Smith was the biggest surprise. Smith had first come to notice earlier in the month when he scored a hat-trick for a Scottish Junior Select against a Hibs-Hearts Select at Beechwood Park, Dundee, and Mr A. Irvine had announced after that game that Hearts, of whom he was chairman, had made arrangements to sign him. Willie McCartney had made no announcement of his intentions, but had travelled to Montrose to discuss the matter with the young centre, and Smith had signed for Hibs in the North British Hotel prior to his debut.

The appearance of Bobby Combe was also unexpected, as he had been training at Tynecastle, and had been watched by a Hearts deputation as recently as two days earlier. The Inveresk Athletic player signed for Hibs immediately after the game. The third youngster was Jock Weir, from Leith Renton. He was the odd one out, as he was not expected to join Hearts.

With their largely trialist attack, Hibs looked likely to succumb to Hearts' pace and punch, and by half-time trailed by one goal by Smith to two by Walker. The second half was sensational. Hibs kept the ball away from the clutches of centre-half Dykes, and ran riot. Smith completed his hat-trick,

The Hibs' party pictured at Hampden following their Summer Cup win of 1941. Back row (l to r) Gallacher, Anderson, Smith, Cummings, Gilmartin, Fleming and Cuthbertson. Middle — Mr. J. Drummond Shiels (Director), Adams, Shaw, Busby, Milne, Kean, Kerr, Hall and McColl (Assistant Trainer). Front — Nutley, Caskie, Mr. H. Swan (Chairman), Baxter, McCartney (Manager), Finnegan, Combe and Shaw (Trainer).

Combe scored his first goal for Hibs, and Adams got his name on the scoresheet too. Hearts' only consolation was a late penalty goal for a silly infringement when it was too late to matter.

There was great glee amongst Hibs supporters about their latest scoop, and more was to follow. Matt Busby of Liverpool joined Hibs, as did Bob Hardisty, an amateur with Wolves but probably better remembered as the balding captain of Bishop Auckland who dominated so many FA Amateur Cup finals in the '50s. Then Everton's Jimmy Caskie became available; Falkirk approached him first but he signed for Hibs.

All were signed in time to help their new club in the last event of the season, the Summer Cup, although it was Milne, with a hat-trick at Parkhead, who was instrumental in seeing off Celtic's challenge in the first round. Clyde posed more of a threat by winning 2–1 at Easter Road in the second round, and things were not going any better in the second leg until a switch between Smith and Milne did the trick, bringing three goals in eight minutes, a hat-trick for Willie Finnegan and a 5–5 tie on aggregate. It was also Busby's debut. Hibs won an Ibrox play-off and a Tynecastle semi-final against Dumbarton to meet Rangers in the final.

Rangers scored twice in the opening twenty minutes, a position from which it was generally considered inconceivable that they would lose — but lose they did. Just before the interval Milne was brought down and Finnegan converted the penalty. From then on Hibs' play was inspired, a switch between wingers Caskie and Nutley did wonders for both, and Finnegan equalised on the hour. There was really no holding Hibs after that, but it took them until the second last minute to score again, by means of a header from Baxter.

The cup was presented by Mr W.C. Cuff of the English association. The competition was obviously not intended to have a long run, as the trophy was to remain the property of the winners. The Hibs players each received ten War Savings Certificates for their efforts, and the men who thus benefited were Kerr; Shaw, Hall; Busby, Baxter, Kean; Nutley, Finnegan, Milne, Combe and Caskie.

The Summer Cup competition was in fact repeated during the next four years, and with the Southern League and League Cup, established the pattern for the rest of the war. Also established was the near-monopoly of Rangers in winning them. The Southern League lasted for six years and the Ibrox side were its sole champions, as well as winners of six of the ten cup competitions that they entered.

There was little doubt either that Hibs were Rangers' most consistent challengers. During the six seasons the Light Blues suffered only 22 League defeats, and five of them were by Hibs — no-one else exceeded three — and the 24 points at stake between the two sides were shared equally. Of the four cups Rangers did not win, Hibs won two, Aberdeen and St. Mirren one each.

Less predictable than the results of many of the games was when exactly they would take place, and the teams that would be fielded. Half the Hibs team on occasion consisted of guests, apart from their longer-term ones like Hall and Baxter, and in the 1944 Rosebery final Hearts found that no fewer than seven of the eleven listed the previous day had become unavailable in the meantime. A further problem was one of equipment, because the clubs had failed to obtain a supply of clothing ration coupons. The Board of Trade's view was that since the level of rationing was far more than sufficient anyway, supporters should donate coupons to buy their clubs' strips. At a time when the more fortunate were able to get a curtain to convert if they required a wedding dress, not everyone agreed with the Board of Trade, and it brought a new meaning to phrases such as a defence being run ragged.

There was a further problem in kick-off times. These were spread over many hours in the first place, but even then the unpredictable travel situation made them no more than a rough guide. Communications

Jimmy Kerr saves from Wallace (Partick Thistle) during the war.

generally were quite primitive, and at Easter Road vital information was disseminated by an elderly retainer bearing a display board round the track at a leisurely pace. On one occasion, by the time those in the south stand and enclosure learned that the kick-off had been put back because of Clyde's late arrival, the Shawfielders had not only turned up but were two goals up.

No-one would say that Rangers had better players than Hibs — no-one reading this book anyway — but they certainly had more, and were able to run a team in the North-Eastern League as well. This enabled them to achieve a level of consistency that their rivals could not match. In particular, Hibs were able to field a reasonably settled defence, but in attack only Smith and to a lesser extent Caskie could be relied on each week.

It was at half-back that Hibs were arguably strongest, and the envy of others. It was during 1941–42 that Busby became recognised as a top-class wing-half, playing behind the young wing of Smith and Finnegan. He was only able to stay for about a year, and then it was Finnegan who stepped back to replace him, a move that had a greater effect on Hibs' forwards than on their half-back prowess. Baxter and Kean completed this division, and later on Hugh Howie began to make his mark. At full-back the partnership was that of Shaw and Hall, with Jock Govan coming in on occasion and taking over when Hall eventually went back to Sunderland.

Govan had his first run when Davie Shaw had his first cartilege operation in 1943, and it was also in this era that Shaw acquired his nickname of 'Faither'. Bobby Baxter, it seems, got wind of a happy event in the Shaw household and had tactfully waited until the whole team was assembled to run out on to the pitch before offering his 'Congratulations, Faither', and the name stuck.

In goal, Hibs had service, apart from Kerr, from Joe Crozier of Brentford, Jock Brown of Clyde and Hamilton, and latterly Mitchell Downie who later went to Kilmarnock. In attack, apart from Smith and Caskie, Nutley, Combe and Cuthbertson all put in appearances when their other commitments allowed, and Hibs always seemed to benefit especially whenever Milne was on leave from the RAF. They were not around too often, and a succession of others helped out at different times. Season 1943–44 was the most unsettled for Hibs, and nineteen different players contributed to their seventy-one League goals.

The most promising of the younger brigade was Willie Bogan, of Renfrew Juniors, who made his debut in October 1943. Bogan quickly made his mark, so quickly indeed that after less than two years' senior experience he was chosen to play for Scotland against England at Hampden. Unfortunately he was carried off injured within a minute of the start, and as he was never honoured in the more competitive post-war years, his stands as the shortest international career ever. A notable guest for some months before his call-up in 1942–43 was Stan Williams, Aberdeen's South African winger, while the names of McGillivray, Colvan, Devlin, Marshalsay, Nelson, Croft from Morecambe and Woodburn from Newcastle may stir the odd memory.

Hibs' Eightsome — Rangers' Reel

Back in 1941, if Rangers' defeat by Hibs in the Summer Cup had come as a shock, it was nothing to what was in store for them in September. Rangers came to Easter Road with a hundred per cent League record, a four-point lead and intent on revenge. Milne put Hibs in front in seven minutes, but Venters equalised from a penalty. It was a harsh award for Baxter's tackle on Smith, and things began to look ominous, but it took more than a soft

Willie Finnegan, Hibs' captain, introducing his colleagues to Mr. Attlee, the Prime Minister, and Mr. Mathers, Lord High Commissioner, prior to the Victory Cuptie with Partick Thistle at Easter Road in May 1946. Chairman Harry Swan is seen in the centre.

penalty to save Rangers this time. Dawson was in top form, but he was beaten twice more before the interval, and, incredibly, five times after it. 'The Ibrox team was cut to shreds by bewildering footwork' and every one of Hibs' eight goals crowned a smart combined move. Combe scored four of them, Smith and Milne two each, and the crowd's pleasure was not diminished by the ordering off of Venters for assaulting Kean.

Few felt that they had not had good value for their thirteenpence admission. Willie McCartney declared that it was his proudest moment and nobody doubted it.

Hibs reacted to their success by losing their next three games, but did not entertain any naive notion that Rangers would adopt a forgive and forget attitude in the return, three months later. A difficult afternoon was in prospect, especially when Baxter and Milne had to call off at the last moment. Rangers set out apparently to run Hibs into the ground, but Shaw and Hall were seen to be holding the Ibrox wingers, and Kean was superb as a stand-in centre-half. Nevertheless when half-time came, it was the harassed defence's first respite, and after it they were as busy as ever. There was a real let-off when Rangers had a goal disallowed, and then suddenly in a quick raid Smith found Combe unmarked, and the inside man coolly put the ball into Dawson's net. Hibs held out after that with much less difficulty.

There had not been much cheer in 1941, but Hibs' supporters had had a generous share of what there was. Hibs never recaptured the form that had routed Rangers, but they finished second. Cuthbertson had been enlisted along with his goalscoring talents, but in his place Smith and Combe each exceeded twenty League goals and sundry others. More than twenty Hibs players were now in uniform, but others were employed in Robb's shipyard and were more readily available, so that Hibs also did well in the resurrected Second XI competitions.

Unfortunately, no-one else was able to find form to rout Rangers either, and so the Ibrox side swept on unchecked until they met Hibs again in the Summer Cup final.

The Summer Cup this year was to be different. The organisers wanted to include the sides in the new North-Eastern League, but the Southern League teams refused and went ahead without them, amid complaints of unfriendly and unsportsmanlike behaviour. Another change was that, of the ten War Savings Certificates, seven were to go to the winners and three to the losers.

Hibs' passage to the final was straightforward, against Clyde, Third Lanark and Motherwell, and the final was another exacting affair as may be imagined. Rangers' defence was 'rather ruthless' and Milne was injured in only four minutes, but the ten Hibs gave as good as they got. Davie Shaw hit the bar, and that was as close as anyone came to a goal. After extra time they were level on corners too, at just two apiece, and so a coin was tossed. 'Rangers jubilation at winning seemed a bit misplaced after their display of spoiling football', but at least Hibs were still ahead, 13–7, in War Savings Certificates.

Cuthbertson reappeared for Hibs in August 1942, home on leave, and Milne too was able to play in more than half the games. With Smith having his best season as far as scoring went — he had twenty-six goals — and Stan Williams on the left, it looked for long enough that Hibs might take the championship. They established a clear lead up to November, but in a poorer run over New Year in which only five points came from six games, they surrendered it to Rangers, and indeed lost second place to Morton when they lost 1–0 in their second last game at Cappielow.

The most dramatic game had been against Rangers at Easter Road on Boxing Day. Hibs' slide had started, and they were desperate to win to keep in touch. Venters had put Rangers ahead, but Baxter had equalised from the penalty spot by half-time. The second half began as vigorously as ever, and after four minutes Cuthbertson scored but the goal was not allowed. This was not the first incident that caused bad feeling, but shortly thereafter Dawson was struck unconscious by a bottle hurled from the terracing, and had to be replaced by Symon in Rangers' goal. Far from helping Hibs, this lunatic act ended their chances as the game died with neither side able to find any appetite for it thereafter. Rangers also eliminated Hibs from the League Cup, and in the semi-final of a Summer Cup that was notable for Tommy Lawton's five-goal display for Morton against Clyde.

The following season was not dissimilar. By October Hibs were top jointly with Dumbarton, but hit a bad patch in the run-in, largely because they seldom had the services of their first choice forwards, and Celtic overtook them to finish second to Rangers. In the League Cup that followed, however, Hibs made amends, and qualified for the only time, in a section that included Third Lanark, Morton and Albion Rovers. They put on a fine show to beat Clyde 5–2 at Tynecastle after being on the receiving end in the opening phase, and qualified for the final against — yet again — Rangers.

The 1944 League Cup final bore a strange resemblance to the 1942 Summer Cup one. It was another hard game and it finished without a goal scored, but this time Hibs had an advantage of six corners to five and so took the trophy. The winning corner was won by Caskie three minutes from time, and acclaimed as if he had got the ball in the net. The parallel with 1942 went further in that the losers had only ten men for most of the game, after Dawson had been injured in a clash with Bogan in seventeen minutes, and in that the winners' supporters were not noticeably sympathetic.

Nothing if not consistent, Hibs had a much better first than second half to their programme in 1944–45. After two initial defeats, they took twenty-three points from twelve games, only dropping one at Parkhead on a day when Smith, Baxter, Milne and Caskie were all playing for Scotland at Wembley. The slump that followed this run was just as dramatic, with only one win in the nine games after the turn of the year, and this allowed Celtic, Motherwell and Clyde to overtake Hibs.

The Edinburgh Select

August 1944 had seen the introduction of the Allison Challenge Cup, for which a Hibs-Hearts select were to do battle annually with a top English club for the benefit of local charities. Aston Villa were the first to answer the challenge, and defeated the Select 4–3 at Tynecastle. Despite this the Rosebery Cup had not yet been discarded — there were enough cases requiring charity to go round — and Hibs and Hearts met to contest it on May 9th. Victory in Europe had finally been achieved the previous day, and so it was a large and carefree crowd that thronged Easter Road. A corner flag thwarted Hearts' hopes of winning a corner in the last minute, and so that was the margin by which Hibs triumphed. To celebrate, the teams were entertained to tea in the boardroom, while 'solos were rendered by Mr. Kenny McCrae, the well known Gaelic tenor' (*Evening News*).

By August, victory against Japan was assured too, but it had been considered impossible to revert to peacetime football for another year at least. The Southern League thus entered its last year, with thirty sides in two divisions. The season was one of adjustment, as the players came home from the war and the guests returned to their own clubs, and clubs also had to contend with the younger men being called up for national service. For the clubs who had shut down during the war there was the task of building a team from scratch.

From Hibs' point of view, Baxter went to Hearts, and Peter Aird took over as Hibs' centre-half; Alec Hall went back to Sunderland, and Govan and Shaw established a partnership which represented not only Hibs but Scotland. During the season Willie Bogan joined Celtic for a fee of £5,000, and Jimmy Caskie went to Rangers, to be replaced in the spring by Johnny Aitkenhead, Queens Park's left-sided player who was noted for his ability to glide past opponents. In addition, Devlin and Downie were transferred to Kilmarnock.

Queen of the South were among those who hastily assembled a team in the weeks prior to the August kick-off for their first game in five years, so it was a blow to Hibs to lose 3–0 at Palmerston Park. It seemed that they had not lost any ground because Rangers had lost too, but as the season progressed the Ibrox side built up a big lead, and Hibs just pipped Aberdeen, that most northerly of Southern League sides, for second place. In the League Cup, it was the other way round, Aberdeen winning their section from Hibs on goal average, and they went on to win the trophy. Arthur Milne was back on a more regular basis, and he shared the main scoring honours with Smith, who reached a century of Southern League goals before the competition finished.

There was keener anticipation of the Victory Cup which replaced the Summer Cup in 1946. It perhaps seemed a little belated, but a qualifying competition had been in progress through the winter, and East Stirlingshire and Clachnacuddin joined the League sides in the two-legged first round. Hibs met Dundee, and a hat-trick by Gordon Smith gave them a three-goal lead at Easter Road. It did not seem any more than was needed, as Hibs had lost 4–1 at Dens Park on Christmas Day, but this time they restricted the Dark Blues to two goals.

Hearts visited Easter Road in the second round, and a 40,000 crowd saw

Arthur Milne clashes with Partick Thistle goalkeeper Steadward during the Victory Cuptie at Easter Road in May 1946.

Aitkenhead make his debut for Hibs, Tommy Walker his return for Hearts and a game full of excitement. Weir scored twice in the first half, but in between Kelly robbed Govan and beat Kerr for Hearts, so the result still hung in the balance. It stayed that way all through a tingling second half until Peat scored Hibs' third with five minutes left.

Hibs were at Firhill for the third round, where neither they nor Thistle deserved a second chance, but a 1–1 draw gave one to both. Mr Attlee the Prime Minister was among the crowd for the replay which Hibs won with late goals by Milne and Wright, and then Milne and Smith (penalty) scored the goals which caused Clyde to lose the semi-final at Tynecastle.

It would not have seemed right if Hibs' opponents had not been Rangers, but this time they simply did not match the Ibrox side. Peat and Aitkenhead were drawn ever deeper to help out, and as a result Smith and Nutley did not get the service that Waddell and Caskie were thriving on, and the writing seemed to be on the wall before Finnegan diverted a shot from Gillick past Kerr in twenty minutes. Hibs equalised at the perfect time, when Aitkenhead hammered Nutley's cross into the roof of the net seconds before half-time, but Rangers had the perfect reply when Duncanson put them ahead again seconds after it without a Hibs man having touched the ball. Hibs fought back, and one goal plus the inspiration it would have brought

151

F

might have seen them through, but Duncanson's speed brought him the only other score in the closing minutes. The Hibs line-up was Kerr; Govan, Shaw; Howie, Aird, Finnegan; Smith, Peat, Milne, Aitkenhead and Nutley.

The final phase of Hibs' wartime programme indicated most clearly that wartime was over — they were able to tour in Czechoslovakia. It was also clear that it was just over, as the Russians were still regarded as liberators and friends. Hibs had had a lot of advance publicity, and lived up to every word of it especially when they beat the local champions, Sparta Prague, by 3–1. They were welcomed wherever they went, which was Brno and Ostrava, although overall they won two and lost two, and a novelty for the supporters at home in Edinburgh was listening to commentary on their two games in Prague as presented by the booming voice of Willie McCartney.

CHAPTER 15

The Famous Five, 1946–52

Scotland's football enthusiasts were happy when football officially got back to normal on 10th August 1946, and none more so than Hibs' supporters, 35,000 of whom watched their team drub Queen of the South 9–1, with four goals for Weir. A sterner test awaited them in midweek at Ibrox, but Hibs won that one too, before a crowd of 60,000, and despite losing a goal in the opening minutes. Aitkenhead equalised and crossed for Weir to head the winner just after half-time. The Hibs' team which kicked off so well was Kerr; Howie, Shaw; Kean, Aird, McCabe; Smith, Cuthbertson, Weir, Buchanan and Aitkenhead.

Hibs' third win was at Hampden, although they scored only once against Ronnie Simpson, at fifteen the youngest ever player to play in a Scottish League game. Curiously, the second youngest, Alex Edwards, years later also made his debut against Hibs, and both later played for the Easter Road club.

Hibs thus early established themselves as Rangers' likeliest challengers, but successive defeats at Aberdeen and Motherwell, both as a result of injuries at Pittodrie, notably to Smith, dampened their prospects. Another defeat, by Hearts in Tommy Walker's last game for them, did not help.

The League Cup sections were played off in October, and Hibs qualified comfortably from Third Lanark, Hamilton and Celtic. Not much was going right for Celtic — they were bottom of the League, and when they did beat Hibs their wild kicking and head-high tackling earned them more criticism than praise. Moreover, Hibs beat them 7–0 in a reserve game.

Back in the League, Rangers had established a gap at the top, and it was important for Hibs to close it when the teams met again in December. The crowd was 40,000 and the game worthy of such, but Hibs had to be content with one point, and depended on a late equaliser by Willie Ormond, recently signed from Stenhousemuir, even for that. Hibs did clear one difficult hurdle with an emphatic win at Tynecastle on New Year's Day, but when they dropped points to Morton and Motherwell in January, the title race was over. Hibs were second, five points ahead of Aberdeen. Apart from Ormond, Hibs had also introduced Eddie Turnbull, whose signing had been Mr McCartney's reward for a late-night excursion to Carronshore.

With the championship settled, attention switched to the Scottish Cup, and the League Cup knock-out stages which took place in March. In the latter, Hibs seemed well placed after drawing 4–4 at Airdrie, but in the second leg, 125 minutes had passed and the moon had appeared by the time Finnegan scored the only goal. Midweek football was banned, so the rule was to play for the first goal in the event of a draw after extra time.

The semi-final was at Hampden, and a crowd of 125,000 saw a determined Rangers score thrice by half-time, and a shaken Hibs able to pull only one back thereafter. Rangers seldom play without determination, but what caused this particular display of it was that Hibs had just put the Ibrox team out of the Scottish Cup. Rangers were fortunate even to draw that one at Ibrox, but in the replay at Easter Road, they looked likely to reach extra time when Hibs put in a rousing finish. Twice in the last six minutes Smith had the Rangers defence at sea, and provided goals for Ormond and Cuthbertson, to the delight of most of the all-ticket 50,000 crowd. The post-war battle between these two was well and truly joined.

Hibs disposed of Dumbarton without fuss, then met Motherwell at Hampden. The Lanarkshire men looked smarter, but Turnbull put Hibs ahead in the first half, and it took a Kilmarnock penalty to take Motherwell into extra time. There were no more goals then either, so it was sudden death again. At last a goal came. The Motherwell goalkeeper cleared upfield and Howie, instead of trapping the ball, lunged forward on tired legs and swung at it, and was as amazed as anyone when it sailed over Johnstone's head into the net. The game had lasted two hours and twenty-two minutes.

Aberdeen had beaten Arbroath in only twelve minutes less, and so met Hibs in the final. Cuthbertson gave Hibs a first-minute lead but Aberdeen swarmed back and in the ten minutes before half-time Hamilton headed the equaliser and man of the match Williams scored another. Hibs were sprightly enough in the second half, but well held, and Aberdeen came nearest when Kerr conceded a penalty then saved it. Hibs had no complaints about the result.

Even without winning a trophy, it had been Hibs' best season for a long time, and the manager had spent it making sure their challenge in future would be even stiffer. Eddie Turnbull's introduction to the first team had been immediate and impressive, and the pressure on Combe and Cuthbertson to hold their places at inside-forward was increased with the expensive acquisition of Leslie Johnstone from Clyde. It was a challenge they met successfully, and within months Johnstone was on his way back to Clyde and then Celtic.

Jock Weir had gone to Blackburn in January, and perhaps the centre-forward potential of an admittedly very young Lawrie Reilly was not fully appreciated, because Hibs signed first Stirling from Dumbarton and then Alex Linwood, the former St. Mirren centre, capped during the war and now of Middlesbrough, to replace him. Reilly meanwhile competed for left-

Hibs' postwar team is usually remembered on account of its attacking capabilities, but there was not much wrong with their defence either. A 'big five' of Kean, Kerr, Shaw, Howie and Govan are seen preceding Gordon Smith out of the tunnel onto a snow-covered Ibrox in February 1947, where they held Rangers to a goalless draw.

wing appearances with Willie Ormond, and Tommy Aitkenhead, who ultimately lost the battle and went to Motherwell.

That only left Gordon Smith as an automatic choice in the forward line, though it is doubtful if Mr McCartney considered even Smith as such. His system was akin to the modern idea of a player pool, but as in any pool, there were larger and smaller fishes, and Smith was never dropped.

Scotland's football enthusiasts were clearly happy again in August 1947, with the innovation of starting with the League Cup. More than 300,000 turned out the opening day, 40,000 of them at Easter Road where Hibs' much discussed new attack did not live up to expectations, perhaps because of an injury to Kean behind them, and Hearts beat them 2–1. Since Hearts also won the return — and for that matter the September league game — by the same score, Hibs had no worries about fitting in the quarter-final ties.

Reilly was given a rare chance at centre and scored a hat-trick against Queen of the South, but then Hibs lost the important game at Ibrox, despite Combe scoring the first goal on their behalf. Partick Thistle were top of the table hereabouts but an inspired spell from Smith led to Hibs' displacing them in November. Even by his standards, Smith's first goal at Motherwell was brilliant, when he beat five defenders en route to goal, and he followed this with five goals against Third Lanark and a last-minute winner at Dundee. Five goals in a League game was a record for a winger.

McCartney's Champions

Hibs beat Hearts 3–1 in appalling conditions on New Year's Day as they were expected to do — Hearts reached bottom place in the table in January, which was at that time unusual — while Hibs stayed ahead of Rangers through the month but mainly because the Glasgow side had games in hand. The showdown between them on January 31st was keenly anticipated, but first Hibs had to deal with Albion Rovers in the Scottish Cup. Cuthbertson scored the only two goals in the match, which was less remarkable than the evidence of bad feeling on the terraces, but neither seemed to matter when it was learned that Willie McCartney had collapsed at Cliftonhill and died later in the day.

The football world mourned, but there was scarcely time to pause, and although Matt Busby's name was mentioned in the managerial context, Hugh Shaw was appointed to succeed McCartney in time for the Rangers' game a week later. It was a game in the best tradition of these clashes, with the Ibrox defence apparently impregnable until, in the last minute, Linwood made a success of a seemingly forlorn chase and Cuthbertson, unmarked for once, headed his cross past Brown. There was hardly time to centre the ball.

Willie McCartney did not see his team win a trophy, and it seemed that no-one else was going to either. Rangers' games in hand seemed destined to count in their favour in the League, and they got the better of another confrontation with Hibs in the Cup. Hibs had eliminated Arbroath, Aberdeen and St. Mirren to reach the semi-final, and the venue of Hampden was well chosen, because the crowd that turned up numbered 143,570. Hibs made their usual assaults on the giant Rangers' defence, but this time the 'iron curtain' did not buckle, while at the other end a single mistake by George Farm, deputising for Kerr, cost Hibs dear. Farm went for a long cross from Waddell on the touchline, let the ball go through his grasp and Thornton sent it into the empty net.

Meanwhile, Hibs made no more slips in the League, and scored four goals at Paisley and Parkhead, and Queens Park did them a good turn by winning at Ibrox. So when Hibs beat Motherwell on April 19th by five goals, they needed just one point from their last game to take the title. The last game was at Dundee, but before it was played Rangers dropped another point, at Motherwell, and so they could no longer catch Hibs. It was just as well, because Hibs lost at Dens Park.

Former Hibs' captain Davie Shaw guards the Aberdeen post while his goalkeeper Curran clears from Reilly and Ormond. An incident from the league encounter at Easter Road in January 1951, in which Hibs beat their nearest challengers for the title by 6–2.

There was much recognition of Hibs' achievement, but none more than when Govan, Shaw, Smith, Combe and Turnbull were all selected to play for Scotland against Belgium. Scotland won 2–0. It also said a lot for Hibs' reserve strength that, minus all five, Hibs started their tour to Belgium creditably enough, only losing to Standard Liège by the odd goal in three.

Hibs' defence of their title was somewhat haphazard. From the outset they dropped points more regularly than prospective champions should, and early on surrendered a three-goal lead to Albion Rovers in the last ten minutes. Later history dictates mention that the equaliser was a penalty goal by Jock Stein. Hibs lost consecutive home games to Celtic and Morton, and lost 5–1 at Motherwell, yet they topped the table at the end of November. It was a three-horse race with Dundee and Rangers who both had games in hand, and though Hibs won at Ibrox in November and beat Dundee at Easter Road in December, it was not enough to counter that advantage. In the return games, Hibs lost by the only goal in the usual hard game with Rangers. Dundee beat them 4–3 with three second-half goals in seven minutes, and it became a two-horse race. Rangers won it by a point, with Hibs, the top scorers, six points behind Dundee.

A major attraction in September 1948 was the McCartney Memorial Match, with FA Cupholders Manchester United the visitors. A crowd of 35,000 saw the English team win by the only goal scored by Buckle, but the man of the match was their goalkeeper Crompton, which gives an indication of the balance of play.

Even bigger crowds turned out for the League Cup matches, with Hibs in the same section as Rangers and Celtic. 55,000 saw Hibs' first game at Parkhead, and 48,000 the second one against Rangers at Easter Road. The section had a remarkable finish, with Rangers winning it after having only two points at the halfway stage, and it also featured a 6–3 win for Clyde against Celtic. A further reason for the League Cup producing Hibs' biggest attendances was that their Scottish Cup ties were against Forfar, Raith and East Fife.

It was only in September that *The Scotsman* had observed that Reilly seemed to be making the outside-left position his own, so it came as a surprise when he was capped in that position just a month later. Alex Linwood went to Clyde in December, but the stocky Angus Plumb, who scored ten goals in eight games, and the experienced Cuthbertson were his replacements before Reilly switched into the middle late in the season. That left the left-wing berth free for Willie Ormond, and a famous footballing jigsaw puzzle was taking recognisable shape.

Then, with the League race lost by the end of March, Hibs introduced two more new faces against Partick Thistle; in goal there was Tommy Younger, whose fearless displays were considered by some to be prejudicial to his own best interests, and Bobby Johnstone, the diminutive inside-right from Selkirk who had been outstanding with the reserves in recent times. It was also about this time that Englishman John Paterson, an elegant player for a centre-half, began to establish himself in the first team.

The Five Come Together

So the 'Famous Five' were all together, but with Cuthbertson and Combe contesting the inside-forward places, it was some time before all five played in the same game. The first occasion was a friendly at Sanquhar against Nithsdale Wanderers on April 21st, when Hibs won 8–1, with goals by Ormond (2), Reilly (2), Turnbull (2), Smith and Mick Gallagher, the Eire

St. Mirren goalkeeper is beaten by Bobby Johnstone and Lawrie Reilly respectively, for Hibs' third and fourth goals in the first half of the replayed cup tie at Easter Road in February 1951.

internationalist half-back. Their second appearance as a quintet was against an Irish League XI in Belfast in aid of the Northern Ireland War Memorial Building Fund in May, but their first in competitive football was delayed until October. Apart from the Belfast engagement, Hibs ended their season by scoring four times in the last ten minutes to beat Tottenham Hotspur 5–2 at White Hart Lane, and set a new trend by flying north to meet a North of Scotland Select at Inverness.

Gordon Smith had been Hibs' top scorer for the last two seasons, and he made it three with a tally of 29 goals, all but four in the League, in 1949–50. He scored over seventy goals in these three years, heavy scoring for an outside-right, as would be shown by comparison with modern wingers, if there were any.

Smith was also Hibs' captain now, having taken over from Davie Shaw who had a lengthy absence following a cartilege operation, and he led his men to their most successful season so far. They qualified easily in the

League Cup from Third Lanark, Falkirk and Queen of the South, and then after losing 4–2 at Firhill took only ten minutes to clear the deficit in the second leg en route to the semi-final. This was against Dunfermline at Tynecastle, and although Reilly gave Hibs a first-half lead, the Fifers fully deserved the win that the two goals by former Hibs player Gerry Mayes gave them.

It was the disappointing display at Tynecastle that prompted more team changes, and inspired they were. The entire half-back line of Gallagher, McNeil and Cairns was replaced by Combe, Paterson and Buchanan, and with Cuthbertson now in Third Lanark's scarlet and Plumb in Falkirk's navy, Combe's step back paved the way for Johnstone to establish himself. So on October 15th, a week after the League Cup failure, Hibs' front line read Smith, Johnstone, Reilly, Turnbull and Ormond, and they beat Queen of the South 2–0. Smith scored in twenty-two minutes when Henderson failed to hold a shot from Ormond, and Turnbull in sixty-two with a 'special' from twenty-five yards.

It seems ironic at this distance that the attention at the time was given to Hibs' 'new' half-back line, which became established with Buchanan on the right and Combe on the left. Bobby Combe had in fact played left-half before — but that was during the war, and under Hugh Howie's name because Combe was home on sick leave at the time!

Hibs had lost at Tynecastle in the League in September, but in a superb run their new-look formation dropped only one more point until New Year. That was against Celtic at Parkhead, where the home side equalised in the last minute. There was great cheer on December 10th when Motherwell hammered Rangers by four goals to nil.

So when the Ne'erday derby came round, Hibs had taken 25 points out of 26. Hearts had won ten games in a row, and the scene was set as never before. Edinburgh's biggest crowd of 65,850 paid to see it, though unfortunately not everyone was able to. Rather unoriginally, the game was of two halves. In the first, Hibs produced as fine a display as they had yet shown, although they scored only once — Ormond sold two priceless dummies, and his cross was headed in by Smith. Then Hearts played so well in the second half that they deserved to win: Conn equalised in seven minutes, and twelve minutes from the end Wardhaugh shot past the unsighted Younger, and so they did so.

Hibs soon regained their winning ways and lost just one more League game. That was the one with Third Lanark, when they were 'a mere gallimawfry of football talent', a word the reporter seems to have shared with Shakespeare.

It was in February that referee Mr. J. A. Mowat, with a display of bravery

The Hibs' team that ran away with the League Championship of 1951. Back row (l to r) — Combe, Paterson, Govan, Younger, Manager Shaw, Buchanan, Ogilvie, Souness and Gallagher. Front — Smith, Johnstone, Reilly, Turnbull, Ormond.

worthy of a Victoria Cross, awarded Hibs three penalties against Celtic, and Turnbull took full advantage of all three. Turnbull also scored Hibs' other goal, and Collins scored for Celtic — from a penalty.

Despite their successes, Hibs had failed to break clear of Rangers. Their final game was at Ibrox, and Hibs had to win to regain the championship. There was another huge crowd, 101,000, and they were disappointed in a rather tame goalless draw. They had yet to learn to treat such things as a victory. Rangers still required a point from their last game with Third Lanark, and they got it when Thirds missed a late penalty with the scores level.

Hibs finished second with 49 points, more than they managed in any of their championship years, and six ahead of Hearts. Hibs and Hearts each scored 86 league goals, 28 more than Rangers, and Hibs' reward this year was a tour of Germany, Austria and Switzerland.

Scotland's soccer anglophobes may like to be reminded that Hibs stopped off en route to the continent to beat Tottenham Hotspur again, and that the only goal came when Alf Ramsey sliced a clearance into his own net. The more notable of their results on the continent were the 4–2 win over the Bavarian side Augsburg, who were reckoned to be about the best team around, and the 6–1 success over Bayern Munich who weren't. The wheel of fortune has spun a bit in Germany too.

There was by now great optimism around Easter Road that Hibs were about to realise their obvious potential, and there was nothing in the League Cup sections to discourage it. Hibs won all five games they played, although they only just made it at Falkirk where they lost three goals in the opening eighteen minutes. In the sixth game at Dens Park, they were leading by two goals by Reilly when the local raingod intervened to save Dundee with a thunderstorm. Dundee could not catch Hibs anyway, so there was no replay.

The quarter-final against Aberdeen was altogether a different matter. Home supporters streaming out of Pittodrie were confident that Aberdeen had done enough in coming back from a goal behind to win 4–1, but a huge crowd at Easter Road showed that Hibs' supporters did not think the tie was lost. In only three minutes the Dons' defence was rattled when centre-half Anderson lofted the ball into his own net, but for all their effort Hibs could not score again in the first half. By that time the crowd had increased to 60,000, and the excitement became unbearable when Johnstone scored on the hour and then Ormond equalised five minutes later. Aberdeen did well to hold out for extra time, but within a minute the stadium was again a sea of green and white when Reilly put Hibs in front. That seemed to be that, but the crowds were silenced on their way to the exits when a speculative shot from Yorston found its way into the top corner of Hibs' net in the gathering gloom.

The replay at Ibrox was another thriller. The only goals came from a Turnbull drive in the first half and a Baird effort in the second, and so the show moved on to Hampden twenty-four hours later. Again there was excitement aplenty. Hibs led 3–1 at half-time but had had the advantage of a strong wind so their lead looked slender. It was then that they showed what they were made of, as they scored twice into the wind to leave Aberdeen without an answer. Johnstone (2), Reilly, Smith and Turnbull were Hibs' scorers at Hampden.

The semi-final between Hibs and Queen of the South took place at Tynecastle in another gale. Queens won the toss and emphasised their success with a quick goal. Thereafter the match belonged to Eddie Turnbull. The determined inside-left did the work of many in turning the game Hibs' way, not least with a twenty-five yard rocket into the wind to level the scores. When Hibs were awarded a second-half penalty, Turnbull's shot was again unstoppable, and his hat-trick completed the scoring.

The final was against Motherwell. Hibs had won a League game at Fir Park a week earlier by 6–2, and for over an hour dominated the final, but without scoring. Turnbull's industry was clearly missed, and Ormond was something of a misfit at inside-forward. So Motherwell held out, and when

Tommy Younger turns a tricky shot over the bar. Tommy won many caps for Scotland and while stationed in Germany on National Service flew more than a hundred trips to play for Hibs.

the pace relaxed in the last quarter of an hour, Young and Forrest headed two goals in three minutes. When Younger then kicked the ground in trying to clear and the ball rolled to Watters who lobbed it into the net, it was a fitting end to Hibs' day.

While Hibs had been romping ahead in the League Cup, their championship ambitions had been jolted by two defeats in the first three games. A superb run then followed this indifferent start, and the only point that was dropped in the next ten games arose from a freak goal at Ibrox. Paterson had the ball near halfway and was under no pressure when he elected to pass back to Younger, but he failed to take into account that the goalkeeper had come out for that very eventuality, and the ball sailed over Younger and into the net.

Hearts beat Hibs again on New Year's Day, one of the factors, which was becoming a feature of these games, being Smith's inability to master McKenzie, who against other opponents was no more than an average back. Hibs were then three points behind joint leaders Dundee and Aberdeen, but with four and three games in hand respectively, and the next day narrowed that gap by hammering Aberdeen 6–2.

That was the start of another good run which included the run-in for the League and also the Scottish Cup ties. Hibs needed two attempts to beat St. Mirren in the Cup, but then did so decisively, to set up another showpiece with Rangers at Ibrox. It was a tie which was to remain long in the memories of those present, and they numbered 106,000. Few sides had survived twice falling behind at Ibrox, and coming back against that redoubtable defence to win. Hibs were rather nervy when it happened the first time, an early goal by Simpson, and it took them almost till half-time to come back, Smith shooting an Ormond cross into the net. Then immediately after the interval they were back where they started, with Simpson getting another quick score. Rangers this time dropped back into defence as they were wont to do, but on this occasion the tactic failed them as a Turnbull rocket blazed past the ranks of blue jerseys into the net. Hibs now had the ascendancy for the first time, and with nine minutes to go they were awarded a free kick not far from the penalty area. The blue wall faced Turnbull apprehensively but instead of the dreaded thunderbolt, Turnbull passed to Ormond, he flicked it to Johnstone, and the diminutive inside man spooned the ball accurately into the top corner of the net for a tremendous victory. The hundreds of Hibs' supporters who had been locked out and listened to the game by crowding around the buses which were equipped with wireless now had the advantage of the space to celebrate and cavorted round the car park. Airdrie were the only side to beat Hibs in the run-in to the League but a week later a hat-trick by Reilly saw Hibs through at Broomfield in the Cup. That took Hibs to the semi-finals, and their opponents were again Motherwell. If Dame Fortune had not exactly smiled on Hibs in the League Cup final, she abandoned them completely this time.

Within a minute, Paterson slipped and let Aitkenhead in to lay on a goal for Kelly, and after fifteen minutes full-back Ogilvie broke his leg and Hibs had to rearrange the side to cover the position. This meant Turnbull and Johnstone going very deep, and Hibs effectively playing with three forwards. Nevertheless, at last they got going, and Reilly burst through to score spectacularly, only for Kelly to score again after McLeod put Motherwell two in front. Smith sent Reilly through for another fine goal, but then Ormond was carried off with ruptured ligaments, and Hibs simply did not have the firepower to threaten again.

However, by now Hibs were running away with the League, and they won it at Shawfield with four games in hand. There was no scoring in the first half, but with only Turnbull of the regular forwards playing, Mulkerrin, Souness (2) and Buchanan scored to give Hibs a comfortable win.

Hibs were a long way ahead, and Rangers were certain of being second, when the two met on the last Saturday in April. With a minute to go, Hibs led 4–0 which could as easily have been fourteen, and Rangers were awarded a free kick. Hibs' wall faced Woodburn when Reilly noticed that the kick was indirect, and he raced upfield to spread the news. As he arrived, Woodburn shot, and the ball sped into Hibs' net — off Reilly's boot. 'The Rangers' supporters' silence which greeted the goal is probably the highest tribute they have ever paid to Hibs.'

Two days later Hibs beat Celtic to finish with a ten-point advantage over Rangers. 'As an Irishman might say, it's not every day that a team defeats Rangers and Celtic in one weekend.'

Champions Again

Season 1951–52 was not so much a new season as a continuation of the old one. Football never really stopped. Hibs went first to France in May, where they drew with the Racing Club of Paris under floodlights, and beat Olympique Nice by a Reilly goal. A third game, with St. Etienne, was cancelled, but Hibs were not home long before they were visited by Rapide Vienna in a Festival of Britain game. The Austrians won 5–3. Hibs next turned up in Inverness in the middle of June to beat the local Thistle 6–1, and then in July there was the St. Mungo's Cup.

This was a knock-out competition for Division A clubs and was also in connection with the Festival of Britain. Hibs beat Third Lanark and Motherwell but lost in a replayed semi-final to Aberdeen. Celtic won the final. St. Mungo also had a quaich which Division B teams competed for and Ayr United won.

When the official season did start, Hibs' main ambition was to become the first side outwith the Old Firm to win the League outright in successive years. There were not too many distractions because they were eliminated from the two cup competitions in the first round. In the League cup, opening defeats by Partick Thistle and Motherwell made qualifying unlikely and Hibs gathered only five points. Their only contribution to Scottish Cup history was in attracting a record gate for their tie at Kirkcaldy.

In the League, however, things were better. Hibs were unbeaten in their first nine games, although there was a close call when Aberdeen came back to draw from three goals down, and when Hibs did lose it was because Morton goalkeeper Jimmy Cowan had one of his unbeatable days rather than that Hibs played badly. At this stage East Fife were top, until Hibs gave one of their brighter displays to beat the Methil men 4–2 and reverse the positions.

It's bath time — Archie Buchanan, Laurie Reilly, John Paterson and Gordon Smith. (Sadly, Archie Buchanan died in 1984).

Rangers, however, were as always the greatest threat, and they came closest to lowering Hibs' colours at Easter Road. Time was short indeed when Jock Govan in a rare gallop upfield reached the byeline and cut the ball back for Smith to equalise.

Every now and then Hibs seemed to have recaptured their form of a year earlier, as when they ended St. Mirren's unbeaten home record with an emphatic 4-0 win, and when they won 5-0 at Cathkin, but there were many games when they were reported to be below their best. Still, they did lead the table at the turn of the year, and the question was whether Rangers' games in hand were sufficient to let them catch Hibs.

Not for the first time, much depended on the two meeting at Ibrox. Hibs gained more than Rangers by the 2-2 draw, which seemed to point to their winning the title, but some opinions on that matter were changed when they lost 5-2 to Queen of the South. Hibs were then three points ahead; they had two home games to go, and Rangers four away ones.

The ball was more in Rangers' court than Hibs', especially as the Easter

Road side had more than three weeks to wait for their penultimate match. Rangers did Hibs more favours than themselves during this time, so that when Hibs beat Dundee, the championship was theirs. The victory was a relief when it came, because for most of the first half Dundee were the masters, and they led by a goal before Hibs at last managed to swing things their way, mainly because of the persistence of Ormond who scored twice.

One of the problems of a small League was that in the absence of bad weather or a good Cup run a team tended to run out of fixtures. This happened quite often to the Division B sides as a whole, and when it did, they played for the exotically named B Division Supplementary Cup. In 1951–52 Hibs had only one Saturday league game after March 1st — the one they lost at Dumfries — and so they played a number of friendlies. These included games with Manchester City (4–1), Manchester United (1–1), Bolton Wanderers (2–2), Doncaster Rovers (3–0) and Tottenham Hotspur (2–1). All except the Bolton game took place in England, and a notable scoring feat was that of Jimmy Souness, the reserve winger, who netted four times at Maine Road.

Hibs were again the League's top scorers, although within the club Reilly had taken over from Smith as the leading marksman. Reilly not only emulated the winger's feat of being Hibs' top scorer three years in succession, but topped the A Division scorers' table in each of them (shared with 'Legs' Fleming of East Fife in 1952–53). In early 1951 Gordon Smith became the third Hibs player to score a hundred competitive goals for Hibs, excluding wartime games, and a year later Reilly became the fourth. By mid-1954 Turnbull, Ormond and Johnstone had joined the list, and all five reached the ton in League games also, although in Johnstone's case it was only achieved during his second spell with Hibs in 1960. Reilly went on to be Hibs' highest-ever League scorer — the author made his total 187 — while Smith, with a career tally of 364 goals in all games, is far and away the country's highest scoring winger. Both of these still stand as club records, but that of Eddie Turnbull, of having 348 League appearances, was overtaken about two decades later by Arthur Duncan.

CHAPTER 16

Return of the Five, 1952–58

When Mr Harry Swan was elected Chairman of Hibs in 1934, he prophesied that given ten years at the helm he would take Hibs to the top. Allowing for the disruption caused by the war, few would disagree that he was largely successful. Apart from his considerable expertise as an administrator and businessman in the running of the club, and indeed country, as he had a spell as SFA chairman, Mr. Swan had an unusual talent for recognising how the game was developing, and so Hibs had been among the first to seek out foreign opposition while the general view in Britain was that continentals could only play across the park and could not shoot.

Likewise Hibs had played under several of the new lighting systems, while trying to assess what would be best for Easter Road. Among those they had visited had been Racing Club de Paris, and in November they had taken part in the first modern floodlit game at Stenhousemuir. 'Flood' might not have been the most appropriate prefix for the Ochilview lights, but the majority of those present were at least able to keep track of the score. For those who were not, the news is that Hibs won 5–3.

There was, however, one project that fortunately did not go ahead; the proposal was to extend Easter Road to take 98,000 spectators by increasing the terracing all round the pitch, except the stand side, to the height of the high part which was added in the '50s and demolished in 1983, as well as a new road and entrances, but there was no mention of covering any of it. Time has shown how unwise an investment the extension would have been — the only team which could ever have filled it would soon be past its best, and attendances throughout the country were soon to start a long decline. But meanwhile the bandwagon continued to roll.

The opening League game of 1952 was Gordon Smith's 500th game for Hibs, but as far as the Easter Road faithful were concerned, that was all that was notable about it. The game's only star was Johnstone, not the youthful Hibs inside-right, but Queens' balding and toothless veteran Charlie, whose perpetual grin must have haunted Jock Govan for many a day.

If that game was soon forgotten, the same could not be said for Smith's benefit match which followed nine days later, when Hibs tackled Manchester United, the English champions. There were goals aplenty, and Turnbull lashed in the first from a headed clearance. Rowley's spectacular shooting for United brought him the next two scores, but Turnbull scored again, this time from a penalty, and at the second attempt. Pearson was the next to be successful, beating Hibs' young goalkeeper McCracken with a low shot, and so United led at half-time.

They did not lead long after it. United missed a second-half penalty, had a goal disallowed and another effort whipped off the line by Paterson, but yet they were trounced. At the other end, Reilly too had a goal chalked off but soon Ormond equalised amid great excitement, and Turnbull put his side in front with another penalty. Smith had an easy score when Wood failed to hold Turnbull's next rocket. A white ball was introduced at this point, and it was quickly headed into United's net by Reilly, and Turnbull finished off the jamboree with another blockbuster (7–3).

It rained goals all week. Two days before the United game, Hibs had scored six in the first leg of their League Cup tie with Morton. Two days after it they got another six in the second leg. A hat-trick by Reilly against Hearts three days after that made it twenty-two goals in eight days, not a record, thought *The Scotsman*, that was likely to be broken. Even by its own standard, the Hibs' goal machine was working overtime, and they also scored seven in five separate League games, including Motherwell twice. Motherwell conceded seven goals to Reilly alone, and the centre ran up a club record of thirty League goals, as well as fourteen in the two Cup competitions. But there were also more occasions when the spark of genius failed to ignite, and Hibs lost six League games, four of them to sides in the lower half of the table. They were also crushed 7–1 by Arsenal at Highbury, watched by the Duke of Edinburgh and a television audience for the first time.

The League was very much a three-horse race, between Hibs, Rangers and East Fife, and they were the only sides to average over a point a game. The Fifers' challenge was finally killed off when Hibs beat them in April, but they finished nine points ahead of Hearts who were fourth. Hibs and Rangers drew their annual 'decider' in January, and by the middle of February Hibs were three points ahead with two more games played. They lost only once more, but it was still not good enough. When Hibs finished their programme, Rangers needed three points from two games, and got exactly that to win on goal average. Had the rules governing goal difference been as they are now, Hibs would have won the League that year.

Hibs supporters who had seen their side win a Cup grew thinner on the ground. Hopes were high in the League Cup after their demolition job on Morton, and even more so when they led by a Reilly goal in the Tynecastle semi-final against Dundee, but twice thereafter the Hibs defence got itself into a fankle which resulted in the Dark Blues playing at Hampden. In the Scottish Cup Hibs beat Stenhousemuir and Airdrie easily enough, but then went out to Aberdeen. An exhilarating game at Easter Road was drawn, and two goals by Hamilton gave the replay to the Dons.

The Coronation Cup

A third Cup chance went abegging too, with the Coronation Cup. The four Scottish sides were to be chosen fairly as the League champions, the Cupwinners and the Old Firm, so Hibs qualified as runners-up to Rangers. There were four English sides too, and Hibs met Tottenham, and drew 1–1 on a day when Hearts were beaten at Pitlochry. The score in the replay was the same with seconds to go when Reilly demonstrated his penchant for last-minute scores. Hibs beat Newcastle United comfortably by four goals and then met Celtic in the final which was watched by 107,000 people.

Celtic's recent form had been impressive, and it continued so in a first half in which Mochan scored from twenty-five yards. In the second half it was Hibs' turn. Many a goal seemed certain, but wasn't, and when one arrived, with two minutes to go, Walsh scored it for Celtic. Howie cleared his first effort off the line, but right back to him, and the Celt made no mistake the second time. The Hibs' team at Hampden was Younger; Govan, Paterson; Buchanan, Howie, Combe; Smith, Johnstone, Reilly, Turnbull, Ormond.

Most Scottish sides still had not been to the continent, but Hibs broke even more new ground in 1953 with a trip to Brazil. They lost twice and drew with Vasco da Gama, and were far from disgraced, especially when one considers that they were without the specialised preparation etc. which fortifies modern expeditions to such places.

Hibs' draw with Vasco da Gama was earned partly by another last-minute goal from Lawrie Reilly, and it was some time before he scored another, because when season 1953–54 opened the centre was in dispute with Hibs, holding out for a benefit match as had been given to Gordon Smith. Reilly was not the next most senior among the Hibs' players — Jimmy Kerr had gone to Queen of the South, where he did not play long because he broke a leg in a domestic accident, but Bobby Combe had signed for Hibs in 1941, and Jock Govan and Archie Buchanan had both joined before Reilly. So had Hugh Howie, whose ill health was imminently to end his career. Howie had fewer caps than Reilly, but he had averaged a goal a game against Wales in 1949 (his only international)!

Reilly refused to be interviewed by English clubs, and not many Scottish ones could afford the £30,000 asked, so presumably he had somebody in particular in mind. Dundee were said to be interested, and it is not known what Reilly thought of Stirling Albion's bid of £17,000, but nothing transpired, and the centre resigned in time to contribute both goals in a 2–2 draw at Old Trafford at the end of September.

Tommy D'Arcy was Reilly's deputy, and Hibs showed other changes too. Willie McFarlane, who had been a teammate of Younger's through school

Eddie Turnbull's drive flashes past Ronnie Simpson to open the scoring in the Coronation Cup match between Hibs and Newcastle United at Ibrox. Hibs won 4–0.

and minor football, renewed the association when he replaced Jock Govan at the back, and as Howie was forced out of the game, Pat Ward took over at centre-half. Before that happened, Howie was involved in a quite disastrous League Cup semi-final with East Fife at Tynecastle. Tommy Younger was responsible for Hibs trailing for half the game, being caught under the very zenith of a looping header from Bonthrone, but with ten minutes to go Reilly charged goalkeeper Curran and the ball into the net to equalise, and three minutes later seemed to have won the game by heading Hibs' second.

It was then that Howie stepped in. First he caught the ball on the penalty spot, and the barrel-like Emery smashed home the spotkick. Three minutes later he handled another pass. This time Younger fearlessly got in the way of Emery's kick, but the full-back crashed in the rebound. Howie had not much chance of getting away with either offence — the offending hand was swathed in new white bandaging.

Bobby Combe was now captain — it had been decided to pass the honour around the senior professionals — and under him Hibs also made an encouraging start to the championship. They were well in contention when they met Raith Rovers at Easter Road in December, and won easily enough by five goals, but Smith broke his leg and Buchanan suffered a nasty knee injury that required a cartilege operation, so that both were out for the rest of the season. In addition, Reilly contracted pleurisy in the new year and was sidelined for many months. With Souness having gone to Hearts a year earlier, Smith's place was taken by Tommy McDonald, while Dougie Moran made a bright impression in Reilly's absence. Nobody overtook Reilly's tally of fifteen League goals, although Bobby Johnstone was the club's top scorer overall, and Hibs finished in fifth position, and by chance level yet again with Rangers. Celtic clinched the title when they won 3–0 at Easter Road in April.

The season petered out somewhat for Hibs. Their supporters felt let down by the Cup defeat by Aberdeen, not so much because of the result as Hibs' failure to hit back after going behind. Aberdeen supporters enjoyed it rather more, but less so than when their side hammered Rangers 6–0 in the semi-finals later on. On the face of it Hibs' close season tour did not bring much greater cheer, but they did get a creditable draw with Sparta Prague, and two of the sides that beat them turned out to be the West German and Czech World Cup teams warming up for the 1954 tournament.

It was to Switzerland in 1954 that Scotland first sent a World Cup party, under manager Andy Beattie, whose duties did not include picking the team. As there were only thirteen players, there was not much picking to do, and with Reilly indisposed they included only one Hibs man, Willie Ormond. It was intended that Ormond should write a piece for the club programme on his return, but the winger seemed to think it an experience best forgotten.

Eddie Turnbull was the next to have a turn as Hibs' captain, for season 1954–55, and Sammy Kean had taken over as trainer from Jimmy McColl, who nevertheless stayed around Easter Road for many a year thereafter. Jock Govan and Mick Gallagher went to Ayr United, and Archie Buchanan, having fought his way back into the team, broke his leg at Pittodrie in September and missed most of this season also.

Of the younger brigade, the first to show was Tommy Preston, who stood in for Reilly, and scored eight goals in the League Cup section games, though not enough unfortunately to prevent East Fife going through. Preston scored another two goals in a memorable game against Sparta Prague, in which Hibs played brilliantly to thrash the Czech champions 6–2.

Preston was not the only newcomer to make his mark — and they all seemed to be half-backs. Preston himself staked a claim for under-23 honours at wing-half, and the same was true of Jimmy Thomson, who had already been capped at three different levels of football. Pat Ward started the season at centre-half, but was soon displaced by the elegant Jackie Plenderleith, while later in the season there were a few appearances by John Grant and Bobby Nicol.

Lawrie Reilly in a duel with Andy Kerr of Partick Thistle. 'Last-minute Reilly' won more caps for his country than any other Hibs player.

Drenchlighting

The major event at Easter Road in late 1954 was the opening of the new floodlights. Hibs had over a number of years tried out the different systems in England, France, Switzerland and Larbert, and had settled for the best there was. Dean of Guild approval was obtained on 3rd September, and the whole system was in operation for the official opening six weeks later. The GEC lighting and control equipment was selected and installed by Miller and Stables of Northumberland Street, and was referred to at the time as 'drenchlighting'. The pylons were 100 feet high, the iight strength 200 kilowatts and the cost to 'light a match' twenty-five shillings.

Hearts were Hibs' guests on October 18th, and the lights were voted the best in Britain, while Hibs' supporters could anticipate 'being able to see, every year, England's most famous sides in action' according to the club programme. The football on that first night won less acclaim, but Tulloch of Hearts scored Edinburgh's first floodlit goal, and his team-mate Whittle the second in a disappointing game.

When Reilly returned for Hibs at the end of October, and the 'Famous Five' reunited, the hope was that the centre's return would reinforce Hibs' challenge in the League. This hope did not last very long as in Reilly's first game back Clyde scored five times in the opening twenty-five minutes against Hibs at Shawfield. A mile away, Hearts were winning the League Cup and emphasised what seemed to be a shift in power in Edinburgh football by winning the Ne'erday derby 5–1, with Plenderleith quite unable to contain Bauld.

Hibs' season then ended rather prematurely when they failed to take any points in January and then visited Tynecastle again in the Cup at the start of February. This time they had a plan, resting Plenderleith and playing the more robust Grant to counter Bauld. The plan did not work, and when Paterson switched to centre-half after the interval, that did not seem to improve matters much either, so that with the Hibs' defence giving a good imitation of panic, Hearts scored another five.

It was therefore a meaningless sequence of games that left Hibs in fifth place. Bobby Johnstone was transferred to Manchester City for £22,000, and fewer than a thousand people saw the game with Stirling Albion at the end of March. Aberdeen won their first League title with a distinctive style of defensive play with quick breaks into attack, and Clyde beat Celtic in a replayed Cup Final, so that for once none of the prizes went to Ibrox or Parkhead.

Scotland toured Austria and Hungary in 1955, Gordon Smith was the tour captain, and on his return he also became Hibs' skipper again. It was appropriate that he first led Hibs out against Aberdeen, where Davie Shaw, who had handed Hibs' captaincy over to Smith the first time, was the new manager. Buckley scored the only goal in a typical Aberdeen breakaway, and then when Hibs failed rather unluckily to beat the Cupholders Clyde at Shawfield, they were three points behind the Dons and unable to bridge the

Tommy Younger saves from Sandberg, the outside left of Djurgaaren, in the European Cup match played at Firhill in November 1955. John Paterson (no. 3) looks on.

gap. But even without the League Cup, there was plenty of interest in Hibs' fare, with the first European Cup competition and the new Anglo-Scottish Floodlit League.

The European Cup

The inaugural European Cup was an invitation affair organised by the French sports magazine *L'Equipe*. Not all the teams invited were national champions, the emphasis being rather on a pro-European attitude and crowd appeal. Hibs fitted the bill as well as anyone, and in any case Aberdeen had shown little enthusiasm for continental involvement. In fact British sides in general were slow to warm to the idea, as they had been to the World Cup, and Hibs were the sole UK representatives.

Their first-round opponents were Rotweiss (i.e. Red and White) Essen. Hibs' achievement against the Germans tends to be played down because Essen have declined as a major force, but they were champions of the country that held the World Cup, and included in their ranks Helmuth Rahn, whose goal in the final had made that the case. Rotweiss were, like Hibs, a much travelled team and had not long finished a tour which had

Rheims goalkeeper Jacquet punches clear during the European Cup semi-final against Hibs in Paris. Willie Ormond is prevented by Zimmy from doing very much about it.

included wins over Independiente and Boca Juniors in Argentina and Penarol in Uruguay.

Hibs' trip to the Rhineland provoked so much interest that not one national newspaper was represented in Essen. They missed a brilliant display in the mud in which Hibs broke through time and time again, and Turnbull (2), Reilly and Ormond scored their four goals. The thousands of British servicemen present were delighted and Hibs were given a great ovation as they left the pitch. The men who performed so well were Younger, Higgins, Paterson, Thomson, Plenderleith, Preston, Smith, Turnbull, Reilly, Combe and Ormond.

It was just as well that Hibs had won so well, because when the return leg was played a month later, Smith, Reilly and Younger had all failed to make it back from an international engagement in Copenhagen, and Jock Buchanan, Mulkerrin and Adams were drafted in at the last minute. Buchanan scored in five minutes, but at the end the crowd went away unhappy with Hibs' line-up, the 1–1 score, the display of the Germans and the overall lack of entertainment.

It was anticipated that the winners would meet Real Madrid next, but it turned out to be the Swedish side Djurgaarden, from the Stockholm suburb which roughly translated means Zoo, and who had eliminated the Polish police side Gwardia Warsaw in the first round. Sweden's football had closed for the winter, and so Djurgaarden played their home leg under Partick Thistle's new lights at Firhill. It did not seem to upset them much. Within a minute Edlund put them in front, and quarter of an hour later Andersson rattled Younger's crossbar. Then Hibs changed to a more direct style than was their wont, and the goals came. Combe took a Smith lob on the drop to equalise before the interval, Mulkerrin took advantage of a kindly bounce to run through to give them a lead, and after Turnbull missed a penalty, he had a shot deflected for Hibs' third goal. A Turnbull penalty was the only score in another disappointing second leg at Easter Road and Hibs were in the semi-finals.

Hibs' opponents this time were the French champions Rheims. It was not clear at first whether the first leg would be in Paris or Nice, which is nowhere near Rheims, but Paris it was, on 4th April. Hibs played well, with wingers Smith and Ormond impressive, and if Reilly got little change out of centre-half Jonquet, the internationalist Kopa got no more from young John Grant. Younger was also in fine form, although he was beaten by a Leblond header midway through the second half. It looked as if Hibs would hold out at 1–0, but Bliard scored a second in the last minute.

A floodlight record crowd of 45,000 urged Hibs on to reverse the position at Easter Road, but it was not to be. At times it was unbelievable that the French defence would survive, but somehow they did, and with twenty minutes to go Kopa sent Glovakic through, apparently offside, to score for Rheims. The heart had gone from Hibs, and Rheims went on to lose 4–3 to Real Madrid in the final.

It was not necessary to have floodlights to play in the European Cup — several East European sides still do not — and indeed it did not even seem necessary for the Anglo-Scottish Floodlit League. Hearts joined and played their home games at Easter Road. There was some difficulty in getting enough sides to play, especially as the authorities had outlawed the competition, and Partick Thistle were the only other Scottish entrants. Hibs beat Newcastle 2–1 (home) and 2–0 (away) and Manchester City 2–0 (home) in the only fixtures which they completed. They also played Manchester United again, Edwards, Blanchflower, Taylor, Viollett and all, and trounced them 5–0.

Although contemporary opinion was otherwise, it may be argued that Hibs might have made a stronger challenge for honours at home had their extracurricular interests been fewer. As it was, by the end of January they were third in the League, two points behind the leaders Hearts, and they finished level on points with the Tynecastle team who were third. The most memorable game, at Ibrox, is remembered for the wrong reasons. Hibs were leading by a lucky goal when Younger was bundled into the net by Simpson, neither of them playing the ball which made its way independently into the net too for the equaliser. Later on, when Younger, holding the ball, braced himself to be charged by the bulky Kitchenbrand, Rangers were given a penalty, and Hibs left Glasgow possibly more indignant than ever before about the quality of justice there.

The 1956 Scottish Cup brought another first for Hibs, their tie with Raith being the first under lights, but the result was less memorable, and few Hibs' supporters will not have been reminded time and again where the trophy ended up.

On the team front, Hibs' aging forward line remained very much the men in possession, but their reign was clearly nearing its end, and what proved most disappointing was that there were few ready to take their places. It was equally true of the defence, nowhere more so than in goal — Tommy Younger had moved on to Liverpool, and his replacement was Jackie Wren, straight into the first team from Bo'ness United. What is surprising about this state of affairs is that while Hibs' first team had more or less ruled the roost for a decade, their second string had known success that was little short of phenomenal. In a period of over eight years since 1945, Hibs' reserves lost only five out of 115 competitive games at home, and, home and away, averaged well over three goals a game over that long period.

It was clear, then, that the manager, Hugh Shaw, shared his predecessor's flair with youngsters, yet they were not there when at last the club depended on them. For this the manager must take some of the blame, inasmuch as it would surely have been in the club's interests to deliberately blend in some younger talent over a period rather than wait until the crunch came, and have to field, for example, a totally inexperienced defence as Hibs had to in 1956–57. On the other hand, Hibs continued to do well in reserve football in the late '50s even while the first team struggled a bit, and manager Shaw might well have felt that some of his second-team stars would have made a greater impression in the first team than they did. Players like Jock Buchanan and Malcolm Bogie come to mind as players clearly too good for the reserves but who consistently failed to take the chances given them in the top team. However, one encouraging sign in 1956 was the form of fifteen-year-old Joe Baker, who had signed from Craigneuk Boys Club and had been farmed out to Armadale Thistle, who acted in some respects as a nursery club for Hibs at the time.

It was exactly ten years since football had restarted after the war, and Hibs had been in the forefront of things throughout that time. The same could be said of the next six minutes. The opening game was at Tynecastle, and in these early minutes Eddie Turnbull scored a brilliant goal, but thereafter Hearts scored five, and Hibs were seen in their poorest light for years. The management recognised that traditional problems assail all sides from time to time, and if Hibs had perhaps been somewhat tardy in starting to deal with the problem, they also did not have their troubles to seek.

During the autumn Wren and Joe McLelland, who had been introduced at left back, were called up for national service, although the goalkeeper, stationed at Middle Wallop, hoped to be available quite often. Archie Buchanan recovered from his leg break, but was never again able to challenge seriously for a place, and Pat Ward had joined John Ogilvie at Leicester. Ward's replacement, John Paterson, then cracked some ribs, while up front Gordon Smith broke his leg, and Preston and Mulkerrin needed cartilege operations. So Hibs brought in the robust Pat Hughes at half-back, and Johnny Frye and John Fraser made more appearances, along with Jimmy Harrower, who gained an under-23 cap a year or two later. A useful signing around this time was that of Lawrie Leslie, a big brave goalkeeper whom Jock Buchanan had met in the forces and recommended to the club.

Halfway through the season, Hibs took the view, publicly at any rate, that their youngsters were doing well enough, and had they scored the half-dozen extra goals that their play merited, they would have been up with the title challengers where they deserved. As it was, they finished in mid-table but they did seem to be over the worst. Lawrie Reilly recovered from his sinovitis in his knee to be the club's top scorer yet again with sixteen League goals and play his fifth game for Scotland at Wembley, a record. His five goals at Wembley also stand as a Scottish record. Gordon Smith came back to such effect that he went on tour with Scotland's party for the World Cup qualifying games, and Jackie Plenderleith was Scotland's centre-half at under-23 level, with Bobby Nicol the reserve for the position. Moran went to Falkirk in time to score the winning goal in the Scottish Cup final, Mulkerrin went to Accrington and Archie Buchanan was freed at his own request. George Boyle, the young defender, and John Baxter, a youth cap from Benburb, were demobbed, and Andy Aitken made his initial appearances. His signing was unusual for an Edinburgh lad, as he was spotted while playing for Cliftonville in Belfast while on national service.

Throughout the season there was one game that stood out. That was the Cup tie with Aberdeen, and although Hearts were playing Rangers at Tynecastle and Scotland were playing Wales at Murrayfield, a crowd of 27,000 watched it. Some, it is true, only stayed for twenty-eight minutes, by which time Aberdeen were four up, but they rued it later. Hibs attacked down the slope in the second half, and in three minutes Smith scored. Hibs swarmed round Aberdeen's goal, but twenty minutes passed before Reilly, almost on the goal line, stabbed the ball so that it swerved viciously into the net. Four minutes more and Nicol scored through a ruck of players and the excitement reached fever pitch. The pressure was relentless, but perhaps Hibs were over-anxious because they could not score again, although Ormond hit the bar in the last minute. At Tynecastle, where Hearts' supporters had cheered the half-time score, Rangers won 4-0, while Scotland beat Wales 9-6.

Joe Baker

By August 1957 there was a greater sense of optimism around Easter Road, although Hibs again failed to qualify in the League Cup, and Joe Baker, just turned seventeen and dwarfed by his opponent Doug Baillie, made his debut at Airdrie. Celtic won the section, and were forgiven by Hibs' supporters when they won an astonishing final against Rangers by seven goals to one.

In the League Hibs had lost just four of the sixteen games by Christmas, and were second in the table. There was not much doubt who was going to win it, as an aggressive Hearts team rampaged through their card losing only once, but even after losing two goals in the first seven minutes of the September derby at Tynecastle Hibs' youngsters were unbowed and their play would have justified a much better return than a 3-1 defeat. John Baxter made his debut when Hibs won 1-0 at Pittodrie in September and Johnny McLeod, a team-mate of Baker's at Armadale and with a similar turn of speed, celebrated the renewal of that association by scoring twice on his debut, a 4-1 win at Kilmarnock.

It was on December 29th that Hibs' cookie crumbled. Not only did Hibs lose 3-1 to Clyde, but Preston, Harrower, Baker and McLeod were all crocked, while Alex Marshall, who seemed likely to be the next to come into the first team, suffered a compound fracture of the leg in the reserve game at Shawfield. Already without Smith and Ormond, Hibs struggled to raise a team for their three remaining New Year fixtures and lost them all. All League aspirations had gone and they won only two more championship games.

The Cup, however, provided more cheer than for some years, if not in the two games it took Hibs to dispose of Dundee United, then certainly in the next round at Tynecastle. In an effort to match the physical approach of

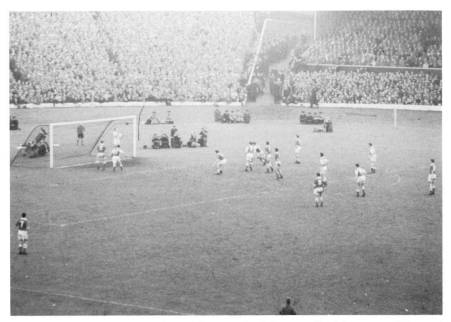

This picture shows the considerable appeal of the cup final between Hibs and Clyde in 1958. Joe Baker has a powerful header well held, with Willie Ormond in close attendance.

Mackay and Cumming, Hibs played John Grant at inside-forward, and this time their plan must be judged to have worked. Even then it was a close-run thing, with Leslie performing heroics in goal to restrict the lethal Tynecastle attack to three, while at the other end an unforgettable display of all-out action brought Joe Baker a personal swag of four goals. It is worth recalling that in the season in which Hearts so often seemed to be invincible, Hibs twice beat them by scoring four goals at Tynecastle — the first occasion had been the opening of the Tynecastle lights in October, a match that also gave Baker his first goal for Hibs.

The next round was scarcely less exciting. Third Lanark were Hibs' visitors, and two goals for Baker and one for Fraser were just enough to beat them. That took Hibs to the semi-finals and their opponents at Hampden were Rangers. Perhaps games between these sides a decade earlier had been fought out more skilfully, but none with more commitment. It took 180 minutes, and the drama lasted to the end. Hibs were leading by two goals to one, after a 2–2 draw, and only a minute remained for them to hold out when Leslie went for a cross ball, failed to hold it and it ended up in Hibs' net. The goal was given, but on the say-so of a linesman; referee Davidson changed his mind and Hibs held out to go into the final. Subsequent photographic evidence showed the linesman to have been correct, with three hands having stretched for the ball, one of them belonging to Brand, the Rangers' inside man thereafter known as 'Hans'.

While Hibs' youngsters were making a name for themselves in the Cup, there were more signs that the old days had gone. Gordon Smith, seventeen years a professional, required an operation to remove bone fragments from his ankle and there were doubts whether he would be back. Hugh Howie tragically died in a car crash in January. Then in March Lawrie Reilly conceded the game to his knee trouble and announced his retirement. On the Monday before the Cup Final, he made a nostalgic final appearance in a League game against Rangers.

There was nothing at stake, with Hearts having won the title by the proverbial mile, but that did not exempt Reilly from the type of treatment that had caused his premature exit in the first place. Telfer was roundly booed for his attentions to the centre as Hibs were so motivated by the occasion that they actually won two points. Aitken scored the only first-half goal with a shot that thundered under Ritchie's bar, then in fifty-six minutes Fraser crossed from the right and Reilly smacked the ball into the net off a post. Each side scored once after that and Reilly left the pitch to a standing ovation.

The Cup Final itself disappointed as a spectacle as well as in terms of the score. The first decisive blow came in thirteen minutes and crippled Andy Aitken, whose electrifying speed was vital to Hibs. Then Clyde scored the only goal, and it was a tragedy for John Baxter who, in a desperate effort to clear a shot from Coyle, diverted the ball past Leslie, who seemed to have had the original shot covered. Turnbull, a tower of strength at right-half, and Ormond, both survivors of Hibs' 1947 team, struggled valiantly to swing the game, but Clyde held what they had and the nearest Hibs came was when Baker handled the ball into the net. There was much sympathy for the two veterans, striving for the Cupwinners' medals which however were not going to come to them.

CHAPTER 17

The Baker Boy, 1958–64

By the time that the '50s became the '60s, Scottish football was finding its celebrities scarcer. The Famous Five were followed by Hearts' 'Terrible Trio' and Rangers' 'Deadly Duo' of Miller and Brand, who only proved that three and two sometimes add up to quite a bit less than five. What was needed to maintain this progression was clearly a Sizzling Solo, and if anyone fitted the bill it was Joe Baker, who seemed to capture every headline going for the next few years. In fact by the autumn of 1959 *The Scotsman* was defending itself concerning the number of column inches which had been devoted to the young centre. The sequence has been maintained even beyond Baker, of course, because as we will see, when he left Hibs there was nobody to follow him, and football has been becoming more and more negative ever since.

Meanwhile the second half of 1958 showed that Hibs had not solved the problems of the first half. They had no complaints about losing their League Cup section to Kilmarnock on goal average, because the Rugby Parkers beat them twice, and when they lost 4–0 at Ibrox in November it was their sixth reverse in ten championship matches and the third by that margin. Hibs had yet to find a good full-back partnership since Govan and Shaw. They had Grant and McLelland. John Grant played for Scotland, but Joe McLelland failed to measure up to the international standard of his predecessor. Smith was still missing, and Turnbull was finding it harder to control the middle of the team and provide service for the young forwards up front, Baker and his two lookalikes Frye and Aitken.

Two factors helped to turn the tide. Despite Hibs' problems, Baker was capped by England at under-23 level, which seemed to do wonders for his confidence. He was not the stand-out that he was at Easter Road, although he played well, but then his inside-forwards at this level were Bobby Charlton, described as a fair-haired youngster for readers who might have wondered, and Jimmy Greaves. In addition, Baker not only had to adjust to the English style of play, but also had a language difficulty, as the regional accents of England differed from the pure form of the language that is spoken in Motherwell.

The return of Gordon Smith did Hibs no harm either. Although never quite the Gay Gordon of yore, his very experience was exactly what Hibs needed, not to mention his incomparable crosses, and they lost only three of their next sixteen games. Baker in particular responded with a purple patch

183

G

The Hibs' team of 1958, taken the day after Lawrie Reilly's final appearance against Rangers. The line-up is: back (l to r) Trainer W. Hunter, Macleod, Grant, McLelland, Leslie, Paterson, Turnbull, Plenderleith, Baxter. Front — Fraser, Aitken, Baker, Reilly, Preston and Ormond.

that brought him eighteen goals in nine games, including hat-tricks against Queen of the South and Celtic.

The good run ended with the Scottish Cup tie against Raith Rovers. The first game at Kirkcaldy was drawn, Hibs' goal being Smith's 364th and last in senior football, a club record and British record for a winger. The replay was tense and exciting, with feelings being vented among both players and the 22,000 onlookers. Smith was at his best, and Turnbull scored from a penalty when he was impeded. Des Fox, who by now shared the inside-forward duties with Davie Gibson, made it two, then in the second half ex-Heart Conn headed past Leslie. Then with ten minutes remaining Baker was carried off after a clash with centre-half McNaught, which sparked off most of the trouble and effectively ended Hibs' season.

Hibs did beat Falkirk and Partick Thistle before drawing a difficult tie at Cathkin. Baker returned, only to show in the early minutes that he was not ready to do so, and he changed with Smith. The veteran played with the dash that had long been missing, but later he too was hurt and he did not play for Hibs again. It was curious that after gracing the right wing for so long his career with Hibs should end in the centre where it began. Behind them, Plenderleith was hurt within two minutes in blocking a shot, and Turnbull laboured like an ordinary mortal, which indicated that he too had been in the wars.

Joe Baker, Hibs' most prolific goalscorer.

Hibs therefore took more interest in the physiotherapist's reports than the semi-final draw, and their single point from their last five League games showed how much Smith, Turnbull and Baker were missed. It was something they were going to have to learn to live with, because at the end of the season Turnbull hung up his boots and became the club trainer, while Smith received a free transfer. It was the club's contention that a further operation on the winger's ankle was too big a responsibility to shoulder, but Smith thought otherwise and had it at his own expense. It was a sad parting, but the player was proved right, and by August was in such fine fettle that he signed for Hearts with a dozen other clubs disappointed. A crowd of ten thousand watched his first appearance for the Tynecastle reserves.

Meanwhile, back at Easter Road, the replacements were Bobby Nicol and Jim Scott. Scott in particular bore a heavy burden as Smith's successor as well as being the younger brother of Alex, Rangers' internationalist winger. A third change was in goal, where the young and raw Willie Wilson from Musselburgh Windsor took over from Leslie who had had tennis elbow for some time. Leslie was in fact transferred to Airdrie in November 1959 for just £4000, a very bad bit of business as not much more than a year later he was chosen to play for Scotland at Wembley. The big goalkeeper missed that game through injury, and must have had mixed feelings about so doing as he watched his deputy, Frank Haffey, beaten nine times.

Under new captain John Grant, Hibs again had no grouse about not qualifying in the League Cup — they lost all six games. Rangers exposed their weaknesses in defence and at half-back by scoring six at Easter Road and five at Ibrox and yet it was Motherwell who topped the section, helped by a hat-trick in two and a half minutes by Ian St. John in their win at Easter Road. It was a strange competition with Hearts reaching the semi-finals in company with Third Lanark, Cowdenbeath and Arbroath, so it was no surprise when Hearts won it.

Hibs tried to buy the experience they needed up front first by bidding for Jimmy Wardhaugh who had asked Hearts for a transfer, and then by signing Bobby Johnstone back from Manchester for £6000. Johnstone's style had changed during his absence — he had been playing centre-forward, but at the club which operated the 'Revie plan' which determined that it was not the centre's job to score goals. This idea evidently caught on in the south, as it was later extended by Alf Ramsey so that it was not anybody's job to score goals. Johnstone therefore played a deeper role than of yore, which in any case his much portlier figure made a necessity.

Johnstome made his second debut against Kilmarnock in a game that was otherwise remarkable in that wing-half John Baxter was cheered by Hibs' supporters. Baxter had hitherto been barracked irrespective of his performance, but against Kilmarnock discovered a little suspected talent for blasting home direct free kicks, which the crowd warmed to. Nevertheless, in the weeks to come the Hibs attack was criticised for slowness, in thought rather than action, except of course for Johnstone who was the other way round, and manager Shaw admitted in the programme for the match with Dunfermline that they were still struggling to find the elusive touch that would transform pressure into goals. Preston and Ormond were brought back to add punch, to surprising effect.

Goals Galore

The game against Dunfermline was a pleasant surprise for those who saw it, with Hibs scoring seven and the Fifers four, and each centre, Baker and veteran Charlie Dickson, having a hat-trick, and it was only a start. Hibs beat Bolton by 5–2 in midweek and then swamped Airdrie 11–1 at Broomfield to end an amazing week. Baker had three, Preston four and even left-back McLelland had one.

The score at Airdrie broke many a record, including the twenty-two goals in a week that the Hibs side of 1952 had run up. The Broomfield ground already held the record for a Second Division score and shared the First Divison one, and there is a theory that this is something to do with a high proportion of the space between the corner flags also being between the goalposts. In British terms, Hibs' eleven was a record for an away team in a League match; only Sheffield United and Dundee had reached ten before, but Hibs did it again eight weeks later.

The goals in the meantime had not exactly dried up, with twenty-three in seven games in the championship, and an exciting 6–6 draw with Middlesbrough, who were led by Brian Clough, a rival for Joe Baker's international spot, but few foresaw the ten-goal barrage with which Hibs demolished Partick Thistle at Firhill. Macleod led the rush with three, while 'the kindest thing that could be said about Fairbairn's goalkeeping was that it had more than a touch of novelty'.

The goals continued to flow. Hibs scored four at Pittodrie and were well beaten, then Hearts' ploy of playing an extra defender to curb Baker paid off in a 5–1 win at New Year. There were four goals in the last seven minutes of a thriller at Motherwell, and ten goals shared in an exciting draw with Clyde. When the championship finished, Hibs were top scorers with 106 but placed eighth. Baker, who had scored his 100th senior goal in little over two years against Ayr United, had 42 of them, twelve ahead of Reilly's club record.

Unfortunately the happy-go-lucky atmosphere which had carried Hibs through big scores for and against was sadly lacking when Rangers got down to stopping them in the Cup game at Ibrox. 'No unbiased observer could deny that Rangers were first to employ violent methods' which together with 'some mysteriously inconsistent refereeing from Mr. Jack Mowat' led to 'some of the crudest brawling seen' for some time. The only other cloud on the horizon concerned Baker. The livewire centre had continued to be shown the favour of England's selectors, and had made the full international team, including the one that played against Scotland at Hampden. Baker subsequently went on tour with England, thereby missing Hibs' own continental tour, and already the question was being posed, how long could Hibs hold on to him?

Hibs' tour was to have included Holland, Germany, Italy and Switzerland, but when arrangements were confirmed it was limited to Germany and Yugoslavia. The game in Germany was against Bayern Munich again, against whom Hibs won to make it five in a row since the war.

Baker stayed at Easter Road for another year, but early in the new season Bobby Johnstone fell foul of the management and the rotund Nicker was despatched back to Lancashire, Oldham this time, rather more ignominiously than five years earlier. Hibs were back where they had been a year before, and failed to take a single point from their opening eight League games.

The solution this time was the signing of Sammy Baird from Rangers for a 'pretty substantial sum'. Baird's languorous and studied style had not been the hallmark of every Ibrox half-back, but it enabled the new man to take over Johnstone's role of playmaker. Baird made his debut at Perth, in another defeat, and he was joined by Ronnie Simpson, the thirty-year-old Newcastle goalkeeper thought to be past his best, and Eric Stevenson, a teenage inside-forward whom Hibs had signed after the SFA had cancelled his registration with Hearts and fined both the Tynecastle club and their manager. Despite these newcomers, Hibs not only lost to St. Johnstone but followed that by a 6–0 home defeat by Celtic before eventually a hat-trick by the hard-shooting Bobby Kinloch, another recent introduction, broke Hibs' duck against St. Mirren.

There were other problems too. John Baxter, the new captain, first fractured his jaw and later was hurt in a car crash, while following Jackie Plenderleith's departure to Manchester City in the summer, it was not until Jim Easton, called up from Drumchapel only at the start of the season, took over from John Young that the centre-half position was again satisfactorily replenished. However, as the new-look team sorted itself out, results improved and Hibs finished comfortably in the top half of the table. It was Hibs' return to the European scene which made 1960–61 a season to remember.

Bedlam at Easter Road. The occasion was the Fairs Cuptie against Barcelona in February 1961 which featured an Entebbe style raid by the police to rescue referee Malka from a violent mob of Spaniards. Bobby Kinloch scored with the penalty which sparked off the trouble.

The Inter-Cities Fairs Cup had started in 1955 along with the European Cup but so far only two competitions had been completed, Barcelona winning both. The competition was supposed to be between cities which had trade fairs, but the rules were interpreted rather loosely depending on who the organisers wanted to include. Hibs qualified for the 1960–61 tournament apparently because of the Edinburgh Festival, and Dunfermline a year or two later on even more dubious grounds. Hibs had in fact accepted an invitation to enter as a select with Hearts in the 1958 competition, but this had fallen through because of Hearts' involvement, albeit brief, with the European Cup.

The Spanish are Madder

By now Hearts had failed twice to make any impression in the European Cup, and in between Rangers had been humiliated by Eintracht Frankfurt's twelve goals against them, so Scottish football prestige could stand a boost.

Hibs had the opportunity to provide it when they drew Barcelona after Lausanne Sports had scratched against them in the opening round. Barcelona were also in the European Cup and had just become the first team to lower the colours of Real Madrid in that competition; they also led the Spanish League from their Castilian rivals.

The first leg was postponed owing to fog at Easter Road, and so the teams met first in Barcelona two days after Christmas. The Spaniards would have known that Joe Baker had scored five against Third Lanark on Christmas Eve, but that did not help them prevent him get another two against them. Preston and Macleod also counted as Hibs rose to the occasion with such effect that they led 2–0 and 4–2 before their hosts scored twice in the final six minutes. Manager Shaw and trainer Turnbull, who had seen a fair part of Hibs' previous successes, agreed it was the club's finest hour, while Sammy Baird went as far as to admit that he and his manager had discussed tactics. The others sang in their dressing room. Possibly the nicest aspect of the event was Baker's appearance after Hibs' next home game with Barcelona programmes for the young fan who had pressed two shillings in his hand after the Third Lanark game for that purpose.

The second leg took place on February 22nd, and Barcelona would know this time that Baker had recently scored nine goals in a Cup tie against Peebles Rovers, perhaps without their appreciating the quality of the opposition. They certainly had something of a Baker complex, especially after the English cap headed home a Macleod free kick in just ten minutes. The 54,000 crowd celebrated, but they gradually quietened as Barcelona ominously began to build up some rhythm, and were silenced altogether when Martinez swivelled to hook in a long throw-in in half an hour. Just before half-time, the Hungarian Koscis reached a cross to steer the ball past Simpson, and Barcelona trooped off looking relaxed for the first time.

Barcelona's composure went with the interval. Hibs' opening onslaught down the slope did not slacken in ten minutes, and the Spaniards were at panic stations trying to curb the aggression of Baker and Macleod. Twice the centre was halted abruptly and illegally within the penalty area, only for indirect free kicks to be given, and Barcelona breathed again, but not for long. With fifteen minutes left, Baird headed on an Ormond corner and Preston beat the goalkeeper to it to equalise. The Spaniards' desperation was now showing ever more wildly, and after another ten minutes they lost the place completely. Baker sent Macleod in on goal, the winger was again scythed down by Garay and this time a penalty was given. The result was the worst players' riot seen in this country.

From the moment that Herr Malka's desision was appreciated, he was in full retreat to midfield from a posse of incensed Barcelona players led by Medrano, the young goalkeeper. Hibs' players first tried to calm their opponents down but then had to leave the protection of the official to the police. Eventually Kinloch was able to take the kick, but his shot had scarcely hit the net when the referee was assailed again by Koscis and others who chased him and battered him to the ground. Dozens of police arrived to the rescue but they were kicked and fully seven more minutes passed before order was restored. There were hurried discussions about possible arrests, but amazingly the game restarted without as much as a name being taken, and the terrified arbitrator was enveloped by police when he belatedly concluded proceedings.

The trouble for which the game is remembered clouded a performance that did Hibs and Scotland enormous credit. The Hibs' team was Simpson; Fraser, McLelland; Baxter, Easton, Baird; Macleod, Preston, Baker, Kinloch, Ormond. Not long after Hibs received a letter of apology from Barcelona, asking to be allowed to return to Easter Road to show everybody that they were really jolly good sports after all, but unfortunately they were unable to return before Baker and Macleod had left Hibs.

Meanwhile Hibs met Roma in the semi-final, and the tie was similar to so many involving Italian teams who like to play a bit on their own grounds and eliminate football altogether on their opponents'. The first game at Easter Road threatened to erupt at times, especially after Hibs' second equaliser eight minutes from the end, and heartier handshakes have been seen than those which concluded the affair.

The second game was only a week later. Hibs were not allowed the use of Roma's pitch, because it was a local holiday. Strange, thought manager Shaw, since the same thing had happened in Barcelona, but the Hibs' boss came up with a ploy of his own — that of Baker and Kinloch changing shirts. It was perhaps surprising that the Italians were fooled by this, because both had played in the first leg, but they were, and Kinloch was systematically assaulted by those assigned to mind Baker. Kinloch nevertheless managed Hibs' first-half goal, and Baker had the freedom to score twice in three minutes after the break to put his side 3–1 in front, but the game, like the first, finished level. Roma won the toss for the play-off venue, and by deferring it until the end of May found Hibs far short of match practice and won easily 6–0.

It seems that when re-signing time came round, Baker had suggested a modest recognition of his exceptional talents which the club refused to countenance and the centre found himself up for sale. Considering the exposure which Joe had had in England, it was surprising that when the bidding got under way, there was not an English club in sight. Roma were there, so Baker, or possibly Kinloch, had obviously impressed them, likewise Torino, as ever leaving no stone unturned in their efforts to keep upsides with city rivals Juventus.

So for a while there was a series of covert meetings and clandestine arrangements between various parties, while Hibs stated that they did not want the centre to go at all, and the Italians bemoaned the wrangling which offended the high ethical standards of Italian football, and which meant that since they were in competition, the price would be higher. Ultimately Roma pulled out and Baker went to Torino. The reader may compare the £12,000 he reportedly received for so doing with the £5 weekly he was said to have been refused by Hibs and decide whether he was right, even although his year-long stay in Italy included two suspensions, a bad car crash, legal trouble with a photographer and ultimately the cancellation of his contract. He was the eighth Hibs player to score a hundred goals, and did so in by far the shortest time, and when he left there were not many vying to be the ninth.

A few weeks later Johnny Macleod left Hibs too, for Arsenal. His career had blossomed with under-23 caps followed by an appearance at Wembley in the 9–3 game, and a year later he teamed up with Baker again at Highbury. Willie Ormond also left, to go to Falkirk after a fifteen-year spell that had much to outweigh the three leg-breaks that had punctuated it. He did return in October with two brilliant goals to earn his new team a point.

The only new signing to replace the departed talent was Ally McLeod, much of whose time had been spent in the colours of Blackburn Rovers, and who displayed some clever wing play. Hibs believed in their policy of paying youngsters the highest rates in the country, and so it was fair that the salvation of the club should in the first instance be left to them. At centre-half, Jim Easton from Drumchapel was being rated a better prospect than Plenderleith, who had gone to Manchester City some time earlier. Easton made a good impression in the Select charity game, as did Davie Gibson, with a first-half hat-trick. Gibson's skill had never been doubted, but he had hitherto seemed to lack strength and stamina.

But despite a lot of promise and thousands of pounds in the bank, there was no direct replacement for Baker; Kinloch was tried at centre, but Hibs struggled and matters came to a head in early November when Hugh Shaw resigned. He was around pension age anyway, but he took over at Raith Rovers. The Hibs job was not advertised, because Hibs knew who they wanted, but the man concerned, Bobby Brown of St. Johnstone, unfortunately did not want Hibs. Second choice was Jock Stein who was doing wonderful things at Dunfermline, but the Fifers would not let him go, so Hibs' next choice was Walter Galbraith.

One of Joe Baker's twenty-three cup goals for Hibs. This one is Hibs' first at Hamilton in 1961.

The Galbraith Gamble

Mr Galbraith was a Scot, who had played full-back for Queens Park, Clyde and Grimsby, and had since managed Accrington, Bradford PA, New Brighton and Tranmere Rovers. At Accrington he had once fielded a team of eleven Scots, while his latest charges Tranmere had been relegated to Division Four and put out of the FA Cup by non-League opposition. Hibs' new boss was a student of continental methods, and had been the guest of the Hungarian FA.

In between managers, Hibs had paid Manchester City £18,000 for Gerry Baker, Joe's older brother, whose lively leadership was enough to put Hibs into a safe position in mid-table. The only other transfer action was the move of Davie Gibson of Leicester City, not, as it was pointed out, that Hibs needed the money, and in any case Mr Galbraith had already identified a replacement. The manager was known as a buyer of good footballers, and one name linked to Hibs was Leeds United's homesick nineteen-year-old, Billy Bremner.

By August Hibs had hardly spent a fortune on Johnny Byrne (Tranmere), Morris Stevenson (Motherwell), Doug Logan (Queens Park) and John Blair (Bradford), yet there was optimism that new skipper McLeod might lead his young charges to the long-awaited revival, and Mr Galbraith hoped to be 'in there pitching among the championship contenders'. A spate of injuries was blamed for this failing to take place, with McLeod missing most of the early games, Falconer all of them, Easton breaking a leg at Airdrie and Eric Stevenson doing likewise at Paisley. The position was so bad that there were debuts for Peter Cormack at Airdrie and Jimmy O'Rourke against Utrecht in the Fairs Cup — both only sixteen, but the former already an amateur internationalist. Many of the points that were won were by dour defensive actions backed up by inspired displays by Ronnie Simpson, and even as the injury position improved, the results did not, and a single point from the last eight League games of 1962 portended trouble in store. Equally discouraging was that only 16,000 had seen what was even for Simpson a superlative display to hold Celtic at Easter Road, and crowds of only 5,000 had turned out for the Fairs Cup ties with Copenhagen and Utrecht.

The portents were not wrong. The worst winter for many years put football in cold storage until March, and when it resumed it was not long before things at Easter Road became desperate. Eddie Turnbull left the club with a suddenness which surprised the chairman and manager, and Ally McLeod asked to be relieved of the captaincy: new player Tommy Leishman took over. Hibs took only one point from three League games then lost a crucial one at home to Airdrie. It was during this game that one disappointed supporter, catching the ball on the main terracing, took it up to the top and dispatched it over the back, for which he was first arrested then given a complimentary ticket by Mr Swan on the grounds that at least he knew what he was going to do with the ball.

The 2–0 defeat by Airdrie was a desperate result because it was followed by four away games at Parkhead, Dens Park, Ibrox and Firhill within a week, and when Hibs lost the first of these they had collected only eleven points from twenty-three games, with Clyde third bottom with nineteen points from twenty-six games, and a better goal average. However, a very sprightly performance, especially by Baker at centre, brought two unexpected points home from Dundee, and a last-minute own goal gave Hibs another at Firhill. A goal by Baker and a tense rearguard action gave Hibs their first home win for five and a half months against Motherwell, and two more draws meant that Hibs had moved onto 18 points from 28 games, four behind Clyde who had played just one game more now.

At this stage Hibs lost 3–0 to Falkirk in a way that showed just how much their position was affecting their play, and although Clyde lost to Motherwell, Hibs seemed to be past the point of no return. Hearts had tried to help Hibs with the loan of players but the move had not been sanctioned by the League, and they now did their utmost with some amazing defensive lapses that allowed Hibs to score three in five minutes and draw at Tynecastle — but Clyde likewise drew, at Dumfries.

Clyde's two games left were with Celtic and Rangers, and when they lost to the former it was still possible for Hibs to stay up. With the newly signed veteran Willie Toner to calm a jittery defence, it was a chance they were able to take. While Clyde were idle, Hibs first beat St. Mirren by the narrowest of margins, then did their confidence and their goal average the world of good with a 4–0 win at Dumfries. This put Hibs level with Clyde, and a large support followed them to Kirkcaldy on May 20th, reminiscent of a similar trip to Dunfermline in the '30s. Happily the outcome was as satisfactory, and the crowd invasion which greeted Baxter's opening goal was born of sheer relief. Hibs went on to win this one by 4–0 too, and Clyde were left to beat Rangers by eight goals to survive.

It had been a close call for Hibs but at least lessons seemed to have been learned, and changes were made and money spent. The changes started at the top, where Harry Swan remained on the board but gave up the chair in favour of William P. Harrower, MBE, a successful bookmaker. Tom McNiven, only 29, was the new trainer, and was a qualified physiotherapist, and one significant addition to the playing staff by the start of the season was that of Neil Martin, a tall inside man from Queen of the South with a particular talent for heading goals. Martin was such an immediate success in his first season as a full-timer that despite breaking a wrist and a nose, he contributed thirty-four goals and played for the Scottish League.

Martin was followed into Easter Road by Pat Quinn, the ex-Motherwell inside-forward from Blackpool, in September, Linfield's classy left-back John Parke in October and Willie Hamilton, the brilliant but tragic Hearts' playmaker who had had a cartilege operation earlier in the season. Gerry Baker and Ally McLeod had moved on, and the former was replaced by Stan Vincent from Cowdenbeath in February.

Despite the lavish expenditure Hibs struggled, and it was late in the season before they were really out of trouble. The main cause was a spate of injuries the like of which the manager had never seen, including another leg-break for Jim Easton and two cartilege operations for John Parke, but another result was the introduction of several of Mr Galbraith's youngsters, Bobby Duncan at inside-right who later made the right-back position his, Billy Simpson, centre-half from Edina, and Pat Stanton and Davy Hogg, both from the same Holy Cross team that had already given Hibs Jimmy O'Rourke.

Eventually the injury position resolved itself, Hibs' league status was confirmed, and at that point manager Galbraith resigned, without acrimony and without another position lined up. He is generally remembered as the man who all but took Hibs to the Second Division, yet the two who succeeded him owed much of their relative success to the players mentioned in the last two paragraphs and others given their spurs by Mr Galbraith. Meanwhile in Fife, Jock Stein had already intimated that he was leaving Dunfermline at the end of the season, and few were surprised when he took over with Hibs.

Hugh Shaw, manager of Hibs, during the Championship successes of the early fifties.

CHAPTER 18

Stein to Turnbull, 1964–70

If Walter Galbraith had brought a lot of good players to Easter Road, Jock Stein made a good team of them. Stein added only one signing of his own, that of John McNamee, a giant of a centre-half who was understudy to Billy McNeil at Celtic Park. McNamee's strength ensured that he provided 80% of the momentum in any challenge; it was liable to get him into trouble with referees and opponents but he was readily accepted by the Easter Road faithful for exactly the same reason.

Success came quickly. A Summer Cup had been introduced to while away the cricket season, on a League Cup basis with regional sections. Hibs were a shade fortunate to qualify in their group, as they finished above only Falkirk, but with Hearts already committed to tour in North America, Hibs beat Dunfermline in a play-off, and then Kilmarnock in an exciting semi-final.

The final with Aberdeen was to have followed at once, but the granite city was laid low with typhoid and so it was held over till August. In the first leg at Pittodrie, Jim Scott twice scored somewhat fortuitously to keep Hibs in the tie and only one behind, but even this deficit was not easily eradicated at Easter Road, where it took a late goal by Vincent to take the game into extra time. It was then that Eric Stevenson seemed to have won it with a close-range header, but this time the Dons had fortune with them when a lazy ball from Cooke bounced high into Wilson's net at the last gasp.

So a third game was needed, and Aberdeen won the choice of venue. Little good it did them. In five minutes Willie Hamilton shot fiercely into the roof of their net, and although Winchester equalised, Hibs were never in trouble. Stanton missed a penalty and Martin struck a post before late goals from Scott and Cormack sealed an inevitable win. Hibs' winning line-up was Wilson; Fraser, Parke; Stanton, McNamee, J. Stevenson; Cormack, Hamilton, Scott, Martin and E. Stevenson. Willie Wilson had displaced Simpson in goal but there was some surprise when Simpson was signed by Celtic.

Meanwhile the League Cup sections had been settled with Hibs edged out by Dunfermline, but it was a measure of their supporters' new expectations that they were barracked for only beating Third Lanark by three goals. Hearts were representing Edinburgh in the Fairs Cup this year, so as a consolation for missing out on Europe, Hibs brought Real Madrid to Easter Road early in October and completely upstaged their rivals. With a heavy guarantee to meet, Hibs had to increase the prices by half to six shillings and still required over 30,000 tickets to go to break even. They failed narrowly to achieve this, but neither the club nor those who paid minded that.

An early memory of the game is of a shot from the legendary Hungarian Puskas, which started off looking like a misplaced pass into the North Enclosure but which had Wilson scrambling to save at the post. Puskas, by now a veteran, attributed his long career to superb fitness, but on the night he was totally eclipsed by Willie Hamilton about whom the same could not be said.

Then in twenty minutes Hibs put together a move up the left which ended with Cormack swivelling to crack home a first-time shot that Real could not have bettered, and the crowd sat back to watch Real step up their game and swamp Hibs. But they tried and could not, and as time passed and defeat loomed, some desperation crept into their erstwhile elegant play, none more so than when Pat Quinn flighted a free kick over their area and Zoco sent the ball into his own net and Real were beaten. The result was probably more of a surprise to John Rafferty (who had forecast a score of seven for the Spaniards) than to goalkeeper Wilson who had vowed they would not get any.

Now on a high, Hibs continued their spree with four goals at Ibrox, and maintained their interest in what was a very unusual title race involving four teams with neither half of the Old Firm in sight. The pattern was already established with a third of the programme gone, with Kilmarnock, Dunfermline, Hearts and Hibs forming the leading group.

It followed that Hibs were also bidding, for the first time in a decade, to redress the balance of football power in Edinburgh. They had failed to prevent Hearts continuing their winning ways at Easter Road in September, so it was more important to do well at Tynecastle in January. Hearts went all out as always for the opening goal which was such an inspiration to them, so when half-time came at 0–0, Hibs, it seemed, were halfway there. Thereafter the game is remembered for the goal which won it. Quinn took a short free kick which left Hamilton in possession but almost on the goal-line, but as Cruikshanks and the world looked for his cross, Hamilton shot with such venom and swerve that the ball was next seen to be rolling along the top of the Hearts' net. Inside.

Hibs had a lot going for them then, and when they met Rangers again, a spectacular headed goal from Neil Martin gave them their first double over the Ibrox side since their championship season of 1902–03. Another feature was that the crowd of 43,000 compared favourably with that of 36,000 at Ibrox in October. Jock Stein might well have led Hibs to the title — they were virtual leaders at this point — but he resigned to take over as manager of Celtic. Stein in fact stayed to guide Hibs to another win against Rangers,

A crowd of 44,300 saw Neil Martin score with this spectacular header to give Hibs a rare league double over Rangers, on a snow-covered Easter Road in February 1965.

this one in the Cup before an Easter Road attendance of 47,000. Beating Rangers obviously brought him great satisfaction, because Celtic while he was in charge of them made a habit of it.

Bob Shankly

An Edinburgh bookmaker quoted Eddie Turnbull, then with Queens Park, as 6-4 favourite to succeed Stein, followed by Messrs Prentice, Baird, Cunningham, Peacock, Cullis, McColl, Young and Waddell, so anyone who put their shirt on Bob Shankly would have been clothed for life. Shankly had been a centre-forward with Falkirk, winning a League cap, and since his playing days had managed Falkirk, Third Lanark and currently Dundee, whom he had taken to the League championship and the semi-finals of the European Cup. More recently, however, he had been rather unhappy about the breaking up of that successful side.

Shankly took over at Easter Road as season 1964–65 was building up to its memorable climax, with Kilmarnock stealing a lead at Tynecastle and holding out for an hour against a Hearts side who themselves required only one goal to be champions, and while Kilmarnock took the League, Celtic were winning the Cup with a last-gasp winner against Stein's first charges Dunfermline. Unfortunately, Hibs had anticlimaxed somewhat a week or two earlier — successive defeats by Dundee and Celtic put the League title beyond them, and they were well beaten by Dunfermline in the Cup semi-final at Tynecastle.

Bob Shankly was Hibs' manager for the next four seasons. He was of the traditional style, perhaps old-fashioned, preferring his teams to play the game the way it came to them, with two wingers wide on the flanks, and with little time for the more defensive and tactical style that was becoming popular — with coaches at least — in England. Kilmarnock were the first Scottish club of any note to take to the new style, and had thereby won the League title playing to miserable attendances. The Ayrshire side provided a striking contrast to Hibs, the most cavalier of sides, who scored far more goals but lost more too, and whose performances, according to mood, varied from brilliant to moderate. Shankly also had an old-fashioned determination to hold on to his best players, and strove Canute-like to stem the drift south. As at Dundee, it was the hopelessness of this that finally made him quit.

Despite the perpetual transfer talk surrounding Peter Cormack and the occasional transfer of a team-mate, Shankly had a talented pool of players at Easter Road and overall did not need to use more than about twenty with any regularity, while at any one time his pool scarcely exceeded a dozen. Willie Wilson remained the first-choice goalkeeper but was so plagued with back trouble that Thomson Allan played fully as many games. Indeed at one time, with third choice Jack Reilly also injured, Allan was playing regularly for the first team and the reserves.

At left-back Joe Davis had the remarkable record of 273 consecutive appearances from late 1964 when he left the sinking ship that was Third Lanark to replace John Parke who, unsettled in Edinburgh, had gone to Sunderland. Davis captained Hibs for three seasons and became a penalty kick expert — his tally of forty-three competitive goals was a great credit to the full-back, and also, of course, to Eric Stevenson who seemed to win most of them.

Davis's partner at right-back was Bobby Duncan, who took over from John Fraser, and whose overlapping style, in the modern way of full-backs, did not disguise the fact that he had originally been signed as a forward. Duncan's cantrips up the touchline came to an abrupt end with a horrific tackle from behind by Celtic's John Hughes in January 1968. It was 347 days before the right-back made another appearance, and his career never picked up thereafter. Billy Simpson therefore had a lengthy spell as deputy, till in 1968–69 both were superseded by Chris Shevlane, the red-haired former Hearts' player freed by Celtic.

At centre-half McNamee remained the man in possession but was ever playing under the constant threat of official disapproval, and so for the player's sake he was transferred to Newcastle to make a fresh start, at the end of 1966. His successor at Easter Road was John Madsen, one of Morton's imported Danes. The new man was short for the position, especially after McNamee, but no softer a touch, and turned out to be one of the manager's most inspired acquisitions. Beside both, Pat Stanton completed a

Hibs beat Rangers three times in 1964–65. Only Willie Hamilton knew whether he dummied or deflected John Fraser's free kick past Ritchie and McKinnon to win the Scottish Cuptie between the sides with just two minutes to go.

formidable barrier, with his astute reading of situations and his apodictic tackles.

Hibs' midfielders through the Shankly era included Pat Quinn and the polished Alan Cousin, who had played under the manager at Dundee. This skill was complemented by the willing industry of John Baxter, now nearing the end of his spell, and from about 1967 the tenacious Allan McGraw, also from Morton. McGraw was signed in 1966 as a striker, having been the Greenock club's best striker for the previous five years, and allegedly the only man ever to score on every senior ground in Scotland, but after struggling for a season to hold a forward position with Hibs he settled in further back.

One of the strikers who caused McGraw such selection difficulties was Peter Cormack, who continued to expend an enormous amount of energy, much of it fruitfully. Cormack was forever involved in transfer talk, but he remained while a succession of partners did move to other clubs. In the autumn of 1965 Willie Hamilton went to Aston Villa for £25,000, and shortly afterwards Neil Martin to Sunderland for double that. Jim Scott had a turn at centre next until the youthful Colin Stein broke through, and was even described as 'gliding gracefully' in one early report. Stein was the last big name to leave Hibs under Bob Shankly, and he was replaced by Joe McBride, a prolific but aging sharpshooter from Celtic. Cormack, Martin, Hamilton, Scott and Stein all played for Scotland, and much credit was due to Hibs' manager that they were still in a challenging position when they had all gone. Jimmy O'Rourke was a first reserve throughout this time, but for so many positions that he was seldom out of the first team for long.

Shankly's Hibs were an exciting team when the mood took them, but that was not by any means always, and in particular they seemed less inclined on heavy grounds in winter, and against defences which were not prepared to give them the space they needed to play. So there was a tendency for Hibs to make a good start to the League Cup and the League, but to fall from grace in the middle section of the championship and the Scottish Cup, so that by the time that grounds were firm again their chances of any honours had gone. In successive years Aberdeen simply rushed Hibs out of the Cup in a replay at Pittodrie, a faint-hearted display never looked like being enough to stop a hard-hitting Airdrie team at chilly Broomfield, and a year after that Hibs were likewise simply too soft to hold Rangers at Ibrox.

In contrast, Hibs reached one League Cup final and one semi-final. They were unlucky to have to replay the 1965 semi against Celtic after the Parkhead side had drawn level in the last minute, but Celtic were too good to give a second chance to, and they won 4–0. Time was equally close three years later at Tynecastle, where Hibs and Dundee were level until in the last moments Allan McGraw, who had been stretchered off but had returned though barely able to walk, managed to force the ball into the net with his massively bandaged knee. Once again Hibs met Celtic, and although the final was deferred to March because of a fire at Hampden, Hibs were six down before O'Rourke and Stevenson scored two late goals.

It was much the same in the League. Celtic were good enough to concentrate on scoring goals themselves not to have to worry about stopping others; Hibs were one of the few to take up their challenge, and what resulted were some of the best games of football seen, with goals aplenty, even if Celtic scored a greater proportion of them than their play merited. The outstanding example of that was in late 1968 when Hibs, at their best, came back from being behind to take the lead with just fifteen minutes to go, only for Celtic to reply with an unbelievable spell of four goals in five minutes.

Against Rangers it was the other face of Hibs that was seen, with the Edinburgh side too often swept aside by the power that seems to be preferred at Ibrox. So for different reasons Hibs failed to register a championship win over either half of the Old Firm, but they did establish an ascendancy over Hearts.

The derby games were ones for the statisticians. Hibs took ten points from sixteen, and at Easter Road scored their first home win in fourteen years in 1966, and their first Ne'erday home win in twenty years in 1968. At Tynecastle in 1965 Hibs scored four times between the third and tenth minutes, Stevenson and O'Rourke each counting twice, and two years later Pat Quinn, ending a goalless spell of twenty-three months, had a hat-trick. Hearts won 3–1 at Easter Road in September 1968, and these goals were their last championship ones for over five years.

Overall it seemed that Hibs were making some progress, as they moved from sixth to fifth to third in the table, but slipped to twelfth in 1968–69. There were two reasons for this. The first was that John Madsen had gone home to Esbjerg to resume his career as an architect, and neither Stanton nor Cousin who teamed up in the middle of the defence was really a 'stopper'. Secondly, Stanton, Quinn, Stein, Scott, Hunter, Cormack and the youngsters Blackley and Marinello were all sent off in a spate of marked indiscipline, and although Hibs were not a hard team — more, as we have seen, the reverse. At the time, orderings off were still something of a rarity and a disgrace.

Nap against Naples

Still, if Hibs had failed to topple Celtic and Rangers, it should be remembered that these two became the first British teams to reach European finals in 1967, the European Cup and the Cupwinners Cup respectively. Hibs were as usual more concerned with the Fairs Cup, and it was in that competition that they brought off their notable win of the era in November 1967. While older fans recall Barcelona, a slightly younger generation still talk about Naples.

Not much had gone right for Hibs in the Stadio Fuorigrotta, where Scotland's World Cup hopes had gone west two years before. Colin Stein did score, but only after the Italians had got four, and in addition Hibs were hit by the sterling devaluation and ran out of money. The Hibs' players were presented with silver cigarette lighters to mark the auspicious occasion, but were nevertheless fit enough to have a go in the second leg.

It was a whirlwind start, and in five minutes Bobby Duncan let fly from near halfway and the ball obligingly dipped under Dino Zoff's crossbar. Then Cormack was upended but Hibs were denied a penalty, and the game seemed to settle into a familiar pattern, until three minutes from the interval Pat Quinn accurately squeezed the ball in at a post.

Downhill second half, Hibs attacked fervently with the 22,000 crowd mostly packed round the bottom goal. After twenty minutes the Italians were still holding out, but then Alex. Scott, who had come from Everton when his brother left Hibs for Newcastle, placed a corner on the near post for Cormack to leap high and head Hibs' third. Bob Crampsey was still debating with his TV audience whether Hibs would rely on the new 'away goals' rule or go for the kill when Scott crossed to the far post and Stanton stooped to head the fourth. The tie was won, but Colin Stein collected a fifth by delicately blasting a shot an inch past Zoff's ear.

Hibs' reward was a tie with Don Revie's Leeds United, not that long out of the Second Division, but recognised as the ultimate method team, and whose style could not have contrasted more with Hibs' own. The first game was at Elland Road and was decided by one early goal scored as a result of a faulty Hibs' goal kick, but Hibs might well have won had not Stein, whose bustling style was causing many problems, been injured in a heavy tackle and carried off.

The return attracted over 40,000 spectators, and their opinion of Billy Bremner caused the television soundtrack to have to be dubbed. In just six minutes Hibs were level when Stein lobbed over the goalkeeper's head from a tight angle. Hibs continued to outplay a team that could match them only in physique, but they failed to capitalise, especially on one occasion when Stein had a clear run in on the goalkeeper. Then Wilson was penalised for infringing the 'four steps' rule, which both custodians had flouted all evening, and as Hibs' concentration lapsed for a moment, Giles chipped the ball in for the unmarked Charlton to score. Hibs were left to score twice in seven minutes and were out.

Leeds went on to beat Rangers and Dundee on their way to win the trophy in the way they liked best, by holding out for a goalless draw after earning a scoring one away from home. They had more trouble with Dundee than Rangers, and the suggestion was made that they were more worried about the Rangers' support than about their team.

Apart from their trips to Europe, Hibs also travelled to North America and Africa. As Toronto City they played in the North American Soccer League, against such teams as Aberdeen, Dundee United, Sunderland, Wolves and Cerro, the famous Uruguayans; and the following summer, 1968, they had one of their more bizarre experiences, in Nigeria.

Nigeria was embroiled in the bloody civil war caused by the attempted secession of the oil-rich Biafran state at the time, and Hibs became involved when the Biafran representative at the United Nations complained to the Security Council that this 'unusually large football team of seventy including T. Stein and E. Stevenson' were really British paratroops on their way to help the federal army against them. John Fairgrieve pointed out that

Dino Zoff did not often concede five goals, but he did so in the Fairs Cuptie between Hibs and Naples in November 1967. This picture shows Pat Stanton heading home a far post cross from Alex Scott to put Hibs four up. Peter Cormack (left) watches approvingly.

Hibs were by no means unprepared for this sort of engagement as a result of tangling with Bremner, Hunter and company, but in the event Hibs' biggest problem was the intense heat, which might well have been foreseen.

Bob Shankly resigned in September 1969 after Hibs had opened their League campaign with a 3–0 defeat by Ayr, but in truth he had been less than happy since the departure of Colin Stein the previous October. Stein had persistently asked for a move, and Hibs had reluctantly agreed terms with Everton for him, which Stein to most people's astonishment turned down. Shankly's joy was short-lived. It was rumoured that Preston had an interest, but although Hibs were even less willing to lose their man to another Scottish side than to an English one, they had to accept Rangers' offer of £100,000, the largest so far between Scottish clubs. It was only then that the awful truth came out — Stein was a Rangers supporter. Over the years, Hibs players who have gone south have generally been welcomed back in their new colours, but the Easter Road crowd did not forgive Colin Stein. Bob Shankly resigned in disgust at the time, and although he was persuaded to carry on, his frustration persisted and he called it a day less than a year later.

The managerial post was advertised this time, and Willie McFarlane was the applicant who most impressed the judges. Since leaving Hibs, he had played for Raith Rovers and most of the Border clubs, and was currently Stirling Albion's part-time boss as well as a manager of a construction plant firm. A confident extrovert, McFarlane announced that he was hopeful that Cormack would stay, and even persuaded the would-be wanderer to sign a one-year contract. Early results were good too, with Hibs winning at Parkhead, Ibrox and Tynecastle, and leading the League at the end of November.

So far Hibs and McFarlane could do no wrong, but the infallibility tag soon started to disappear. On December 30th, the manager announced that there would be no move for Peter Marinello, who was exciting selectors and scouts alike and had even impressed Archie McPherson with a two-goal display at Ibrox in October. But Marinello was an Arsenal player by the time Hibs met Hearts on New Year's Day, and Cormack's frustration was evident in the manner of his ordering off in the derby game. He was sent off again at Paisley in his second game back after suspension, and Hibs cut their losses by selling him to Nottingham Forest.

Hibs' performances slipped a bit too, although they finished third, and much of the cause was the constant transfer talk which had even the new captain Pat Stanton feeling unsettled. Hibs had already spent £30,000 bringing Airdrie's centre-half Jim Black to Easter Road at the start of the season, and now they bought the services of Arthur Duncan, Partick Thistle's speedy left-winger, for a third of the Marinello proceeds — and who is to say that that was a bad deal? In his time Duncan was to get over a hundred goals for Hibs, while Black scored only three, and one of them was while Black was still with Airdrie. However, he did form a lengthy partnership with John Blackley in the middle of the defence, with a style best described as complementary to the subtle play of the latter.

In between, McFarlane had introduced Erich Schaedler, whom he signed from Stirling Albion with much less publicity. Schaedler won the battle for the left-back position from Mervyn Jones, who was not Welsh, but *was* the nephew of Rangers' skipper John Greig. Schaedler's start was not entirely auspicious, in that an own goal was the most notable contribution of his debut for the reserves, and with his very first tackle for the first team he had team-mate Peter Cormack carried off, in the friendly against Gørnik Zrbzre. Erich Schaedler never learned the art of making a compromising tackle, but four years later he played for Scotland against his father's native Germany.

CHAPTER 19

Turnbull's Tornadoes, 1970–75

'I want Aberdeen to be great — and we're almost there'. Eddie Turnbull said that in February 1971, and certainly he had built a good team at Pittodrie. Aberdeen were Scottish Cupholders and were challenging Celtic furiously for the League championship, and yet in July of the same year Turnbull left the granite city to take over Hibs, whose season had been very different.

The period 1970–71 had above all been one of change at Easter Road, and the changes had started at the top in September when William P. Harrower was bought out as majority shareholder by Tom Hart, a successful East Lothian builder whose company had amongst other things put up 'The Right Wing' in Willowbrae Road for Gordon Smith. Hart brought two former goalkeepers to the board with him, Tommy Younger and Jimmy Kerr, who was also a director of his construction business.

The new administration got off to a sensational start by accepting the resignation of their manager as early as December. He was replaced by Dave Ewing, who had recently joined the club as a coach, and was considered to be something of a capture in that capacity. A Scot from Perth, Ewing had been a centre-half with Manchester City in Bobby Johnstone's time there, and had joined Hibs from Sheffield Wednesday.

The change in manager brought changes on the field too. The new boss fielded some formations whose cautious approach was alike foreign to Hibs' teams and supporters, and as the results did not get any better, they were not readily accepted. Hibs had not had a particularly good start to the season, but by the close they had settled down to twelfth place. They did reach the semi-finals of the Cup, but in the League games leading up to that, seemed to be doing no more than passing time.

Dave Ewing also had a preference for different players to follow his plans than had McFarlane. Out went Erich Schaedler, replaced by Mervyn Jones and out went McBride and Graham, the two players involved in the row which led to McFarlane going, as well as Jim Blair, who had come from St. Mirren the previous year for a substantial fee and soon went back to Paisley for about half as much. And out went Marshall and Shevlane, to be replaced by Roy Baines, a teenaged goalkeeper from Derby, and John Brownlie, who had impressed one and all with his aptitude for attacking from right back. These last two changes were imminent anyway in view of the ages of the players involved.

To replace McBride, Hibs brought back Joe Baker, who had been working his passage home from Italy with stops at Arsenal, Nottingham Forest and latterly Sunderland, and who returned to Hibs to an emotional welcome and the winning goal against Eddie Turnbull's Aberdeen, who had not conceded a goal for about three months. Jimmy O'Rourke found favour, with his high work-rate, and youngsters Alex Cropley, Kenny Davidson and John Hazel all began to make the grade.

By the time the long-awaited semi-final with Rangers came off, therefore, Hibs had a much changed look about them. The game itself was a shambles, with weak refereeing allowing only the strong to survive, and with skill eliminated, few chances and no goals were witnessed. It was at this point that Dave Ewing made a name for himself by expressing the opinion 'Rangers are rubbish' in public, and apparently without heed to the fact that Hibs had not actually beaten them. Hibs' last big game of the season was the replay which Rangers deservedly won by two goals to one by O'Rourke, and once it was over Mr Ewing packed his bags for some coaching appointment in England.

Eddie Turnbull therefore found Hibs in a state of some disorder, and his first season was largely one of consolidation, which was sufficiently successful for his new charges to move eight places up the table to fourth and reach the Cup final. His Aberdeen side had been built from the back, and likewise with Hibs Turnbull started by finding a goalkeeper. It was somewhat unfortunate for Roy Baines that he was injured at this time, because his chance was thereby lost and before too long he went to Morton. Hibs meanwhile signed Jim Herriot from Birmingham City, a former Scottish internationalist, at the time conveniently playing in Durban. Herriot had the unusual habit of blacking his eyes with soot, apparently to cut down the glare from the sun, which tended to give him the appearance of a photographic negative of Geronimo.

With Herriot, Hibs had a defence in which only Jim Black was not an actual or future internationalist, and up to the Cup final they lost as many as three goals only once, at home to Airdrie. The forward line was not entirely as satisfactory, but then they lacked a centre-forward for most of the time. Joe Baker was continually out with muscle problems which ultimately required surgery, so that O'Rourke and Hazel filled in until January when Alan Gordon joined Hibs. Gordon had found success first with Hearts, notably on account of his heading ability, but had been with Dundee United for some time before going to Easter Road. Hibs had also signed Bertie Auld on a free transfer from Celtic at the start of the season, and Alex Edwards from Dunfermline in October, on the same day that Eric Stevenson left the club to join Johnny Graham at Ayr.

A Hibs squad picture with Eddie Turnbull in charge. Back row: Duncan, Shevlane, Black, (trialist), Baines, Gillet, Brownlie, Baker, Fraser. Middle row: McNiven, Mathison, O'Rourke, Stanton, Grant, Gordon, Blackley, (trialist), Hazel, Nelson, Turnbull. Front row: Davidson, Pringle, Graham, Hamilton, McEwan, Schaedler, Cropley, Auld, Young, Stevenson.

The team was not entirely settled even then, because Edwards was sent off at Methil and missed eight weeks thereafter, but Hibs did reach fourth in the table, and by the end of the season could claim to be the second-best team in Scotland, since they beat the two above them, Aberdeen and Rangers, in the Cup, and took three points out of four in the return League fixtures.

It was, however, difficult to claim any more after Celtic had beaten them 6–1 in the Hampden final. Hibs' one crumb of comfort came from Gordon's equaliser of a second-minute goal by Billy McNeil, but thereafter they had the joyless experience of watching 'Dixie' Deans score the first Cup final hat-trick for about eighty years. It was uncanny how Deans, otherwise no more than an average centre, seldom failed to score against Hibs and Jim Black in particular.

Turnbull's Tornadoes

Hibs obviously learned some lessons from that wretched afternoon, such as that Celtic were there for the beating, because when the two teams met again at the same venue as early as August they showed no inferiority complex — not that any was justified. This was in the Drybrough Cup final, a curtain-raising tournament for the four top scorers in each division of the League, so it was clear that Hibs' forward problems were not too acute. Hibs reached the final by trouncing Rangers in a semi-final remembered for Colin Stein's headstand in an attempt to outwit Brownlie near a corner flag, and their performance at Hampden was a strangely relaxed one for a Hibs team in a Cup final. Confidently they built up a three-goal lead with some first-rate play, and although they as quickly surrendered this advantage to have to play an extra half-hour, a twenty-yarder by Jimmy O'Rourke and a solo from Arthur Duncan brought them home in the end. The Hibs' line-up was Herriot; Brownlie and Schaedler; Stanton, Black, Blackley; Hamilton, Hazel, Gordon, Cropley and Duncan, with O'Rourke appearing as a substitute.

Hibs' supporters had not yet become bored by an endless succession of Cup successes, and so there was some anticipation of their new trophy being paraded three days later, when West Bromwich were Hibs' guests at Easter Road. A 'special motorised vehicle' was being prepared to do the occasion justice. It was then with some humour that the assembled throng watched the club's lawnmower, with some plywood superstructure, painted green and with the sponsors' name spelt wrongly on the side, being driven impressively round the track.

The supporters' humour, however, continued as Hibs swept through the months that followed, almost invincibly, especially on Wednesdays. A consolation for their Cup final debacle was entry to the Cupwinners' Cup, where they first met the Sporting Club de Portugal, usually known here as Sporting Lisbon, and their performance in the Portuguese capital was as good as was seen anywhere, although their hosts won 2–1. Hibs took a while to get going in the second leg — Sporting were clearly the happier at half-time with the score one apiece — but in the second half they cut loose and scored five times without reply to give Sporting their heaviest European defeat. Jimmy O'Rourke had three, one of six trebles he was to record during the season.

The Albanians of FC Besa were next in the firing line, and were trounced 7–1 in a complete mismatch, and it suited Hibs to leave nothing to chance in the return leg. Conditions were primitive, Hibs were confined to their hotel, and when they reached the ground at Durres to find the pitch markings inaccurate and the crossbars too low, the solution offered was to dig a trench under the bar to make up the shortfall in height. Hibs settled for a diplomatic draw in the hope that it would help an easy exit from the country.

Interleaved with these European engagements were the knock-out stages of the League cup, and compared to their experience in Albania, Hibs' jaunts in this one were pleasant indeed, even the one to Airdrie. First, though, they had to go to Tannadice, and trailed by a goal at the interval before swamping Dundee United with another five-goal flourish after the

Jimmy O' Rourke (no. 8) and Alan Gordon (right) watch as Pat Stanton drives home the opening goal in the League Cup Final of 1972. The ball flashes past Connolly, goalkeeper Williams and Jimmy Johnstone, who seems to be in the centre-half position.

break. Then at Broomfield Hibs were again behind at half-time, but this time hit back with six thereafter. Duncan had three and Brownlie his first double, and again Hibs were through with the second game still to come.

Hibs' final Wednesday showpiece of 1972 was the League Cup semi-final with Rangers, inevitably at Hampden. Their one-touch football, especially that of the right-wing triangle of Brownlie, Stanton and Edwards, and their composure, gradually drew the speed and harassment with which Rangers tried to offset their obvious disadvantages elsewhere. As often as not it was Brownlie who broke through, and it was no surprise when the goalminded full-back went all the way to slip the ball into Rangers' net for the only goal. Inevitably, Hibs' opponents in the final were again Celtic.

It was a measure of Celtic's respect for Hibs at this time that their right winger Johnstone, usually regarded as a potential matchwinner, was deployed on the left where it was clearly hoped he would inhibit Brownlie's attacking. So when the Hibs man first 'read' a Johnstone backheeler and then drove upfield past the diminutive redhead, Johnstone's own menace vanished and Hibs had scored an important point.

Nevertheless for an hour the final did little to excite. But Hibs were holding Celtic at all points and then in a ten-minute spell they pulverised them. It started with McNeil fouling Gordon. Edwards' chipped free kick found Stanton inside the penalty area, but to the unbelieving he seemed to be going the wrong way, away from goal, until he abruptly turned and slotted the ball past Williams. Six minutes later Edwards split the Celtic defence to find Stanton on the right, and the skipper's near-post cross was tailored for Jimmy O'Rourke, racing on to head the second. The hectic spell continued with McNeill clearing off the goalline from Gordon, and Stanton striking the base of a post, so that although Dalglish scored late on for Celtic, they were well beaten. The side that beat them was Herriot; Brownlie, Schaedler; Stanton, Black, Blackley; Edwards, O'Rourke, Gordon, Cropley and Duncan. This cup was paraded round Easter Road too, but to prevent any embarrassment, it was carried by young reserves on foot.

A Pleasant Day at Tynecastle

Hibs' Saturday form was impressive too, and they were challenging Celtic at the top of the table. Ayr United were caught up in the euphoria a week after the League Cup final and lost 8–1, and although Hibs were held to a draw in an important game at Celtic Park, they were still on a high when they went to Tynecastle on New Year's Day. Hearts were also doing well, and had been third in the League as recently as mid-December, and, as their club programme pointed out, were one ahead in the last hundred League derbies.

Hearts did not hold that advantage much longer. After Park missed an early chance for the maroons, the roof quickly fell in on them. First a long throw-in was allowed to bounce to O'Rourke in front of goal and in it went. Then Gordon controlled a pass from Edwards, slipped but had the time to steer the ball past Garland. When Cropley intercepted a Hearts' clearance, his header found the home defence too square and Duncan ran on to make it three. A Cropley volley and a Duncan header both went in off Garland's right-hand post, and Hibs were easing off before half-time. In the second half, there was much crossfield play as Hibs were satisfied to pass time, but O'Rourke tapped in a sixth after Stanton had drawn the goalkeeper out, and Gordon made it seven with a header off both posts. Hibs had required a six-goal win to jump over Celtic who were not playing, and so were top of the League, as were their second string in the reserve table. Jimmy O'Rourke had scored thirty-two goals so far and Alan Gordon twenty-nine.

As a fitting reward for his efforts, Pat Stanton holds up the League Cup, while Jim Herriot collects his medal.

Unfortunately Hibs were brought right back to earth just five days later. East Fife were the visitors, and Hibs won by a late Alan Gordon header, but by then John Brownlie had broken his leg in two places in an accidental clash with an opponent and was out of the game for almost a year. Alex Edwards was cautioned for throwing the ball in frustration at the attentions of the East Fife defender Love and the reluctance of the referee to keep them in check. Hibs missed the influence of Edwards, suspended for eight weeks.

Not surprisingly Hibs' form shaded off, even on Wednesdays, when they lost a Cup replay to Rangers after being seemingly well placed with a draw at Ibrox, and when they went down by three goals to Hajduk Split (Split Bandits) in the Cupwinners' Cup and could only afford one. Likewise in the League, Hibs' previously formidable attack could only muster two goals in their last seven outings and finished third, though qualifying for the Drybrough and UEFA Cups.

As usual (for the four years the competition ran) the Drybrough Cup came first, and Hibs won it again, although this time they beat both Rangers and Celtic in extra time, and it was only in the last minute of the extra thirty that Alan Gordon scored the only goal of the final. What was important to Hibs was that they had won without Brownlie, and that Tony Higgins, Bobby Smith and Des Bremner had come of age as first-team players. Bremner's task was the hardest, that of taking over from Brownlie only a few weeks after coming from Deveronvale. Bremner's game was more cautious than Brownlie's — after all, so were those of many a striker — and he improved quickly as he learned to stick to it and not try to emulate his illustrious predecessor.

It was in September that Hibs met Hearts again, also at Tynecastle, and Hearts ended a disastrous spell by winning 4–1. These were Hearts' first League goals against Hibs for a day over five years, but as they had managed only two home League goals following their defeat at New Year, they were still behind Hibs by 8–6 on goals at Tynecastle in 1973 — or 9–5 if one takes account of their first goal having been put into his own net by Erich Schaedler!

However, the excitement at Tynecastle at this result was short-lived, and it was soon clear that time and tide had not yet turned against Hibs. By the end of the season it was they and not Hearts who beat Dundee United 4–1 at Tannadice to pip Rangers for second place in the table, and much earlier than that — in the autumn, while Burnley, newly promoted to the English first division, were administering an 8–0 aggregate trouncing to their city rivals — Hibs were engaged in another titanic struggle with the English league pacemakers, Leeds United, in the UEFA Cup.

As six years before, the first leg was in Yorkshire, and Hibs, with Black and Blackley superb in countering the aerial attacks aimed at the big Leeds strikers, gave as good as they got, and, at least in the case of Pat Stanton driving through the midfield, much better. A goal did not result, but Hibs seemed well placed for the return. Another huge expectant crowd assembled for it; Leeds were supposedly weakened by injury, so that people like Joe Jordan were brought in, but they held out against all the odds and as concerted a ninety minutes of attack as Easter Road has witnessed. Several times it seemed inevitable that their goal would fall, and afterwards even Billy Bremner, the visiting captain, was of the opinion that his side had been outplayed, and that a brilliant Hibs' performance should have earned a substantial victory. But in truth, the brilliant performance came from Bremner himself, controlling his side from some distance behind the back four, and often behind his goalkeeper too. Stanton hit the post in the penalty shoot-out that followed, the only one on either side to miss, and it was fitting that it fell to Bremner to hit his side's fifth and winning kick.

A happy occasion at Tynecastle, on New Year's Day 1973. Alan Gordon's header flies past Garland to put Hibs seven goals in front.

Losing like that to Leeds was scarcely a failure, and Hibs kept playing impressively; by Christmas they were second in the table, and *The Scotsman* thought, after a five-goal thrashing of Morton, that the side was 'certainly better than the Famous Five of a decade or two back' on the grounds of the attacking abilities of their defenders, and the midfield of Stanton, Edwards and Cropley. Certainly Jim McArthur, who had taken over from Jim Herriot but missed the early games with a damaged hand, was back, as at last was John Brownlie.

Joe Harper

Jimmy O'Rourke had come back into favour too, against Dundee in November, and scored nineteen goals in fifteen games, for which feat he found himself dropped, to make way for Hibs' most ambitious signing ever, Joe Harper. Harper had had a chequered career, failing with Huddersfield and returning thence to Morton, where he refound his scoring touch, and

H

was transferred first to Aberdeen, and then to Everton, where he had been for thirteen months, scoring only 14 goals in 48 games, and only six since August. Aberdeen had received £180,000 for him, and were prepared to take him back, but were outbid when Hibs stepped in with £120,000, by far and away a club record. Meanwhile, Jimmy O'Rourke had bounced back for the last time, because he went to St. Johnstone at the end of the season, much to the disgruntlement of a large section of the Hibs' support with whom he was always a favourite, and who never really took to Harper in the same way. Meanwhile Deans scored another couple against Black as Hibs' League challenge to Celtic petered out, and, as mentioned above, Hibs were second.

By August, with Harper having settled in, it seemed that Hibs might at last be poised to take over from Celtic, and early form was encouraging. By mid-October they had qualified for the League Cup final — against Celtic of course, and had lost only once in the League, by the only goal to St. Johnstone, and that scored inevitably by Jimmy O'Rourke. It was at this stage, a week before the League Cup final, that Hibs travelled to Parkhead on League business, and the game was widely considered as a title decider, despite the fact that Rangers were above both.

As things turned out, it was as black a week as Hibs have had. Derek Spalding had by now taken over from Jim Black, who had gone back to Airdrie, but Dixie Deans was unperturbed, scoring five times as Celtic won 5–0 at Parkhead and 6–3 at Hampden. And in between, on what was proving an emotional night as Hibs fought back from a goal down to lead Juventus in the UEFA Cup, the atmosphere went completely flat as Hibs were caught going for more and paid a high price of three late goals.

For all that, and with Rangers' challenge still largely being discounted by those who knew, Hibs were still the second-best team in the country, and it was sheer bad luck that they drew Celtic in the first round of the Cup. The tactic this time was for Stanton to take out Deans, with Spalding only having to look after Kenny Dalglish, but this did not work either, and Deans was again on the scoresheet as Celtic won 2–0.

But by now Hibs had as a matter of policy altered their whole approach. Spurred by the dreadful week in October, but also in anticipation of the tighter Premier League which was coming, it had been decided that a much harder line was called for. The first change in personnel, that of selling Alex Cropley, who had not asked for a transfer, to Arsenal, and bringing Ally McLeod from Southampton in his place, did not seem to be a product of this masterplan — Cropley was no heavyweight, but was a tenacious tackler — but rather a move to balance the books which had got more out of step than usual with the purchase of Harper. And McLeod did come with some worthwhile credentials — he had once scored four goals at Ibrox for St. Mirren in a League Cup tie.

It was more the signing of Roy Barry which confirmed Hibs' change of attitude. And when Hibs met Celtic again and beat them 2–1, Barry stood for absolutely no nonsense from Deans and snuffed him out completely, and the crowd started to warm to him. Hibs managed to sneak in front of the Parkhead side in the League, only to find Rangers in front of both of them, and in fact the Ibrox men took the title with a fortuitous draw at Easter Road — not that there was much chance of their being caught by that time anyway.

This single goal by Joe Harper was enough to win the league cup semi-final for Hibs against Falkirk at Tynecastle in October 1974.

CHAPTER 20

The Premier League, 1975–80

Nineteen seventy-five was a big year in Scottish football, with the biggest reorganisation since the introduction of leagues over eighty years before, and the introduction of a ten-team Premier Division. For Hibs, the year also marked the club's centenary.

The first of two major events was a game against Derby County, the champions of England. The football was not memorable, and the game is less often recalled than Hibs' tussles with Leeds or Liverpool. Derby played a competent 'away' game, and once Bruce Rioch had put them in front shortly after half-time, they rather unexcitingly contained Hibs until time was called.

The second function was a reception for those connected most closely with the club through the years, and among those in attendance were many former players, of whom pride of place went to Willie Harper who had made the journey from Plymouth for the occasion.

This august do took place in October, so the new leagues were well under way. The set-up was the brainchild of, as much as anyone, Tom Hart of Hibs and Willie Waddell of Rangers, and was seen as the salvation of the bigger city clubs, who found it unprofitable to play the lesser fry who had made up the numbers in the old First Division. They now made up the numbers in a new First Division. The plan had been hatched about eighteen months earlier, so that 1974–75 had for many teams been a season of playing for places. Much was expected of it — fewer meaningless games between teams with little at stake, and also the eradication of Scottish teams' tendency to lose 'silly' goals in Europe by having tighter competition at home. The Premier League has had its critics, but by and large these expectations have been fulfilled.

Two of the main criticisms have been the high financial cost of being relegated, and the probability of that happening, with two out of ten going down. The first is an obvious corollary of the financial benefit of playing in the top league, but the second seems to have some substance if it implies that teams are relegated in favour of others who are not in fact any better. This is not the place for an in-depth analysis of the Premier League experience, but during the first five years of it, not once did the promoted sides both stay up.

Anyway, having been joint instigators of these re-arrangements, Hibs could have no complaints about having to play under them, and after two years of coming second there was a conviction at Easter Road that Hibs

The generation gap — Pat Stanton admires the cup medals that Jimmy McColl won half a century before.

might just go one better and become the first Premier League champions. As things turned out, of course they were not, but the competition was voted a huge success by all the clubs early in the new year, and no wonder. At the top, Celtic led by a single point from Rangers, Hibs and Motherwell, while at the other end, any one of Aberdeen, Dundee, Hearts, Dundee United and Ayr seemed as likely to go down with St. Johnstone, who had seemed doomed since August.

Some thought that Motherwell would win the title — mostly Motherwell supporters — until a single headed goal by Bobby Smith won two important points for Hibs at Fir Park and reduced the championship aspirants to three. But next came Hibs' annual decline, by now as predictable and as depressing as the Eurovision Song Contest, according to Ian Wood in *The Scotsman*, and it was all Hibs could do to stay ahead of Motherwell and qualify for the UEFA Cup.

The other competitions had gone less well. Hibs embarked on what has become too habitual for comfort by losing in the League Cup to lower league opponents, in this case Montrose with the deciding goal in extra time the result of Jim McArthur misjudging a punt from the other half of the field.

Montrose thus won 3–2 on aggregate after losing the first leg 1–0, and by coincidence Liverpool eliminated Hibs from the UEFA Cup by exactly the same score. Pat Stanton, by now playing even further from his best position at the back, was made the scapegoat for the defeat at Montrose, and incredibly Hibs went to Anfield to defend their slender advantage without him in the team. Their next mistake was to pay scant attention to Toshack's ability in the air, and the big Welshman was thereby able to head his first-ever hat-trick for Liverpool.

Happily, Stanton was soon restored to the side, withdrew his request for a transfer, and went on to score some memorable headed goals in his forward role in the ensuing weeks — the one at Tynecastle was memorable because it came well into injury time after everyone except the referee thought the game was due to end, and another two won the points from Rangers in an exciting game at Easter Road.

Challenging strongly for the top, Hibs made another move to strengthen their pool in January by buying Mike McDonald from Stoke. McDonald had not had much first-team experience in the Potteries, understudying both Gordon Banks and Peter Shilton during his time there, but was considered to have learned a lot from them. While that was undoubtedly true, there was always a suspicion that big Mike had been playing truant for the lesson on cross balls.

There was more transfer activity to follow. By the previous November Joe Harper had been denying that he wanted to go back to Aberdeen, so it was no surprise when he moved back there in April, in the wake of some unmotivated displays. Hibs only received something under £40,000 for him, so that his forty-five goals had cost the club around £2,000 each. Even so, he seemed to have been better value than his successor at centre, Ally Scott, from Rangers, who with Graham Fyfe formed one half of a swap deal which took Iain Munro to Ibrox. Scott had shown little at Ibrox, and after counting four times in his first four League Cup ties for Hibs, contributed only another five in the remaining time — more than a season — during which he held his place. It was rumoured that Fyfe's form in Glasgow was only one factor in his move, but he did not prove a great asset either, never becoming a first-team regular, whereas Munro later played for Scotland, and was still playing Premier League football a decade later.

Joe Harper had never been accepted as a satisfactory substitute for Jimmy O'Rourke on the Easter Road terraces, but it nevertheless seemed a bad

A reunion of the Famous Five at Easter Road in the seventies. Gordon Smith in particular seems to have hung up his boots too early.

move to let him go, and the disgruntled supporters became downright depressed in September when Pat Stanton went to Celtic in another exchange deal, this one for Celtic's Jackie McNamara. Hibs had already conceded their League Cup section — and three points — to Rangers when the news of the transfers made the teatime headlines, and so it was a small and stunned crowd that were subjected to a featureless draw with Montrose in the final sectional game. The move was roundly condemned, for football supporters are not to be faulted in taking a long-term view of matters.

The shorter term proved as bad as anyone had feared, however; Hibs failed to average even one goal per League game, and Scott at centre managed only three. Their first home win came only on Christmas Eve, and then from an own goal by Ayr's Fillipi before fewer than four thousand enthusiasts. They did not beat that total of one in a home game until March when they scored twice against Kilmarnock. By the turn of the year Hibs were far from clear of relegation, but the return of Ally McLeod, who had been injured for some months, made enough difference. McLeod returned to score the only goal in the vital rearranged derby game in late January, and his run of eight goals in twelve games was prolific in comparison with what had gone before.

Fortunately the defence, bolstered by George Stewart who had been bought from Dundee on the Dens Parkers' demotion in 1976, had restricted Hibs' opponents to about the same meagre scoring rate, and so Hibs finished sixth, seven points clear of Hearts who were relegated for the first time. It was therefore clear how important the seven points out of eight won from the Tynecastle side had been. As for the others, with so few goals for and against, it is not surprising that Hibs drew a half of their thirty-six championship games. The four with Aberdeen yielded but a single goal.

As the other highlights of the season were a UEFA Cup defeat by the unknown Oesters Vaxjo (apparently with or without an 'e') from Sweden, and a Scottish Cup one by Arbroath at Easter Road after Hibs had been lucky enough to draw at Gayfield, it was truly one best forgotten.

What's in a Name?

The next season hardly started any better, with Queen of the South being too good for Hibs over two legs in the League Cup, but at least this year there was a colourful aside to hold some attention. Harry Swan had foreseen the advent of sponsorship a quarter of a century earlier, and also probably the innate reluctance of the various authorities to accept inevitable change. It was only in 1977 therefore that Hibs became the first team to sign a deal for shirt advertising with the sportswear company Bukta, with the blessing of the football powers but not with that of the television moguls. It was true that they were happy to publicise the investments of Gillette in cricket and Coca-Cola in athletics, but were unwilling to compromise whatever principle they thought was at stake by showing Hibs' 'Bukta' jerseys.

Hibs had not previously seen the necessity of having a change strip — since they tended to play in their normal colours even when their opponents were also in green and white — but they came to an agreement with their sponsors to wear a new purple strip for games which were to be covered on television. The purple shirts had white sleeves with green and yellow on them and apart from their general unattractiveness quickly ran into more problems. They were all right as first shown against Celtic and then Ayr, but on the next occasion Hibs' opponents were Rangers and the new shirts clashed with Rangers' blue — as in fact they were liable to do with Dundee, Aberdeen, Hearts etc. So this time the solution was another set of strips, and Hibs turned out looking like a team of goalkeepers in yellow with white shorts.

Hibs' colour problems were causing more comment than their football, and they came to a head in January, with a Scottish Cup game against East

Fife. The intended television treat for the evening was frozen off, so the cameras rolled up at the last moment at Easter Road, where unfortunately the purple togs were not to be found. Eventually a pre-sponsor set of green and white shirts was found, the long-suffering Bukta agreed again, and Hibs were able to take the field — against opponents whose own shirts were emblazoned with 'Cannon Valves' under a somewhat less publicised agreement.

Among their lesser problems Hibs still had that of scoring goals, and to that end had had Jim McKay of Brora and Martin Henderson of Rangers on trial, but neither seemed to entirely solve the problem, so that the next move was to swap Erich Schaedler for Dundee's Bobby Hutchinson. This was not entirely a gain for the Hibs' attack because it meant Bobby Smith, the previous season's leading League goalscorer, taking over from Schaedler at left-back. In addition, John Blackley joined Newcastle in the autumn for a six-figure cheque, allowing Jackie McNamara to discover his best position at the back.

The arrival of Hutchinson certainly made some difference. By November Hibs had been in second-bottom place and playing with as little spirit as success, but they finished well with fifty-one League goals, half as many again as the previous year. This included an unexpected run of nineteen goals in five games, and the mercurial Ally McLeod contributed sixteen, exactly twice as many as Smith had done in 1976–77. It was enough for Hibs to draw their last game with Aberdeen to pip Celtic for the last UEFA Cup place, and they also beat the Parkhead side in a testimonial for Pat Stanton.

There is a general feeling among Hibs supporters that the club has been in steady decline since about 1975, largely on the grounds that the levels of skill seen in the early '70s had been sacrificed in the interests of organisation, as has indeed been the case. But by 1978–79 Hibs were playing in Europe again, reaching the semi-finals of the League Cup and the final of the Scottish Cup, and were unbeaten longer than any of the other nine Premier League sides. It was all attributed to their new-found 'professionalism'.

What this meant was that Hibs were able to remain unbeaten for many weeks by exactly the same methods that others had been criticised for — notably in a League game at Parkhead and a UEFA Cup tie in Norrkoping, where concerted rearguard actions produced better results than games. Even then some luck was needed, as at Tynecastle, where Ally McLeod's equaliser against a Hearts team minus two players ordered off vied with Pat Stanton's of a year or two earlier for lateness. Against such a skilful side as Racing Strasbourg, the clear leaders of the French league, new-found professionalism was not enough, and Hibs fought hard but predictably in vain to redress a two-goal deficit from the first leg in France.

The Norwegian Affair

However, Hibs did make strenuous efforts to ally more desirable attributes to their organisation, involving another drawn-out wrangle with officialdom, this time HM Government. This was over a laudable arrangement to bring two Norwegians, Svein Mathisen of Start Kristiansen and Izaak Refvik of Viking Stavanger, to Easter Road for three months with a view to permanent signings. The negotiations were somewhat protracted, but the pair were finally here to face Morton in the League Cup quarter-final.

Morton had already gained a one-goal advantage at Cappielow, but for the diminutive Refvik in particular, whose legs seemed to move incredibly often to make up for their brevity, it was something of a dream debut. For Ralph Callachan too it was a good night, the best he had had since joining Hibs from Newcastle in exchange for John Brownlie in August. Callachan provided the pint-sized Norwegian with two goals, and in between the elated crowd was delighted to watch Morton's dead-ball wizard, Andy Ritchie, nonchalantly place a penalty kick a yard over the bar.

The most notable thing about Hibs' semi-final against Aberdeen was that Rangers and Celtic were contesting the other one. There was not much between the teams at Dens Park, but in the second period of extra time Aberdeen full-back Kennedy hoisted yet another cross which seemed to be far too near the goalkeeper. But it turned out not to be, as it went over McDonald and into the net off the post. It was hereabouts that the patient Jim McArthur regained his place after three years in the reserves.

Meanwhile most of the interest was in Refvik and Mathisen, mostly because they were not playing for Hibs. The two Norwegians were welcome in Scotland, welcome to the players, spectators and football authorities alike, but Her Majesty's Government at Westminster refused to grant work permits.

The final — in this episode — non-recognition that Scotland had interests different from England's came with the compromise solution, that only full internationalists would be able to come to Britain to play. What this meant was that Manchester United and Liverpool could afford them, but most Scottish sides could not, and in particular Hibs were being penalised by recognising the talent of Refvik, still only an under-21 cap, before the Norwegian selectors. In any case, by the time this generous concession was made, both Scandinavians, mightily sickened, had gone home.

They were gone therefore by the time Hibs started out on their Cup run. The first two ties, against Dunfermline and Meadowbank, should have been formalities, but Hibs were by now well into the way of losing to teams from lower leagues, and it took two tries to beat the Fifers. In the third round at Tynecastle, Hibs were organised enough to counter Hearts. The semi-final was again against Aberdeen, this time at Hampden, on a dreadful night and before fewer than ten thousand spectators. All three goals came in the first half, and Hibs got two of them.

The final was against Rangers, and the first final involving Hibs and the Ibrox side. On the evidence, previous generations had not missed very much. To a large extent this was the fault of Hibs, who played the game very carefully, avoiding giving the large Rangers following any reason to raise much clamour in support of their side. The plan nearly came off, for when Hibs had contained and frustrated for eighty-odd minutes and decided it was time to go for a goal, young Colin Campbell got past his cover, and delivered a hard swerving shot that all but beat McCloy in Rangers' goal.

The second game was no more conclusive; Hibs played less nervously and a little less cautiously than four days earlier, creating the opportunity to score on a number of occasions only to reveal their chronic inability to do so, and the two hours' play finished with them once again defending in some depth.

So a third game was required, and those who had stayed the course were at last treated to a game which had all the highs and lows that are looked for in Cup football. McCloy failed to hold a cross from Rae, and Higgins put Hibs ahead, but McArthur did likewise in Hibs' goal to give Johnstone the equaliser.

The second half was level pegging too. Johnstone scored again, on the hour, from a cross by Russell, but then Hutchinson, racing into the opposing penalty area, was flattened by Jackson, and McLeod levelled the scores from the spot.

And so into the final act, extra time. Hibs seemed in some danger, being a spot-kick decision ahead but not a goal in front, but that was sorted out when Rangers were given their penalty for a tackle by Duncan on Parlane, only for McArthur to save from Miller. Campbell nearly broke the stalemate when he tricked two defenders, but his well-placed shot struck the post; then Davie Cooper, out on the left, sent over a high cross which Arthur Duncan, dashing back to intercept, headed cleanly into the roof of his own net to give Rangers the trophy.

The end of the season could not come quick enough for poor Arthur, but what followed cannot have seemed very much better.

The experience of the Premier League has been one of a leading group aiming to be among the major honours, one or two stragglers at the bottom, and in between, the remaining half of the League, sometimes competing for the last UEFA Cup place, sometimes to avoid the second relegation place, and sometimes both. With ten teams in the division, and a lot of drawn games, the credentials for fifth place do not generally amount to much more than a point a game, and those for eighth not much less. A consequence of this is that, for a team stranded at the bottom, the gap above cannot be closed quickly since the middle group will be averaging their point per game, and to be closed at all requires form which if turned on a little earlier would have meant certain qualification for Europe. So far, the team in tenth place as early as October has always gone down.

By the end of October 1979, Hibs had won just one of their eleven League games and so their fate was virtually sealed. Away points are always hard to come by for teams in trouble, whereas Hibs had Celtic and Rangers in their early home games, and points are never certain against these two either. McLeod missed a vital penalty when Hibs were leading Celtic, and Hibs lost 3–1 to both. When they also went down at home to St. Mirren their goose, if not cooked, was certainly in the oven.

In addition, Des Bremner went to Aston Villa, the latest in a list of sales which brought in badly needed cash, but inadequate replacements. To be fair to Hibs, Bremner was determined to go south, and past experience has shown the impossibility of holding a player in that frame of mind. On the other hand, by accepting an £80,000 reduction in the transfer fee received in consideration of Joe Ward, a former Clyde forward, Hibs were making surely the worst of a bad series of buys. With Joe Harper, forty-five goals had seemed expensive for an £80,000 drop in transfer value, but Joe Ward had scored not once when he was sent on his way.

With Bremner gone and the Premier League statistics so set against Hibs, it therefore seemed that only a miracle could save Hibs — and since the next thing was the acquisition of George Best, it is clear that one miracle was not enough.

Nothing but the Very Best

It was Stewart Brown's suggestion in the *Evening News* which sent Messrs Hart and Turnbull to see the itinerant Irish star, lately returned from America. He was virtually unemployed, but Hibs had to pay Fulham for his registration before what had seemed a mission impossible became a possibility with the appearance of Best and his wife in the Easter Road stand.

A week later came the first sight of George Best in a Hibs jersey, at Love Street, where twice the normal attendance saw him score in the last minute. A week after that, over twenty-one thousand went to Easter Road to see Best play against Partick Thistle, despite Hibs' position and Partick's mindbending displays away from Firhill. On the same day, only twelve

George Best returned to Easter Road to play against Newcastle United in Jackie McNamara's testimonial match in August 1984.

thousand saw the League Cup semi-final at Hampden. Moreover the occasion gave Hibs their second win, albeit by a penalty and an own goal, and in their next home engagement they beat Rangers.

All the same, it would not have been the real George Best if everything had gone smoothly. The high wages which Tom Hart was personally paying Best were a private matter between the two of them, but they caused resentment, and it took a little while for some of the other players to realise that they needed Best as much as he needed them. Also, old habits die hard, and George missed a number of games and earned a suspension by the club for his trouble.

What Best provided from the viewpoint of Hibs' supporters was a focus for interest and spirits which would otherwise certainly have flagged in a wretched season. As it was, there was even a Cup run as a diversion, with victories over Meadowbank, Ayr United and Berwick — after a replay — before the crunch arrived, in green and white hoops. It is fair to say that not much money was riding on Hibs in the semi-final with Celtic, and before the end they were justifying their generous odds. It might have been different if Gordon Rae had been able to equalise with Hibs' best chance just on half-time, but a further three goals in six minutes on resumption rather dampened the enthusiasm.

That was the final straw for Eddie Turnbull, and he left after nearly ten years as manager, in which Hibs had won one major honour and been runners-up for five others. For a few years it had apparently been his job to find a successor, and had he done so he would certainly have retained the seat on the board that Tom Hart had given him. He would also have left the side apparently in a healthier state, but history would have compared him to Alex Maley, who took the plaudits when things went well and left to his successor the results of an inadequate refurbishing policy. Turnbull stayed to pay his own penalty.

Turnbull's successor had in fact been known to him for over thirty years — his old left-wing partner Willie Ormond, who had been a successful manager with St. Johnstone and Scotland, and not unsuccessful since then with Hearts, who had recently sacked him. The affable little winger was therefore in charge when Aberdeen scored five at Easter Road to win the championship, and when Partick Thistle concluded Hibs' season of woe before about one thousand onlookers.

CHAPTER 21

Into the Eighties, 1980–85

The most disconcerting thing about Hibs' position in 1980 was not that they had finished tenth — it was the first time in a decade that they had finished so far down, but that was a pretty good run for any side outwith the Old Firm. And indeed Hibs' average placing during the first ten years of the Premier League set-up — slightly above seventh — was higher than their average during the previous twenty.

Of more concern was the current state of the playing staff; during the previous five years or so, Hibs had received substantial cheques for the services of Cropley, Blackley, Brownlie and Bremner, but neither the resources thus realised nor the club's scouting policy had produced many who were likely to bring in as much in the future. Of Hibs' signings in the second half of the '70s, only Craig Paterson, a centre-half like his father in the '50s, and tall and elegant for the position, showed that level of promise, and only Ally Brazil, Hibs' first Under-21 international, and the rugged Gordon Rae of the other young players had established regular places.

In addition, as we have seen, Hibs had not fared too well in their market acquisitions, so that a series of stopgap arrangements with players well past their best was necessary to bolster the side in the short term, and when Hibs did make an ambitious move by agreeing terms of over £100,000 for St. Johnstone's prolific goalscorer John Brogan, the deal fell through at the last moment over a signing-on fee wrangle. All the more galling then to think of some of the men who might have been wearing Hibs' colours.

First there was Willie Pettigrew, an east of Scotland youngster who was actually on Hibs' books at one time. Pettigrew has largely flattered to deceive during a chequered career, but he did reach a considerable transfer value at one point of his stay at Motherwell, and Bayern Munich were apparently poised to acquire his services. Secondly there was Gordon Strachan, and it is comparatively common knowledge — especially since Strachan's autobiography was published — that Strachan too was at Easter Road until his father and manager Eddie Turnbull had a row.

There was also Eamonn Bannon. Bannon was 'discovered' by a friend of the author displaying his considerable skills with a tennis ball in a school playground and so joined Edinburgh Thistle, but despite playing throughout his youth with that most Easter Road-orientated of clubs, he too slipped through the net.

However, even with the players they had, there was little doubt that Hibs

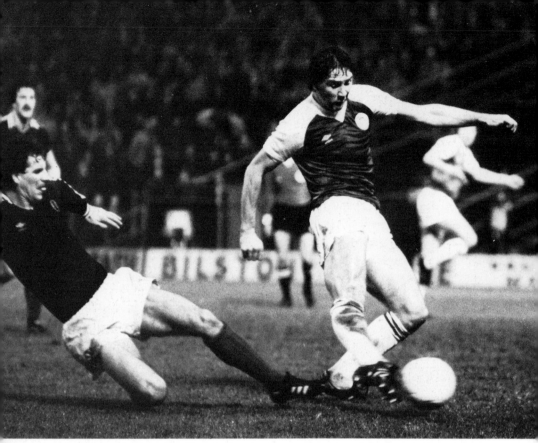

Gordon Rae shrugs off a challenge from a Dundee defender during a league game in early 1982. Cammy Fraser and the television camera are duly impressed.

would return to the Premier League in one attempt, even after a surprise opening defeat at home by a last-minute goal by Raith Rovers. It seemed that Hibs' main challengers for the title would be Motherwell, Dundee and Ayr United, and so it was an important week in September when Hibs had to play all three, and only Motherwell at home. A goal from Willie Jamieson, a tall dark-haired striker who made quite an impression in the First Division, was enough to beat Motherwell, a fleeting visit from George Best which included the pass to Gordon Rae for the latter to score a late winner put paid to Dundee, three goals in the last fifteen minutes by McLeod, Jamieson and Rae secured a victory at Ayr, and Hibs were almost there with thirty-three games remaining. When they won again at Ayr in March, no-one else had done so in between.

Hibs simply had too much class for the First Division. Not only did they have experienced players like Callachan, McLeod, Duncan and McNamara who were largely unrivalled in the division, but they were helped out by John Connolly, the former St. Johnstone and Everton international inside-

The Hibs' pool for 1984–5. Back row (l to r) McManus, Hunter, Jamieson, Rough, R. Rae, Sneddon, McKay, Collins.
Middle — Manager Stanton, trainer McNiven, Thomson, Rice, Brazil, G. Rae, Irvine, Harvey, Youth Coach Neely, Asst. Manager Blackley.
Front — McGachie, Weir, Schaedler, Callachan, McNamara, Kane, McKee.

forward, and Peter Cormack, back from playing in the red shirts of Nottingham Forest, Liverpool and Bristol City and on the look-out for a start in a career in management. There was also a Sinatra-style series of farewell appearances by George Best of which the final one was against Falkirk. Cormack scored only one goal during his run of appearances in the autumn, but that one, against Stirling Albion at Annfield, enabled him to join the elite who have scored a hundred goals for Hibs.

Unfortunately, Willie Ormond's role in Hibs' success was limited to the first third of the campaign. It seemed that although he had been willing enough to help out his old partner Eddie Turnbull, the likeable Ormond no longer had the appetite for the position that he now found himself in, no matter how much he would have enthused after it some years earlier, and was perhaps happier among his regulars in Musselburgh. Furthermore, his

27th April 1985. St. Mirren's first goal at Easter Road scored by defender David Winnie. Paul Kane looks on as Alan Rough goes down in vain. Hibs lost this match 4–0.

health was already giving cause for concern, and the sadness when he left Easter Road towards the end of 1980 was exceeded only on the news of his decease three and a half years later.

As always, however, the affairs of state could not be postponed, and within a short time of his predecessor's exit, Bertie Auld moved into the manager's office. Auld had been the midfield brain behind Jock Stein's Celtic's spectacular successes of the late '60s, and had since made a name for himself in football management with Partick Thistle. Auld had kept Thistle in the Premier Division with a strategy reminiscent of the Great Wall of China, and while his defensive know-how was obviously a useful cushion on which to fall back when necessary, it was to be hoped that his more creative talents would be to the fore with the greater resources at his disposal at Easter Road.

Hibs' run at the top of the First Division continued smoothly under the new management, and the title race developed into a two-horse race between Hibs and Raith Rovers, who were the only team to take four points out of six against the Easter Road side. The third game between the sides, in

Willie Irvine, Willie Jamieson are prominent in this Hibs attack in a match against Hearts.

April, was something of a carnival occasion at Easter Road, with Hibs assured of promotion and looking for the two points to land the championship. This they did with goals from Gary Murray and Ralph Callachan either side of half-time, and thereafter Raith Rovers slipped so badly that they were overtaken in the run-in by both Dundee, who won the second promotion place, and St. Johnstone.

Gary Murray, a strong-running and powerful striker from Montrose whom Hibs had first noticed on their League Cup exit at the hands of the Links Parks club some time before, was one of two major signings that manager Auld made to equip Hibs for the harder challenges ahead, and the other was Alan Sneddon, the Celtic full-back who had impressed one and all with his display in the 1978 League Cup final. Sneddon soon showed his willingness to be involved in Hibs' attack, and also why he had been honoured at Under-21 level, and as a member of Hibs' championship winning side achieved the unusual distinction of receiving championship medals in different divisions with Hibs and Celtic in the same season.

Hibs' record-breaking days perhaps seemed far behind them, but there were a few oddities apart from Alan Sneddon's in 1980–81. There was the

Hibs' defenders looking anxious following a free-kick from Rangers. Callaghan, Schaedler, Sneddon are all involved in the defensive wall.

unfortunate Ian Hendry who broke his leg within the first twenty seconds of his debut for Hibs at Berwick, did not play for the club again, and earned a mention in the Guinness Book of Records for the brevity of his career. There was the East of Scotland Shield, where Hearts' defeat by Berwick caused some jocularity until Hibs suffered likewise at the hands of Meadowbank Thistle. Thus Hibs and Hearts were both eliminated before the final, and the last time that had happened, Thistle had won the trophy because 3rd ERV had not turned up. On a more constructive note, Hibs had become the first Scottish club to install undersoil heating, a sound investment entirely consistent with their entrepreneurial role over the years, and largely paid off in one afternoon when Manchester United were glad to come north for a game during the inclemencies of December 1981.

Impressed as he may have been by these records, Bertie Auld was unquestionably more concerned with seeing Hibs equipped for the struggle ahead, and his efforts in this direction were soon evident. Hibs were quickly seen to be a more tenacious and committed side than the one that had been relegated; they started with an important win against Dundee with goals by Gordon Rae and Gary Murray, a strike force which was indicative of Hibs' greater reliance on power than before. They finished the first quarter by beating Celtic, and by the halfway stage were still averaging a point a game. Manager Auld, who enjoyed the limelight more than most, celebrated with a succession of larger and larger caps, and the cigars which were habitually clamped between his teeth were likewise ever more extravagant.

Gordon Durie scores against Celtic in the match played at Easter Road on 26th January, 1985.

It was true that not all opposing crowds took to what they considered to be 'Partick Thistle' football, but when Dundee manager Donald Mackay remarked that Hibs were boring, it was clearly more a criticism of the system which required such safety-conscious football to be played rather than the club which had successfully adapted to it, and he admitted that he would gladly have changed places with Hibs in a minute. There was some truth in the view that the Premier Division was now producing exactly the unattractive fare that it was intended to prevent, and its former champion Tom Hart was now advocating a switch back to a two-division set-up.

Much less note was taken on this occasion of what Tom Hart thought about the league organisation than of his opinion of the antics of John McDonald of Rangers, following the latter's convincing of the referee that he had been unlawfully brought to earth in the later stages of a game at Easter Road, to earn his side a penalty kick and an undeserved win. Television evidence suggested that the Hibs' chairman had been factually correct, but he was nevertheless fined £500 when the authorities got round to discussing his remarks at the end of January. It was to be the last time that the forthright Mr. Hart was to tangle with authority because in March he collapsed at Pittodrie and died shortly afterwards. Tom Hart is rightly

Hibs' chairman, Kenneth Waugh.

remembered with affection, not only by Hibs' supporters as the man who brought Eddie Turnbull back to Easter Road to bring about the good times of the early '70s, but also by the Scottish footballing public at large as the man who vigorously took up any cause in which he believed irrespective of the opposition, from the wider issues of sponsorship and the importing of foreign players to the ban on Scottish supporters travelling to Wembley.

Hibs meanwhile continued to pick up points in 1982 as they had finished 1981. They averaged one per game, took five out of eight from Celtic, and finished just one adrift of St. Mirren who qualified for Europe. In the end Dundee made it too, the first time both promoted sides had done so, to the exclusion of Partick Thistle and Airdrie. Hibs even survived a cup trip to Tannadice, and looked like winning the replay at Easter Road until in injury time Ally Brazil elected to pass back to Jim McArthur and lost a corner. This led in turn to United's equaliser, a second replay and three more goals for United without reply.

Chairman Waugh

Although Tom Hart's death had been a shock, the transitional phase in Hibs' affairs which necessarily resulted was short and smooth, because a

Hibs in a friendly against Moscow Dynamo. Gordon Durie steers the ball into the net for Hibs' second goal.

short time before, Kenny Waugh, another successful local businessman, had joined the board under an amicable arrangement with Mr. Hart by which the chairman was to sell his interest in the club to the younger man. Kenny Waugh had been brought up not far from Easter Road, in Bingholm, and had been working as an engineer in Portobello power station in the early '60s when he had been among the first to see the potential benefits of the legislation which legalised betting shops for the first time. He had backed his intuition with such determination and enthusiasm that now, two decades on, he not only had a sizeable chain of these establishments, but had branched into the licensed trade, snooker and leisure facilities and property development. Alan Hart, the late chairman's son, and the two former goalkeepers Tommy Younger and Jimmy Kerr, completed the new board.

The first priorities had to be the ensuring of Hibs' longer-term welfare, even at the expense of some short-term popularity. Hibs' stay in the First Division, although mercifully brief, had cost the club dear, and even their comparative success in their first season back upstairs had not brought back the crowds who remembered the more cavalier side of a decade before. So a number of economies were essential, of which the most notable was the transfer of Craig Paterson to Rangers. Paterson was looking for terms that Hibs could not meet in any case, and neither side could be faulted, but the player has of course since been the target of the inevitable criticism following a defection to Ibrox.

It was not long before this became evident, because Rangers were Hibs' first guests when the League Cup started season 1982–83. A spectacular volley by Gordon Rae, who fell back to take over at centre-half, gave Hibs a point, and though they could only draw their other two home games as well, a win at Clydebank meant that they had still a chance to qualify. A win at Ibrox was needed to prolong this hope, however, and it was the more disappointing when they had to settle for the draw which suited Rangers better than them. This draw was much more disappointing than the inconsequential defeat at Airdrie that followed. How much these results hastened the events which followed is debatable, but the following morning Bertie Auld found to his astonishment he was out of a job.

Auld's surprise seemed genuine, but it was certainly true that the Easter Road support had never taken to his survival style of football, as a crowd of little over 2,000 at one of Hibs' home League Cup ties bore witness. In addition, although both Auld and his assistant Pat Quinn had played for Hibs, each was better known as a player with other clubs, and neither lived in the Edinburgh area. The new chairman, who was better able to associate himself with the views of the rank and file support than most, thought that the fans would give their support more readily to men who were local and already closely associated with the club. Waugh hit the nail on the head in this respect; Pat Stanton, along with Jimmy O'Rourke and George Stewart as assistants, was appointed later the same day, and a much larger and enthusiastic attendance welcomed him at his first game in charge, against St. Mirren.

Stanton of course had always been hugely popular at Easter Road, even when finishing his playing career with Celtic, and since then had gained considerable experience in management, firstly as assistant to Alex. Ferguson at Aberdeen, where his boss spoke very highly of him, and then running his own show. He was only five months at Cowdenbeath before Dunfermline appointed him as manager at East End, and his young side there seemed to be coming on in leaps and bounds. There was a general acceptance that Pat would at some time be Hibs' boss, especially since his contemporaries Billy McNeill and John Greig had been given the Old Firm jobs.

Unfortunately all the good will in the world did not give Stanton and his team an easy start. Money was available to strengthen the squad, but the

Alan Sneddon is prominent in this Hibs' attack against Dundee at Easter Road. Colin Harris is backing up.

manager was properly unwilling to pay prices far above his valuation of the players concerned. The Premier League was on him at once, and with Hibs failing to win any of their opening six games, their play developed the anxiety characteristic of sides fearful of being left behind in the table. The home defeat by Morton in particular had no other cause. Eventually Stanton got his man, Mike Conroy, recognised as a very useful midfield man but unable to command a regular first-team spot at Parkhead, and he also transacted a good swap deal, which brought Willie Irvine to Easter Road in exchange for Bobby Flavell, a player who had come to Easter Road a year or so earlier, apparently from a minor Swedish side. Irvine had developed a reputation for spectacular goals at Motherwell, and it was hoped that with this talent of his, Hibs would find goalscoring a little easier. In addition, for the grim encounter with Motherwell, anchored with Hibs at the foot of the table, Hibs fielded Malcolm Robertson, the former Hearts winger, as a result of a chance meeting with Hibs' manager in Waverley Station.

The game with Motherwell was every bit as thrawn as expected, but ultimately a goal did come, and the assembled enthusiasts were mightily relieved to see Gordon Rae come forward from his new defensive role to strike home a low drive from around twenty yards to give Hibs victory.

The prospect of defeat by Motherwell had been unthinkable, and the points a blessing, but the relief was temporary. The next problem was a goalkeeping crisis. Jim McArthur had by this time been keeping goal safely for a decade, so that a dependable last line of defence had become more or less taken for granted — so much so that when he was injured during a bizarre match at Ibrox, in a collision with Alan Sneddon and Rangers' Derek Johnstone, Hibs were caught short of a suitable replacement. McArthur therefore played on in difficult games against Aberdeen and Kilmarnock before being injured again, at Tannadice. Clearly Hibs' league position dictated swift action, and they went into the market at once to sign Alan Rough, the Partick Thistle goalkeeper whose record number of international appearances included those in the 1982 World Cup finals in Spain.

As manager of Partick Thistle, Bertie Auld had singled out Rough from his other ten defenders as being worth a dozen points a year to his side, and Rough soon started showing his worth to Hibs. It was the goalkeeper's brilliant display which was the major factor in Hibs' winning a point at Greenock, and another helped Hibs to draw with Rangers, but for all that, Hibs had to wait until they played Motherwell again to record their second championship win. The situation was much as before except that Motherwell had ground advantage, but again Hibs scraped through by the only goal, this one coming from Gary Murray just before half-time.

The confidence that Rough inspired soon began to show in some relaxed play, and in a three-month spell Hibs lost only to Celtic and Aberdeen. Morton were already beyond hope, and as Kilmarnock gradually fell behind the pack to join them in the First Division, Hibs emerged well clear of trouble. By way of celebration, they took the Rugby Parkers by storm to score eight times and equal the Premier Division record, and if their subsequent seven games produced the more modest tally of two, there was little doubt that Hibs had reason to be satisfied with the manner in which they had played themselves out of a difficult situation following the change of manager. They could afford to sit back and watch the most exciting end to a season for many a year, with Dundee United taking the championship from Celtic and Aberdeen on the final Saturday of the season, and Aberdeen winning both the European Cupwinners' Cup and the Scottish Cup, and both in extra time.

At the end of the season, Jimmy O'Rourke and George Stewart left the club, because of their business commitments, and by the start of the next

Bobby Thomson and Willie Irvine causing a spot of bother in the Rangers goalmouth in a match at Easter Road in 1983.

one, 1983–84, they had been replaced by another weel kent face, that of John Blackley, who had been with Preston North End and Hamilton since his days with Newcastle, and was only too pleased to link up with his former club skipper again. Moreover, Blackley proved a first-class stand-in on the field when the situation demanded — who else could have stepped in at short notice at Ibrox after such a while on the sidelines and turn in such a confident display? Blackley had maybe shed a yard of pace since leaving Easter Road some years earlier, but he still retained his uncanny ability to position himself so well that it seemed he had a magnetic attraction for the ball.

As well as strengthening his playing and backroom staffs at one stroke, Pat Stanton took great satisfaction from the progress of some of his younger players, the first fruits of the youth policy on which Bertie Auld had been so keen after some barren years for recruitment in the late '70s. Auld had in fact been a driving force behind the Scottish Professional Youth League during his time at Easter Road, and under his guidance Hibs had won it.

From Pat Stanton's point of view, the survivors of that side who were now

241

making the grade in the first eleven were Brian Rice, Kevin McKee and Paul Kane. The first two of these three both hailed from Whitburn, both being products of St. Kentigern's High. Rice was the one who had made most impact, and had earned Under-21 honours. The slim red-haired inside man bore more than a passing resemblance to Steve Davis, and like the snooker champion his game was calm and unhurried, with accuracy a top priority. Very much a left-sided player, Rice's studied approach disguised a fair turn of speed, and his left foot also packed a venomous shot, both from the dead ball and on the volley. Kevin McKee has developed into a neat and dependable right-back, and has played some first-rate games against such players as Davie Cooper and Peter Weir. His promotion has had the added advantage of releasing Alan Sneddon to use his powerful running in the midfield area.

The third player to have established his place was Paul Kane, a right-sided midfield player who has quickly shown a maturity beyond his years, and seems the kind of reliable professional essential to a successful side. Paul Kane's father was also with Hibs, having signed in the mid-50s during his national service, but unfortunately his promising career as an inside-right was interrupted when he broke his leg in a clash with Aberdeen goalkeeper 'Tubby' Ogston. He later played professional football in South Africa. Paul was signed from the prolific Salvesen's Boys Club, and also possesses a useful shot; his goals tend to come from well-placed drives rather than just strongly hit ones. In addition to Rice, Kane and McKee, it seemed likely that Robin Rae, the youth international goalkeeper from Musselburgh Windsor, and Mickey Weir, a diminutive midfield dynamo who was already gaining the popularity reminiscent of Jimmy O'Rourke, would be ready to seize on any opportunities offered.

With these additions to the pool, there was little despondency when Hibs lost their first three League games, including the one at Tynecastle — the first Premier League derby in Edinburgh for four seasons. There was a general realisation that Hearts' better start owed a lot to a comparatively easy opening set of fixtures, and no less to good fortune, and so Hibs set out to overhaul them. They managed it too, albeit briefly, and thanks largely to a purple patch by Willie Irvine, whose goal at Tynecastle on New Year's Day was his twentieth of the season, and who had struck up a telling partnership with Bobby Thompson, the ex-Morton utility player whom Bertie Auld had signed from Middlesbrough for £80,000 and who was now justifying the outlay.

Irvine scored a hat-trick against Dumbarton in the League Cup — the first treble by a Hibs player for seven years, and two headed goals from the same player beat Aberdeen in a highly charged game at Easter Road in

Hibs against Rangers — always an exciting fixture. Here Willie Irvine stands tall.

October, and after the Dons had led at the interval. A second hat-trick came against the doomed St. Johnstone, but this one was marred by the dismissal of Thompson for pushing a linesman in the heat of the moment. Thompson was suspended for six months for his indiscretion, which all but finished his career because he failed to regain his place in Hibs' team, and was subsequently again to be seen in Morton's blue and white. Irvine suffered nearly as much, because, minus his helpmate, his goal rush dried up as suddenly as it had begun, and Hibs finished the season modestly in seventh place, while Hearts made the last place in Europe.

The second half of the season which produced this outcome was a little disappointing after some stirring football earlier, and Hibs struggled to find another scoring partnership up front. Little fight was seen in the two Cup games with East Fife which ended in an inglorious exit at Bayview, and cost Alan Rough a broken bone in his foot. The final six games included defeats from Motherwell and St. Johnstone, the relegated pair, as well as Meadowbank Thistle in the East of Scotland Shield. The impression was that some of the existing staff would have to make room for the younger men coming through, and the free transfers at the end of the season included Gary Murray and Mike Conroy who between them represented £100,000 — a large part of Hibs' recent investments. Also released with regret was Arthur Duncan, the evergreen and popular winger, midfielder, full-back and even emergency goalkeeper, whose career of fourteen years with Hibs, a testimonial match, well over a hundred goals and an assortment of international honours ended sadly with a broken collarbone sustained in the Shield game with Meadowbank.

Having cleared the way for fresh talent, manager Stanton again found it difficult to get the men he wanted. Tommy McQueen, Clyde's bright young left-back, was one target, and Hibs seemed on the point of completing his transfer after the clubs had agreed terms when Aberdeen came late into the lists, requiring a left-back following their internationalist Rougvie's transfer to Chelsea, and the player chose Aberdeen, obviously attracted by playing for the League Champions in Europe. Hibs also made an attempt to bring Jamie Doyle to Easter Road, but were unable to convince Partick Thistle that their valuation for the Under-21 international midfielder was a generous one. Nevertheless Hibs started the season in some hope, with the men who had looked the part for the greater part of the previous one.

Things this time could hardly have started worse. Successive defeats from Hearts and Meadowbank Thistle, with the immediate prospect of trips to Pittodrie and Ibrox, set up Hibs' next home game — against Dumbarton — as a relegation battle — in September! It looked like being a long hard winter — and it got worse. Pat Stanton was sent from the dugout at Pittodrie for a remark to a linesman, and then at Ibrox Kevin McKee was attacked on the pitch by a Rangers supporter and required stitches. Then, at Easter Road, Dumbarton scored three times in twelve minutes and took both points. Pat Stanton resigned.

When things go badly, they really go badly, and there followed a dark spell in Hibs' fortunes. Pat Stanton was fined £500 for talking out of turn at Aberdeen around the same time as McKee's assailant at Ibrox got off with one fifth as much. Then, the SFA, making a commendable effort to eliminate crowd trouble at games, considered the attack on McKee, and an earlier incident in which the Hibs-Hearts derby had been stopped by an invasion of Tynecastle supporters, and recommended that either the games be replayed or that Rangers and Hearts respectively forfeit the points. Unfortunately the League was unable to follow these recommendations, but the incidents have helped to establish a code of practice to deal with any future problems of that kind. However, Hibs' immediate problems were not alleviated, and their next disappointment was their failure to attract former Celtic boss Billy McNeill away from his lucrative post with Manchester City.

Alan Rough shows how he feels as a hundred yards away, Colin Harris has just scored the winning goal at Ibrox.

Beset it seemed from all sides, Hibs' reaction at this difficult time was calm and sensible. John Blackley was appointed temporary manager while the permanent position was advertised, and by the time applications had been received and considered, he had made such a favourable initial impression that he was selected from among many others with greater experience.

There was little doubt that Blackley's first task was to keep Hibs in the Premier Division, and, with Dumbarton and Dundee, the two sides immediately above Hibs, picking up points, it was clear that time was not on his side. However, the new manager had sized up the situation already, and in a short space of time had made two significant signings. The first was Gordon Durie, who cost Hibs in the region of £70,000 from East Fife, and quickly showed a strength and resolution beyond his eighteen years. Despite coming straight into Hibs' first team from two divisions lower, Durie made light of the transition, opened his account with two goals in two minutes to earn Hibs a vital point at Dumbarton, and, with Willie Irvine missing much of the season, finished Hibs' top scorer.

The second signing was that of Tommy Craig as assistant manager. The little inside-forward had formerly played for Aberdeen and once for Scotland, since when he had played for various sides in the north of England. He was player-coach of Carlisle United when Hibs made their approach, and Carlisle were understandably reluctant to release him. Hibs were successful, however, and, like Blackley himself, Craig was also a valuable addition to the playing staff of the club.

Meanwhile, on the field, the results gave little cheer. Alan Rough said on television that Hibs would not go down because they had too many good players, but while there was no doubt that on paper Hibs' pool was far ahead of Dumbarton's, now their only rival for the dreaded ninth position, they continued to play neat football without a single break until in early January they were five points adrift of the Boghead side, and the Dumbarton manager was talking of the relegation issue being settled before Hibs' second visit to Boghead in the fifth last round of matches.

Then on January 12th Hibs got their first break for many months, and the tide turned dramatically. The game was at Ibrox where Hibs had no reason to expect good news, and the result hinged on the performances of the two goalkeepers. Peter McCloy of the home side started it when he let slip a shot from Brian Rice some thirty-five yards from goal, to give Hibs an early lead and a huge boost in confidence. Then Alan Rough turned in one of his truly international performances as Hibs held Rangers with commendable calm, and even although he was beaten once, Hibs took both points with a late goal from newcomer Colin Harris, who came on as substitute and gleefully hammered the ball home from close range in the closing minutes. Harris had

Morton's Dougie Robertson and Hibs' defender Eric Schaedler battle for the ball, but Gordon Rae and Alan Rough are relieved to see it slip past. An Easter Road match on February 9th, 1985. Hibs 5 Morton 1.

come to Hibs from Dundee, in exchange for reserve forward Graeme Harvey, and Hibs clearly hoped that he would find the goalscoring form that he had shown for Raith Rovers and persuaded Dundee to pay £80,000 for him.

One week later there was another important psychological boost when Hibs beat Dumbarton with something to spare at Easter Road, and another seven days after that when a five-goal thrashing of Morton brought Hibs level on points with Davy Wilson's men. Even narrow defeats from St. Mirren and Dundee worked to take Hibs ahead on goal difference because Dumbarton's defence was now being beaten regularly, and the Sons' last chance surely came with Hibs having to play Celtic and Aberdeen in successive games.

Dumbarton were relieved to scramble a one-goal win over Morton while Hibs were at Parkhead, and were mightily disappointed that a Paul Kane goal had given the Edinburgh side a similar success, and then they were unable to take advantage when Hibs crashed to Aberdeen. Dumbarton had failed to pull away, and the writing was on the wall.

J

Hibs were now in buoyant mood, and not even the gross injustice of their defeat by the champions was allowed to dent it. They had a midweek test at Tynecastle to follow, and their spirit was such that they fought back to draw after being two down with just six minutes to go. The goalscoring hero this time was another newcomer, Joe McBride, the son of the former goalscoring ace of Celtic and Hibs. Joe Jr. came from Oldham Athletic, where he had gone from Everton after six years at Goodison which included Under-21 caps. McBride is at home playing as an orthodox left-winger, and so is something of a rarity in the Premier Division, as well as at Easter Road where the position had been more or less unused since Arthur Duncan had become a full-back.

And so Hibs reached the crunch with Dumbarton already in front, with a much easier run-in to come, and with a large travelling support subsidised by the club to will Hibs on at Boghead. It was not the tense relegation type of game that might have been expected — instead Hibs took command from the start, Brian Rice and Willie Irvine scored spectacular first-half goals to put the issue beyond doubt, and thereafter Hibs were content to expose the large gulf between the two sides. At the end of the campaign, the eight-point advantage that Hibs held over Dumbarton reflected the relative ability of the two teams; Hibs in fact took 17 points from their last 16 games, and had they managed that through from August, then a place in Europe would have been theirs.

It was sad at the end of it all to see the departure of two more long-serving and popular players on free transfers. Erich Schaedler, who had been at Easter Road for two lengthy spells since first signing in the late '60s, finally retired, although it is to be hoped that his experience will be exploited at the ground for some time to come, and Jackie McNamara, having been troubled frequently in recent seasons by a knee injury, was released and went with good wishes to Morton.

Coming alive in '85

John Blackley's — and Hibs' — first priority had been achieved, and in the end with something to spare, but the longer-term objective of course is to ensure that the situation does not occur again. 'Coming alive in '85' is the club's slogan to emphasise their determination that this aim is going to be met too.

Hibs are a limited company, that is, a business, and gone are the days when a football club can be run as a hobby by a chairman with only the occasional hand-out needed to top up gate receipts. The finances of the game

Three of Hibs' first team squad for season 1985–86. From left, Joe McBride, Paul Kane, Micky Weir.

as a whole have determined that clubs are run as businesses, and Kenny Waugh has gathered together a management team equipped to do that job.

At board level, changes were necessary following the sad death of Tommy Younger and the retirement of Jimmy Kerr; three new directors, all already members of Hibs' New Fifty Club, replaced them to form, with Waugh and Alan Hart, a team of five. Alan Young is the managing director of two national construction companies, and has shown in his career that he is ambitious and progressive, and not afraid to take opportunities when they arise. A quiet and thoughtful person, he does not have specific duties at Easter Road, but is rather in general terms the chairman's right-hand man and adviser. Gregor Cowan, sole partner in his own accountancy firm, is a local man and a lifelong Hibs' supporter, and fulfils his natural role of finance and administration within the club. John Douglas, born in the Lawnmarket and another Hibs' supporter from birth, is a publican, and it is his responsibility to look after the stadium and its appearance. And finally of course there is Alan Hart, a popular figure around Easter Road (and a fair footballer himself), who works on the commercial side as well as representing Hibs on the SFA. In keeping with the modern requirements of running a football club, the Hibs' board is a working board, and their list of achievements is already impressive.

Two appointments in particular stress Hibs' determination to rise again. The first of these is Raymond Sparkes as Marketing Manager, following his dramatic success in selling basketball to the townsfolk of Falkirk. Despite this experience, Sparkes is still the youngest commercial manager in the country, and likewise the most dynamic. Quite apart from their lucrative sponsorship deal with Insave Associates Ltd., Hibs will have deals with Nike, Eastern Scottish, Umbro, Falcon Holidays, and Renault, with yet more underway. The Insave deal in particular is the biggest of its kind outwith the Old Firm, with the investment company's name carried on the players' shirts in season '85–86. In addition, of course, Hibs are the only Scottish club to have an electronic scoreboard at present, entirely in keeping with the club's tradition of establishing trends rather than following them — a tradition the new board are keen to extend.

Closely allied to the marketing side of the club is the effort to increase gate receipts by the refurbishing of the stadium; patrons are already aware that the huge main terracing which had become something of a white elephant in recent times has been reduced to a more appropriate level, and the work of providing a cover for it is, at the time of writing, under way. In addition, green and white paint has been applied liberally to brighten the scene at Easter Road, and provide an eye-catching panorama of alternate banks of colour.

The second major appointment is that of Gordon Neely, who had already earned a fine reputation for his work with young players which is being enhanced presently in the shape of several international honours for the club's S-signings under his guidance. In addition, Hibs have established training schools throughout Scotland in order to cream off as much of the country's bright young talent as possible, and divert it to Easter Road. The fruits of this project will not be seen in Premier League terms for some seasons, but again the determination of the directors to work for the long-term benefit of the club is evident. In the shorter term, a further pair of good young players are making the grade, and will take over from Erich Schaedler and Jackie McNamara, to leave John Blackley with a nicely balanced pool as he necessarily moves away still further from dependence on the players of his own generation.

The players at present breaking through are Gordon Hunter, John Collins, Micky Weir and Calum Milne. Hunter is a current youth cap who was signed while still attending Musselburgh Grammar School, and who has already impressed many people in his few first-team outings. He has the makings of a first-class centre-half, more in the Jackie Plenderleith mould than the John McNamee one, and, under the current tactic of playing three central defenders to let any one of them and the full-backs join the attack as opportunities arise, Hunter's skills would seem to complement those of the rock-like Gordon Rae, and Ally Brazil's dependably high work-rate.

It is behind them that Calum Milne seems set to compete with the experienced Ian Munro for a place at full-back alongside Kevin McKee or Alan Sneddon. Milne is a confident young player with a lot of skill for a defender, and should be a real asset. The last line of defence is of course Alan Rough who requires no further commendation from me.

The midfield section of Hibs' team will show a contrast of styles; the right-hand area of midfield will be the province of Paul Kane, and Ralph Callachan, while on the left, Joe McBride uses his pace on the touchline to good effect. Hibs have also the most potent combination of strikers for some time, with the top scorers of the last two seasons, Willie Irvine and Gordon Durie, and the latter can be expected to play an even greater role now that he has been accustomed to playing in the higher league. In addition, Colin Harris has all the physical attributes desirable for a striker — physique, speed and height — and will be looking to regain the form that made him such a prolific goalscorer in Kirkcaldy.

Munro of course featured with Hibs some years ago, and manager Blackley was glad to find him available to boost his squad during the season just ended. The pool is a nice blend of youth and experience. A player quick to make his mark was young John Collins, impressing everyone with his talent in a promising opening to season 85–86 at Aberdeen. In addition, there are more young players who will hope to emerge into the first team from the reserves: Alan Peters, Steve McIlhone, Danny Lennon, Eddie May, David Fellinger, and Paul McGovern. What price some of them playing in Europe in 1986–87?

At the time of going to press Hibs purchased Steve Cowan from Aberdeen and Mark Fulton from St. Mirren to strengthen the squad for the season ahead.

CHAPTER 22

The Hall of Fame

The meander through the journalism of a century and more has been an interesting one, a transition from stories previously encountered only in history books to those within the recall of older relatives and friends and hence to personal childhood memory. On the narrower but more relevant football front, the game has changed almost beyond recognition from the days when crowd encroachment at the Meadows was a problem, and to watch it requires an outlay of £2 or more compared to 6d (or 2½p as it is nowadays) a century ago. On the other hand, spectator amenities have also improved, to an extent undreamt of in the 1880s.

The overall impression has been one of change, and a consequent awareness of the impossibility of adequately comparing players or teams of different generations. It has nevertheless been a pleasant diversion to select a Hibernian Hall of Fame, without making the further attempt to place the selected few in order of achievement, or for that matter to catalogue their doughty deeds which are described in the foregoing chapters. Suffice it to say that each was a giant in his own time.

A glance at the lists of internationalists in the Appendix will remind the reader of the many fine players who have worn Hibs' colours, and claimants for selection can be found along the whole range from those whose contributions were a whole career of distinguished service to those who became footballing legends in their own time, much of which unfortunately was spent in colours other than Hibernian green. Amongst the former whom I have regretted omitting are Paddy Callaghan, Bobby Templeton, Johnny Halligan, Peter Kerr, Bobby Combe, Arthur Duncan and especially Jimmy McColl, while among the latter Sandy McMahon, Matt Busby, Willie Hamilton and more recently George Best and Alan Rough have delighted Hibs supporters for all too brief a time. A third group worthy of mention have been the 'characters' of the game, such as Harry Ritchie, Jock Govan and, again, Arthur Duncan, who were popular even beyond the extent of their not inconsiderable talents. The list then is long, but the following is a personal selection of those who stood out even in such company.

The first two represent the 'old' Hibs who won the Scottish Cup in 1887, Jim McGhee, who not only captained them but who alone of Hibs' established stars resisted Celtic's bribes, and more than once thereafter set out for an away game with a couple of friends and the hamper to recruit a team en route, and Willie Groves, who was almost unstoppable at a time when nearly any method of stopping an opponent was allowed, and who was recognised as Edinburgh's finest footballing son, despite leaving the city while still a teenager. Groves is an English family name, and it is interesting that it came to Edinburgh in the shape of a London police sergeant who was sent north to help apprehend the notorious Deacon Brodie, and settled in the city.

My third choice is Harry G. Rennie, goalkeeper extraordinary and representing the league and cupwinning side at the turn of the century, a side which was not together very long. Rennie started off in midfield, a position he did not give up on becoming a goalkeeper, and in addition he was the first player to write his own contract and present it to the club to sign — that was how he came to fall out with Hearts and join Hibs in the first place. It is a strange feature of this parade of great Hibernians that no fewer than six either played for or managed Hearts. Rennie took more than a usual interest in his games against Hearts because he had a standing ten-shilling bet — a significant amount at the time — with his great friend Bobby Walker that the Tynecastle idol would not score.

Next comes Willie Harper, another brilliant goalkeeper and orthodox only in comparison with Rennie. My father, whose youth was spent watching Bo'ness FC in the Second Division, remembers just two things about Hibs in the '20s — that they were not nearly as rough a team as Hearts, and that 'Harper of the Hibs' was the best goalkeeper in the land. Although he was at Easter Road for only five years, he won fame and most of his caps there, and his career ran into little but trouble thereafter. During his army days Harper knocked out Joe Beckitt, at one time the British heavyweight boxing champion.

The Hibs' team of the '20s is well represented, with Jimmy Dunn, who achieved the immortality denied to so many by being a Wembley Wizard, and Hugh Shaw, despite the latter's also playing for Hearts *and* Rangers. Shaw came to Hibs as a centre-forward, and not a very good one, but became a top-class wing-half. He also served with distinction as trainer and manager, and it was felt to be fair to include all managers who led Hibs to three League championships.

If Hugh Shaw's inclusion indicates acknowledgement of the importance of the men behind the scenes, the next two emphasise it. It was Harry Swan's drive and determination that lifted Hibs from the mediocrity of the '30s and presented them for almost the first time as a 'big' club, and his success in doing this was of course interdependent with that of his irrepressible manager Willie McCartney.

Of the team that McCartney and then Shaw managed, more in a moment, after a brief consideration of those that followed it. Only two of my selections come from the 'post- Famous Five' period, probably in part because so many fine players have crossed the Border at early stages in their careers. This was true of the first of these two, Joe Baker, as well, but he made an impact during his four seasons with Hibs to 1961 that was comparable only to Willie Groves. His record of English under-23 and full caps while playing in Scottish League football, as well as his rate of scoring goals — 141 in 159 competitive games — brook no argument, and Baker was unquestionably the most *exciting* player I have seen.

The most recent inclusion is inevitably Pat Stanton, whom most readers will recall as a great player and captain, even if his quiet type of authority on the field was not the type to ensure a successful managerial career thereafter. After Reilly and Smith, Stanton remains Hibs' most capped player, despite playing so much of the time out of his best position at the back, to accommodate John Blackley. Pat Stanton was enormously respected, and is the only Hibs player to be Scottish 'Player of the Year'.

There only remains now to consider the one really great Hibs team, that of the early '50s, and that has posed the most difficult problem of all. Without even considering the defence, most of whom played for their country, it is difficult to see who to omit, whereas to include five members of one team seems unjust to some others whose only crime was not to coincide chronologically with such playing partners.

Not many would leave out Gordon Smith, arguably the finest player ever to play for Hibs, and not even counting his European appearances for Hearts and Dundee later on that gave him yet another record. Even in the '80s I have met old men in the pubs of Easter Road who remembered going just to watch Smith — and I have never met any who went each week just to watch Matthews or Finney!

No less an automatic choice would be Lawrie Reilly, who won thirty-eight full caps while restricting such a rival as Bauld of Hearts to three. No forward at the time had played oftener for Scotland, despite his being unlucky in missing three World Cup competitions because of, in order, Scotland deciding not to go, illness and premature retirement.

Then there is Eddie Turnbull, who provided the industry in that famous line, and was probably its most important member when things were *not* going well for it — which of course was not too often, but was also the manager behind Hibs' most successful team since, in the early '70s. And could one include Turnbull and not his partner Willie Ormond, whose career with Hibs lasted even longer, despite an incredible catalogue of serious injury, and who, while Turnbull was finding managerial success at Easter Road, was doing likewise with Scotland's national squad?

Finally there was Bobby 'Nicker' Johnstone, who came into the side latest, and left earliest, but it is impossible to include all but one of a line who were known and are remembered as a unit — the 'Famous Five'. However, the solution is at hand — taking as a precedent BBC TV, whose 1984 Sports Personality of the Year was two skaters, my final selection is the Famous Five, the best club forward line that Scottish football has witnessed, and whose exploits were on occasion beyond belief.

Hibs: The Vital Statistics

Scottish League —   Champions — 1902-03, 1947-48, 1950-51, 1951-52
Runners-up — 1896-97, 1946-47, 1949-50, 1952-53,
1973-74, 1974-75
Division 1 Champions — 1980-81
Division 2 Champions — 1893-94, 1894-95, 1932-33

Scottish Cup —   Winners — 1886-87, 1901-02
Runners-up — 1895-96, 1913-14, 1922-23, 1923-24,
1946-47, 1957-58, 1971-72, 1978-79

Scottish League Cup —   Winners — 1972-73
Runners-up — 1950-51, 1968-69, 1974-75

Record attendance —   Easter Road — 65,800 (v. Hearts 2/1/1950)
Any Hibs game — 143,570 (v. Rangers at Hampden,
27/3/1948)

Biggest wins —   Scottish League — 11-1 v. Airdrie (a) 24/10/1959
11-1 v. Hamilton Academicals (h) 6/11/1965
Scottish Cup — 15-1 v. Peebles Rovers (h) 11/2/1961
Scottish League Cup — 11-2 v. Alloa Athletic (h) 22/9/1965
European Competitions — 9-1 v. Rosenberg Trondheim (h)
2/10/1974
All recorded matches — 22-1 v. 42nd Highlanders (h) 3/9/1881

Biggest defeats —   Scottish League — 0-10 v. Rangers (a) 24/12/1898
Scottish Cup — 1-9 v. Dumbarton (h) 27/9/1890
Scottish League Cup — 1-6 v. Hearts (a) 11/8/1956
1-6 v. Rangers (h) 8/8/1959
European competitions — 0-5 v. Valencia (a) 13/3/1963
All recorded matches — 0-10 v. Rangers (a) 24/12/1898

Most league points — 57 (1980-81)
Most league goals — 106 (1959-60)
Most league appearances — Arthur Duncan (446)
Longest undefeated run — 17 games (29/11/1947 - 19/4/1948)
League goalscorers in successive games — Joe Baker (10)
(17/10/1959 -19/12/1959)
Leading goalscorer (all games) — Gordon Smith (364)
First official substitute — Pat Quinn (12/11/1966)

League Record Year by Year

Season	Div.	Place	Season	Div.	Place	Season	Div.	Place
1893-94	2	1	1933-34	1	16	1973-74	1	2
1894-95	2	1	1934-35	1	11	1974-75	1	2
1895-96	1	3	1935-36	1	17	1975-76	P	3
1896-97	1	2	1936-37	1	17	1976-77	P	6
1897-98	1	3	1937-38	1	10	1977-78	P	4
1898-99	1	4	1938-39	1	13	1978-79	P	5
1899-1900	1	3	1939-40	E	8	1979-80	P	10
1900-01	1	3	1940-41	S	3	1980-81	1	1
1901-02	1	6	1941-42	S	2	1981-82	P	6
1902-03	1	1	1942-43	S	3	1982-83	P	7
1903-04	1	10	1943-44	S	3	1983-84	P	7
1904-05	1	5	1944-45	S	5	1984-85	P	8
1905-06	1	11	1945-46	S	2			
1906-07	1	11	1946-47	A	2			
1907-08	1	5	1947-48	A	1			
1908-09	1	6	1948-49	A	3			
1909-10	1	8	1949-50	A	2			
1910-11	1	9	1950-51	A	1	1 : Division 1		
1911-12	1	13	1951-52	A	1	2 : Division 2		
1912-13	1	6	1952-53	A	2	A : "A" Division		
1913-14	1	14	1953-54	A	5	E : Regional League —		
1914-15	1	11	1954-55	A	5	Eastern Division		
1915-16	1	19	1955-56	A	4	P : Premier Division		
1916-17	1	17	1956-57	1	9	S : Scottish Southern		
1917-18	1	16	1957-58	1	9	League		
1918-19	1	18	1958-59	1	10			
1919-20	1	18	1959-60	1	7			
1920-21	1	13	1960-61	1	7			
1921-22	1	7	1961-62	1	8			
1922-23	1	8	1962-63	1	16			
1923-24	1	7	1963-64	1	10			
1924-25	1	3	1964-65	1	4			
1925-26	1	16	1965-66	1	6			
1926-27	1	9	1966-67	1	5			
1927-28	1	12	1967-68	1	3			
1928-29	1	14	1968-69	1	12			
1929-30	1	17	1969-70	1	3			
1930-31	1	19	1970-71	1	12			
1931-32	2	7	1971-72	1	4			
1932-33	2	1	1972-73	1	3			

EUROPEAN RECORD

Season	Tournament	Opponents	Venue	Score	Tie-break
1955-56	European	1 Rot-Weiss Essen (WG)	a	4-0, 1-1	
		2 Djurgaarden (SWE)	a	3-1, 1-0	
		S Stade Reims (FR)	a	0-2, 0-1	
1960-61	Fairs	1 Lausanne Sports (SWZ)	a	w.o.	
		2 Barcelona (SP)	a	4-4, 3-2	
		S Roma (IT)	h	2-2, 3-3,	0-6(a)
1961-62	Fairs	1 Belenenses (POR)	h	3-3, 3-1	
		2 Red Star Belgrade (YUG)	a	0-4, 0-1	
1962-63	Fairs	1 Staevnet Copenhagen (DEN)	h	4-0, 3-2	
		2 Utrecht (HOL)	h	2-1, 1-0	
		3 Valencia (SP)	a	0-5, 2-1	
1965-66	Fairs	1 Valencia (SP)	h	2-0, 0-2,	0-3(a)
1967-68	Fairs	1 Porto (POR)	h	3-0, 1-3	
		2 Napoli (IT)	a	1-4, 5-0	
		3 Leeds United (ENG)	a	0-1, 1-1	
1968-69	Fairs	1 Olympia Ljubjana (YUG)	a	3-0, 2-1	
		2 Lokomotive Leipzig (EG)	h	3-1, 1-0	
		3 Hamburg (WG)	a	0-1, 2-1, away goals	
1970-71	Fairs	1 Malmoe (SWE)	h	6-0, 3-2	
		2 Vitoris Guimares (POR)	h	2-0, 1-2	
		3 Liverpool (ENG)	h	0-1, 0-2	
1972-73	Cup Win	1 Sporting Lisbon (POR)	a	1-2, 6-1	
		2 Besa (ALB)	h	7-1, 1-1	
		3 Hajduk Split (YUG)	h	4-2, 0-3	
1973-74	UEFA	1 Keflavik (ICE)	h	2-0, 1-1	
		2 Leeds United (ENG)	a	0-0, 0-0, penlts. (lost)	
1974-75	UEFA	1 Rosenborg Trondheim (NOR)	a	3-2, 9-1	
		2 Juventus (IT)	h	2-4, 0-4	
1975-76	UEFA	1 Liverpool (ENG)	h	1-0, 1-3	
1976-77	UEFA	1 Sochaux (FR)	h	1-0, 0-0	
		2 Oesters Vaxjoe (SWE)	h	2-0, 1-4	
1978-79	UEFA	1 Norrkoping (SWE)	h	3-2, 0-0	
		2 Racing Strasbourg (FR)	a	0.2, 1-0	

LEADING GOALSCORERS YEAR BY YEAR

The following is a list of Hibs' leading goalscorers year by year from 1893 to the present day. It has been compiled from newspapers and contains some figures which are slightly different from those produced from other sources. In particular, for the seasons up to 1900, the symbol * indicates that the information available is incomplete but that the player mentioned was nevertheless almost certainly the correct one.

The competitions included are the Scottish League, the Eastern League (1939-40), the Southern League (1940-46), the Scottish Cup, the Scottish League Cup, the Summer Cup (1941-45 and 1964-65), the Anglo-Scottish Cup, the War Emergency Cup (1940), the Victory Cup (1946) and the three European competitions.

Prior to 1893, the only one of the competitions in force was the Scottish Cup. Much of the information on scorers for this period is, not surprisingly, unavailable, but what there is is enough to establish that Jim McGhee is the Club's leading scorer of all time in that competition, with a total in excess of Joe Baker's 23 goals, the highest Scottish Cup figure since. The top scorers in the other major competitions are as follows:

Scottish League — Lawrie Reilly (187)
League Cup — Willie Ormond (41)
European competitions — Alan Gordon and Joe McBride (8)

League		All Competitions	
1893-94 Allan Martin	*	Allan Martin	*
1894-95 Allan Martin	*	Allan Martin	*
1895-96 John Kennedy or Willie Smith	*	Willie Smith	*
1896-97 John Price	10	John Price	*
1897-98 Allan Martin	*	Allan Martin	*
1898-99 Bobby Atherton	7	Bobby Atherton, Andy McGuigan	7
1899-00 Andy McGuigan	*	Andy McGuigan	*
1900-01 Hamilton Handling	7	Bobby Atherton	10
1901-02 Willie McCartney	7	John Divers	12
1902-03 Bobby Reid	13	Paddy Callaghan	16
1903-04 George Stewart	7	George Stewart	7
1904-05 Paddy Callaghan	11	Paddy Callaghan	12
1905-06 Paddy Callaghan	8	Patrick Hagan	9
1906-07 Tommy Findlay	10	Tommy Findlay	10
1907-08 Richard Harker	20	Richard Harker	20
1908-09 Jimmy Peggie	11	Jimmy Peggie	12
1909-10 Jimmy Peggie, John Sharp, Willie Smith	5	Jimmy Peggie	7
1910-11 Matt Paterson	17	Matt Paterson	17
1911-12 Harry Anderson	8	Harry Anderson, George Rae	8
1912-13 Jimmy Hendren	18	Jimmy Hendren	20

	League		All Competitions	
1913-14	Jimmy Hendren	18	Jimmy Hendren	19
1914-15	Jimmy Hendren	14		
1915-16	Sam Fleming, Henry Hutchison	9		
1916-17	Tommy Kilpatrick	12		
1917-18	Willie Miller	16		
1918-19	Bobby Gilmour	6	Bobby Gilmour	6
1919-20	Jimmy Williamson	21	Jimmy Williamson	21
1920-21	Davy Anderson	17	Davy Anderson	17
1921-22	Archie Young	10	Archie Young	12
1922-23	Jimmy McColl	12	Jimmy McColl	14
1923-24	Jimmy McColl	21	Jimmy McColl	22
1924-25	Jimmy Dunn	24	Jimmy Dunn	24
1925-26	Jimmy Dunn	17	Jimmy Dunn, Harry Ritchie	17
1926-27	Jimmy McColl	16	Jimmy McColl	16
1927-28	Jimmy McColl	24	Jimmy McColl	25
1928-29	Jackie Bradley	13	Jackie Bradley	14
1929-30	Jimmy Dobson	11	Jimmy McColl, Jimmy Dobson	11
1930-31	Andy Main	15	Andy Main	17
1931-32	Jimmy Dobson	14	Jimmy Dobson	14
1932-33	Jimmy Wallace	20	Jimmy Wallace	22
1933-34	Peter Flucker	12	Rab Walls	13
1934-35	Rab Walls	11	Rab Walls	14
1935-36	Tommy Brady	18	Tommy Brady	19
1936-37	Willie Black	12	Willie Black	12
1937-38	Arthur Milne	17	Arthur Milne	17
1938-39	Arthur Milne	22	Arthur Milne	23
1939-40	Johnny Cuthbertson	22	Johnny Cuthbertson	23
1940-41	Johnny Cuthbertson	27	Johnny Cuthbertson	32
1941-42	Bobby Combe	22	Bobby Combe	27
1942-43	Gordon Smith	26	Gordon Smith	31
1943-44	Gordon Smith	14	Gordon Smith	20
1944-45	Gordon Smith	21	Gordon Smith	27
1945-46	Gordon Smith	16	Gordon Smith	22
1946-47	Jock Weir	14	Jock Weir	23
1947-48	Gordon Smith	19	Gordon Smith	27
1948-49	Gordon Smith	15	Gordon Smith	18
1949-50	Gordon Smith	25	Gordon Smith	29
1950-51	Lawrie Reilly	23	Lawrie Reilly	36
1951-52	Lawrie Reilly	27	Lawrie Reilly	30
1952-53	Lawrie Reilly	30	Lawrie Reilly	44
1953-54	Lawrie Reilly	15	Bobby Johnstone	23
1954-55	Lawrie Reilly	15	Lawrie Reilly	15

	League		All Competitions	
1955-56	Lawrie Reilly	23	Lawrie Reilly	26
1956-57	Lawrie Reilly	16	Lawrie Reilly	18
1957-58	Joe Baker	14	Joe Baker	22
1958-59	Joe Baker	25	Joe Baker	30
1959-60	Joe Baker	42	Joe Baker	46
1960-61	Joe Baker	21	Joe Baker	44
1961-62	Duncan Falconer	12	Gerry Baker, Eric Stevenson	13
1962-63	Gerry Baker	13	Gerry Baker	18
1963-64	Neil Martin	19	Neil Martin	34
1964-65	Neil Martin	25	Neil Martin	33
1965-66	Peter Cormack	15	Neil Martin	18
1966-67	Peter Cormack, Joe Davis	13	Peter Cormack	16
1967-68	Colin Stein	21	Colin Stein	29
1968-69	Joe McBride	19	Joe McBride	24
1969-70	Joe McBride	20	Joe McBride	22
1970-71	Joe Baker	8	Arthur Duncan	16
1971-72	Arthur Duncan, Jimmy O'Rourke	11	Jimmy O'Rourke	15
1972-73	Alan Gordon	27	Alan Gordon	37
1973-74	Alan Gordon	16	Alan Gordon	22
1974-75	Arthur Duncan	13	Joe Harper	21
1975-76	Arthur Duncan	13	Arthur Duncan	16
1976-77	Bobby Smith	8	Ally Macleod	11
1977-78	Ally Macleod	16	Ally Macleod	23
1978-79	Ralph Callachan	9	Ally Macleod	17
1979-80	Ally Macleod	8	Ally Macleod	10
1980-81	Ally Macleod	15	Ally Macleod	19
1981-82	Gordon Rae	11	Gordon Rae	12
1982-83	Gordon Rae, Gary Murray, Bobby Thompson	6	Gordon Rae	10
1983-84	Willie Irvine	19	Willie Irvine	24
1984-85	Gordon Durie	8	Gordon Durie	8

Hat Trick Heroes

The following players have scored hat-tricks for Hibs in competitive matches since 1900:

7.9.01	H. Handling (3 v Queens Park, League)
30.11.01	W. McCartney (3 v Dundee, League)
22.1.02	A. McGeechan (3 v Queens Park, Cup)
	J. Divers (3 v Queens Park, Cup)

10.1.03	P. Callaghan (3 v Morton, Cup)
24.1.03	P. Callaghan (4 v Leith Athletic, Cup)
31.1.03	R. Reid (3 v Port Glasgow Athletic, League)
24.10.03	G. Stewart (3 v Port Glasgow Athletic, League)
25.1.08	J. Docherty (3 v Abercorn, Cup)
1.2.08	R. Harker (3 v Airdrie, League)
10.3.09	J. Gildes (3 v Partick Thistle, League)
7.1.11	M. Paterson (3 v Third Lanark, League)
25.1.13	W. Smith (3 v Dundee, League)
18.3.14	J. Hendren (3 v St. Mirren League)
10.4.15	J. Hendren (4 v Queens Park League)
17.3.17	T. Kilpatrick (3 v Queens Park, League)
20.8.19	J. Williamson (3 v Hamilton Academicals, League)
18.10.19	J. Williamson (4 v Partick Thistle, League)
18.8.23	J. McColl (3 v Third Lanark, League)
22.11.24	J. Dunn (3 v Aberdeen, League)
20.12.24	J. McColl (3 v St. Johnstone, League)
22.8.25	J. Walker (3 v Kilmarnock, League)
5.12.25	H. Ritchie (3 v Hamilton Academicals, League)
10.2.26	H. Richie (3 v Morton, League)
1.10.27	J. McColl (3 v Partick Thistle, League)
29.10.27	J. McColl (3 v Hamilton Academicals, League)
28.3.28	G. Murray (3 v Queens Park, League)
14.12.29	J. Dobson (3 v Dundee United, League)
18.10.30	H. Brown (3 v Morton, League)
22.11.30	A. Main (3 v Kilmarnock, League)
4.2.31	J. McColl (4 v Hamilton Academicals, Cup)
11.3.31	A. Main (4 v Queens Park, League)
26.12.31	J. Dobson (3 v Forfar Athletic, League)
23.8.32	J. Hart (3 v Montrose, League)
17.9.32	J. Wallace (3 v Brechin City, League)
15.10.32	P. Flucker (3 v Edinburgh City, League)
18.2.33	R. Walls (3 v Edinburgh City, League)
25.3.33	J. Hart (3 v St. Bernards, League)
29.4.33	J. Connolly (3 v Forfar Athletic, League)
4.11.33	R. Walls (3 v Cowdenbeath, League)
3.2.34	J. Malloy (4 v Alloa Athletic, Cup)
12.1.35	P. Flucker (3 v Clyde, League)
23.1.35	P. Flucker (5 v Vale of Atholl, Cup)
9.2.35	H. Anderson (3 v Clachnacuddin, Cup)
28.12.35	W. Black (3 v Clyde, League)
5.9.36	W. Black (3 v Hamilton Academicals, League)
7.11.36	W. Black (3 v Motherwell, League)
18.9.37	A. Milne (3 v Clyde, League)
	T. Egan (3 v Clyde, League)

16.10.37	A. Milne (3 v Arbroath, League)
10.9.38	T. McIntyre (3 v Hearts, League)
24.9.38	A. Milne (3 v Aberdeen, League)
9.12.38	R. Nutley (3 v Dundee United, Eastern League)
1.1.40	J. Cuthbertson (3 v Hearts, Eastern League)
2.4.40	J. Cuthbertson (3 v Dundee, Eastern League)
5.10.40	J. Cuthbertson (3 v Partick Thistle, Southern League)
9.11.40	J. Cuthbertson (4 v Falkirk, Southern League)
23.11.40	J. Cuthbertson (4 v Queens Park, Southern League)
1.3.41	J. Cuthbertson (4 v Clyde, S. League Cup)
22.3.41	H. Yorston (3 v Clyde, S. League Cup)
28.4.41	G. Smith (3 v Hearts, S. League)
7.6.41	A. Milne (3 v Celtic, Summer Cup)
28.6.41	W. Finnegan (3 v Clyde, Summer Cup)
23.8.41	R. Combe (4 v Albion Rovers, S. League)
13.9.41	R. Nutley (3 v Dumbarton, S. League)
27.9.41	R. Combe (4 v Rangers, S. League)
1.11.41	W. Finnegan (3 v Airdrie, S. League)
6.12.41	R. Baxter (3 v Albion Rovers, S. League)
19.9.42	J. Cuthbertson (3 v Third Lanark, S. League)
23.1.43	G. Smith (3 v Airdrie, S. League)
30.1.43	G. Smith (3 v Partick Thistle, S. League)
5.6.43	J. Mcgillivray (3 v Partick Thistle, Summer Cup)
18.9.43	G. Smith (3 v Dumbarton, S. League)
4.12.43	G. Smith (3 v Albion Rovers, S. League)
8.4.44	L. Nelson (3 v Morton, S. League Cup)
3.6.44	T. Bogan (3 v Airdrie, Summer Cup)
21.10.44	J. Devlin (3 v Partick Thistle, S. League)
11.11.44	G. Smith (3 v Airdrie, S. League)
13.1.45	G. Smith (3 v Falkirk, S. League)
31.3.45	J. Weir (3 v Albion Rovers, S. League Cup)
	J. McMullen (3 v Albion Rovers, S. League Cup)
2.6.45	J. Weir (3 v St. Mirren, Summer Cup)
10.2.46	J. Weir (3 v St. Mirren, S. League)
20.4.46	G. Smith (3 v Dundee, Victory Cup)
10.8.46	J. Weir (4 v Queen of the South, League)
23.11.46	E. Turnbull (3 v Partick Thistle, League)
18.1.47	E. Turnbull (3 v Kilmarnock, League)
25.1.47	J. Weir (4 v Alloa Athletic, Cup)
1.3.47	G. Smith (3 v Airdrie, League Cup)
16.8.47	G. Smith (3 v Clyde, League Cup)
27.8.47	L. Johnstone (4 v Airdrie, League)
11.10.47	L. Reilly (3 v Queen of the South, League)
8.11.47	G. Smith (5 v Third Lanark, League)
	A. Linwood (3 v Third Lanark, League)

29.11.47	W. Ormond (3 v St. Mirren, League)
17.1.48	J. Cuthbertson (3 v Queen of the South, League)
1.9.48	L. Reilly (3 v Albion Rovers, League)
31.8.49	L. Reilly (3 v Third Lanark, League Cup)
3.9.49	R. Combe (3 v Queen of the South, League Cup)
10.12.49	G. Smith (4 v Falkirk, League)
4.2.50	E. Turnbull (4 v Celtic, League)
18.2.50	G. Smith (3 v Motherwell, League)
1.4.50	G. Smith (3 v Stirling Albion, League)
15.8.50	L. Reilly (3 v St. Mirren, League Cup)
19.8.50	G. Smith (3 v Falkirk, League Cup)
9.9.50	L. Reilly (4 v Falkirk, League Cup)
7.10.50	E. Turnbull (3 v Queen of the South, League Cup)
25.11.50	E. Turnbull (3 v Airdrie, League)
10.3.51	L. Reilly (3 v Airdrie, Cup)
2.1.52	L. Reilly (3 v Third Lanark, League)
5.1.52	L. Reilly (3 v Stirling Albion, League)
	R. Combe (3 v Stirling Albion, League)
9.8.52	L. Reilly (3 v Partick Thistle, League Cup)
20.9.52	L. Reilly (3 v Hearts, League)
27.9.52	L. Reilly (4 v Motherwell, League)
22.11.52	L. Reilly (3 v East Fife, League)
20.12.52	G. Smith (3 v Queen of the South, League)
3.1.53	L. Reilly (3 v Motherwell, League)
24.1.53	W. Ormond (3 v Stenhousemuir, Cup)
7.2.53	L. Reilly (3 v Queens Park, Cup)
21.2.53	G. Smith (3 v Airdrie, Cup)
28.2.53	R. Combe (4 v Airdrie, League)
25.4.53	R. Johnstone (3 v Third Lanark, League)
12.9.53	R. Johnstone (3 v Third Lanark, League Cup)
16.9.53	T. d'Arcy (3 v Third Lanark, League Cup)
17.10.53	L. Reilly (3 v Falkirk, League)
6.2.54	R. Johnstone (3 v Clyde, League)
27.3.54	E. Turnbull (3 v Airdrie, League)
27.11.54	R. Johnstone (3 v East Fife, League)
12.2.55	L. Reilly (3 v Kilmarnock, League)
28.1.56	E. Turnbull (3 v Motherwell, League)
25.2.56	E. Turnbull (3 v Dunfermline Athletic, League)
25.4.56	L. Reilly (3 v Celtic, League)
8.9.56	L. Reilly (3 v Falkirk, League)
2.11.57	J. Baker (3 v St. Mirren, League)
1.3.58	J. Baker (4 v Hearts, Cup)
27.8.58	J. Baker (3 v Aberdeen, League Cup)
8.11.58	J. Baker (3 v Third Lanark, League)

29.11.58	J. Baker (3 v Celtic, League)
10.1.59	J. Baker (3 v Queen of the South, League)
17.10.59	J. Baker (3 v Dunfermline Athletic, League)
24.10.59	T. Preston (4 v Airdrie, League)
	J. Baker (3 v Airdrie, League)
5.12.59	J. Baker (3 v Arbroath, League)
19.12.59	J. Macleod (3 v Partick Thistle, League)
9.1.60	J. Baker (3 v Third Lanark, League)
23.1.60	J. Baker (3 v Clyde, League)
20.8.60	J. Baker (4 v Airdrie, League Cup)
29.10.60	R. Kinloch, (3 v St. Mirren, League)
24.12.60	J. Baker (5 v Third Lanark, League)
11.2.61	J. Baker (9 v Peebles Rovers, Cup)
1.9.62	G. Baker (3 v Third Lanark, League Cup)
8.4.63	G. Baker (3 v Dundee, League)
7.3.64	N. Martin (4 v Queen of the South, League)
15.4.64	S. Vincent (3 v East Stirling, League)
20.5.64	N. Martin (3 v Falkirk, Summer Cup)
15.8.64	J. Scott (3 v Airdrie, League Cup)
29.8.64	P. Cormack (3 v Airdrie, League Cup)
19.9.64	J. Scott (3 v Aberdeen, League)
14.11.64	N. Martin (3 v Third Lanark, League)
2.1.65	N. Martin (4 v Falkirk, League)
22.3.65	N. Martin (3 v Celtic, League)
22.9.65	J. Scott (4 v Alloa Athletic, League Cup)
	N. Martin (4 v Alloa Athletic, League Cup)
25.9.65	N. Martin (4 v Falkirk, League)
6.11.65	E. Stevenson (3 v Hamilton Academicals, League)
9.9.67	P. Quinn (3 v Hearts, League)
28.10.67	C. Stein (3 v Airdrie, League)
27.1.68	C. Stein (3 v East Stirling, Cup)
27.4.68	C. Stein (3 v Kilmarnock, League)
13.11.68	J. McBride (3 v Lokomotive Leipzig, Fairs Cup)
16.11.68	J. McBride (4 v Morton, League)
7.12.68	P. Cormack (3 v Aberdeen, League)
6.9.69	J. McBride (3 v Partick Thistle, League)
21.3.70	J. McBride (3 v St. Johnstone, League)
16.9.70	J. McBride (3 v Malmoe, Fairs Cup)
23.1.71	J. O'Rourke (3 v Forfar Athletic, Cup)
24.4.71	J. O'Rourke (3 v Clyde, League)
23.10.71	A. Duncan (4 v Falkirk, League)
20.9.72	J. O'Rourke (3 v Dundee United, League Cup)
29.9.72	J. O'Rourke (3 v Sporting Lisbon, Cupwinners Cup)
11.10.72	A. Duncan (3 v Airdrie, League Cup)

14.10.72	J. O'Rourke (3 v Airdrie, League)
25.10.72	J. O'Rourke (3 v Besa, Cupwinners Cup)
11.11.72	J. O'Rourke (3 v Morton, League)
16.12.72	J. O'Rourke (3 v Ayr United, League)
	A. Gordon (3 v Ayr United, League)
10.2.73	A. Gordon (4 v Airdrie, League)
7.3.73	A. Gordon (3 v Hajduk Split, Cupwinners Cup)
3.11.73	P. Stanton (3 v Clyde, League)
22.12.73	J. O'Rourke (3 v Morton, League)
16.2.74	J. O'Rourke (3 v St. Johnstone, Cup)
9.3.74	A. Gordon (3 v Dundee, Cup)
17.4.74	A. Gordon (3 v Dumbarton, League)
15.3.75	I. Munro (3 v Dunfermline Athletic, League)
12.4.75	J. Harper (3 v Airdrie, League)
29.11.75	A. Duncan (3 v St. Johnstone, League)
24.8.83	W. Irvine (3 v Dumbarton, League Cup)
19.11.83	W. Irvine (3 v St. Johnstone, League)
9.2.85	G. Durie (3 v Morton, League)

LEADING GOALSCORERS 1946–85

	League	League Cup Summer Cup Anglo-Scottish Cup	Scottish Cup	European Tournaments	Total
1. Lawrie Reilly	187	31	15	1	234
2. Eddie Turnbull	149	37	9	4	199
3. Willie Ormond	133	41	18	1	193
4. Gordon Smith	125	33	12	—	170
5. Joe Baker	114	16	23	6	159
6. Bobby Johnstone	100	27	9	—	136
7. Jimmy O'Rourke	81	19	15	6	121
8. Arthur Duncan	73	25	7	7	112
9. Peter Cormack	77	16	4	3	100
10. Ally McLeod	71	14	13	1	99
11. Neil Martin	53	31	2	—	86
12. Eric Stevenson	53	20	2	3	78
13. Jim Scott	48	23	4	1	76
13. Alan Gordon	51	10	7	8	76
15. Pat Stanton	50	14	4	7	75
16. Bobby Combe	54	9	5	1	69
17. Joe McBride	44	6	—	8	58
18. Colin Stein	40	8	3	4	55
19. Gordon Rae	42	7	5	—	54
20. Tommy Preston	35	11	1	2	49

	League	League Cup Summer Cup Anglo-Scottish	Scottish Cup	European Tournaments	Total
21. Alex Cropley	28	13	1	5	47
22. Joe Harper	25	15	2	3	45
23. Joe Davis	34	4	2	3	43
24. Gerry Baker	28	11	2	1	42
25. Johnny Cuthbertson	29	6	6	—	41
25. Tony Higgins	24	10	4	3	41
27. Johnny Macleod	28	4	6	2	40
28. John Fraser	25	5	5	2	37
29. Ralph Callachan	25	4	5	—	34
30. Alex Linwood	22	7	4	—	33
31. John Baxter	22	5	3	2	32
32. Bobby Smith	20	8	2	1	31
32. Willie Irvine	26	5	—	—	31
34. Willie Jamieson	25	2	—	—	27
35. Pat Quinn	19	5	1	1	26

36. Willie Hamilton (24); 37. Jock Weir, John Brownlie, Des Bremner (23);
40. Bobby Kinloch (22); 41. Archie Buchanan, Allan McGraw (21);
43. Johnny Graham (20).

Roll of Honour
Full International Appearances — Scotland

J. Blackley (5)	74 v CZ, ENG, BEL, ZAI; 76 v SWZ
D. Bremner (1)	76 v SWZ
B. Breslin (1)	97 v WAL
J. Brownlie (7)	71 v RUS; 72 v PER, NI, ENG; 73 v DEN (2); 76 v ROM
P. Callaghan (1)	00 v NI
R. Combe (3)	48 v ENG, SWZ, BEL
P. Cormack (4)	66 v BRA; 69 v DEN; 70 v EIR, WG
A. Cropley (2)	72 v POR, BEL
A. Duncan (5)	75 v POR, WAL, NI, ENG, RUS
J. Dunn (5)	25 v WAL, NI; 27 v NI; 28 v NI, ENG
R. Glen (1)	00 v NI
J. Govan (6)	48 v ENG, WAL, BEL, SWZ, FR; 49 v NI
J. Grant (2)	59 v WAL, NI
A. Gray (1)	03 v NI
W. Groves (1)	88 v WAL
W. Hamilton (1)	65 v FIN
J. Harper (1)	76 v DEN

W. Harper (9)	23 v ENG, WAL, NI; 24 v ENG, WAL, NI; 25 v ENG, WAL, NI
H. Howie (1)	49 v WAL
R. Johnstone (13)	51 v ENG, DEN, FR; 52 v NI, ENG; 53 v ENG, SWE; 54 v WAL, ENG, NOR, FIN; 55 v NI, HUN
J. Kennedy (1)	97 v WAL
P. Kerr (1)	24 v NI
J. Lundie (1)	86 v WAL
W. McCartney (1)	02 v NI
J. McGhee (1)	86 v WAL
J. McLaren (1)	88 v WAL
J. Macleod (4)	61 v ENG, EIR (2), CZ
J. Main (1)	09 v NI
N. Martin (2)	65 v FIN, POL
P. Murray (2)	96 v NI; 97 v WAL
R. Neil (1)	96 v WAL
W. Ormond (6)	54 v ENG, NOR, FIN, AUS, URU; 59 v ENG
J. Pryce (1)	97 v WAL
L. Reilly (38)	49 v ENG, WAL, FR; 50 v WAL, NI, SWZ, FR; 51 v WAL, ENG, DEN, FR, BEL, AUS; 52 v NI, WAL, ENG, USA, DEN, SWE; 53 v ENG, WAL, NI, SWE; 54 v WAL; 55 v HUN (2), POR, YUG, AUS, ENG; 56 v ENG, WAL, NI, AUS; 57 v ENG, NI, WAL, YUG
H. Rennie (11)	01 v ENG; 02 v ENG, WAL, NI; 03 v ENG, WAL; 04 v NI; 05 v WAL; 06 v NI; 08 v NI, WAL
H. Ritchie (2)	23 v WAL; 28 v NI
W. Robb (1)	28 v WAL
E. Schaedler (1)	74 v WG
J. Scott (1)	66 v HOL
D. Shaw (8)	47 v WAL, NI; 48 v ENG, BEL, SWZ, FR; 49 v WAL, NI
G. Smith (18)	47 v ENG, NI; 48 v WAL, BEL, SWZ, FR; 52 v ENG, USA; 55 v POR, YUG, AUS, HUN; 56 v NI, WAL, ENG; 57 v SP (2) SWZ
P. Stanton (16)	66 v HOL; 69 v NI; 70 v EIR, AUS; 71 v DEN (2), POR, RUS, BEL; 72 v POR, BEL, HOL, WAL; 73 v WAL, NI; 74 v WG
G. Stewart (2)	06 v WAL, ENG
E. Turnbull (8)	48 v BEL, SWZ; 51 v AUS; 58 v HUN, POR, YUG, FR, PAR

D. Urquhart (1)   34 v WAL
T. Younger (8)   55 v POR, YUG, AUS, HUN; 56 v ENG, WAL,
                       NI, AUS

England
J. Baker (5)   60 v YUG, SP, HUN, NI, SCO

Northern Ireland (previously Ireland)
P. Farrell (1)   38 v WAL
W. Gowdy (1)   36 v WAL
J. Jones (4)   36 v WAL; 37 v ENG, SCO, WAL
J. Parke (3)   64 v ENG, SP; 65 v SWZ

Wales
R. Atherton (2)   99 v NI, ENG

Eire
P. Farrell (2)   37 v SWZ, FR (see also Northern Ireland)
M. Gallagher (1)   54 v LUX

Under-23 Appearances — Scotland
J. Baxter (1)   59 v WAL
J. Blackley (4)   70 v FR, ENG, WAL; 71 v ENG
D. Bremner (3)   75 v ENG, WAL, SWE
J. Brownlie (2)   72 v ENG, WAL
P. Cormack (6)   65 v WAL, ENG; 67 v WAL, ENG; 68 v WAL,
                       ENG
A. Cropley (3)   72 v WAL; 73 v ENG; 74 v WAL
A. Duncan (1)   71 v ENG
J. Easton (1)   64 v WAL
J. Harrower (1)   58 v NOR
N. Martin (1)   64 v FR
P. Marinello (2)   70 v FR, ENG
J. Macleod (2)   61 v ENG, Army
R. Nicol (2)   56 v ENG; 58 v NOR
J. Plenderleith (5)   57 v ENG; 58 v NOR (2), ENG; 60 v WAL
P. Stanton (3)   67 v WAL, ENG; 68 v ENG
C. Stein (1)   68 v ENG

England
J. Baker (5)   59 v POL, CZ; 60 v FR, NOR; 61 v IT

Under-21 Appearances — Scotland
A. Brazil (1)   78 v WAL
A. McLeod (3)   79 v NOR (2), POR
L. Muir (1)   77 v CZ

C. Paterson (3)	81 v SWE, IT (2)
B. Rice (1)	85 v WG
P. Stanton (1)	77 v CZ

Scottish League Appearances

J. Blackley (1)	72 v ENG
B. Breslin (4)	98 v ENG, NI; 99 v ENG; 00 v NI
D. Bremner (1)	76 v ENG
J. Brownlie (1)	72 v ENG
P. Callaghan (2)	00 v NI; 03 v NI
R. Combe (4)	49 v ENG, EIR; 54 v ENG, EIR
P. Cormack (6)	67 v ENG, EIR; 68 v NI; 69 v ENG; 70 v ENG, NI
J. Cuthbertson (1)	48 v ENG
A. Duncan (3)	71 v EIR; 73 v ENG; 76 v ENG
J. Dunn (1)	23 v NI
R. Glen (2)	00 v ENG, NI
J. Govan (1)	53 v EIR
J. Graham (1)	71 v EIR
J. Grant (6)	59 v ENG, NI, EIR; 60 v NI, EIR; 62 v EIR
A. Gray (1)	03 v ENG
W. Hamilton (1)	65 v ENG
W. Harper (3)	25 v ENG, IRE; 25 v ENG
R. Johnstone (6)	51 v EIR; 52 v ENG, NI; 53 v EIR, ENG; 54 v EIR
S. Kean (1)	47 v NI
J. Kennedy (1)	97 v NI
P. Kerr (2)	24 v NI; 27 v NI
A. Linwood (1)	49 v NI
W. McCartney (2)	02 v ENG; 03 v ENG
T. McFarlane (1)	97 v NI
W. McGinnigle (1)	25 v NI
A. McLeod (1)	80 v EIR
J. Macleod (1)	61 v ENG
J. McNamara (1)	80 v NI
J. Main (1)	08 v ENG
N. Martin (2)	64 v ENG; 65 v EIR
P. Murray (1)	97 v NI
R. Nutley (1)	40 v NI
W. Ormond (9)	47 v NI; 48 v NI; 49 v ENG; 50 v NI; 51 v ENG; 53 v EIR, NI; 54 v ENG; 58 v ENG
A. Raisbeck (1)	97 v NI
L. Reilly (13)	49 v NI; 50 v ENG, EIR; 51 v NI, EIR; 52 v ENG; 53 v ENG, EIR, NI; 56 v ENG, EIR, NI; 57 v EIR

H. Rennie (6)	01 v ENG; 03 v NI; 04 v ENG; 05 v ENG; 06 v ENG; 08 v ENG
H. Ritchie (5)	22 v NI; 23 v ENG, NI; 24 v NI; 27 v ENG
D. Shaw (2)	49 v NI, EIR
G. Smith (9)	48 v NI; 50 v ENG, EIR; 51 v ENG; 53 v EIR; 55 v ENG; 56 v ENG, EIR, NI
W. Smith (3)	12 v NI; 14 v ENG; 13 v STH LGE
P. Stanton (7)	66 v ENG; 68 v NI; 69 v EIR; 70 v ENG, NI; 71 v EIR; 73 v ENG
C. Stein (2)	68 v ENG; 69 v ENG
E. Stevenson (1)	70 v NI
G. Stewart (1)	06 v ENG
E. Turnbull (4)	49 v ENG; 51 v ENG; 53 v NI; 59 v ENG
W. Watson (1)	34 v NI
T. Younger (4)	56 v ENG, NI, EIR, DEN

'B' Internationals

T. McDonald (1)	54 v ENG
J. Mulkerrin (1)	56 v ENG
E. Turnbull (1)	56 v ENG

Wartime Internationals

R. Baxter (2)	Apr. 44 v ENG; Oct. 44 v ENG
T. Bogan (1)	Apr. 45 v ENG
M. Busby (2)	Oct. 41 v ENG; Apr. 42 v ENG
J. Caskie (5)	Oct. 41 v ENG; Jan. 42 v ENG; Feb. 44 v ENG; Apr. 44 v ENG; Oct. 44 v ENG
S. Kean (1)	Apr. 43 v ENG
A. Milne (1)	Oct. 44 v ENG
D. Shaw (2)	Apr. 46 v ENG; May 46 v SWZ
G. Smith (2)	Oct. 44 v ENG; Jan 46 v BEL

R. Baxter, M. Busby and J. Caskie are sometimes listed with Middlesbrough, Liverpool and Everton respectively, the clubs with whom they were registered at the outbreak of war. The above caps were won while they were regular members of the Hibs' team and would otherwise have been playing for Hibs.

The following abbreviations have been used (except for League Internationals)

ALB	Albania	NOR	Norway
AUS	Austria	PAR	Paraguay
BEL	Belgium	PER	Peru
BRA	Brazil	POL	Poland
CZ	Czechoslovakia	POR	Portugal
DEN	Denmark	ROM	Romania

EG	East Germany	RUS	Russia
EIR	Republic of Ireland	SCO	Scotland
ENG	England	SP	Spain
FIN	Finland	SWE	Sweden
FR	France	SWZ	Switzerland
HOL	Holland	URU	Uruguay
HUN	Hungary	USA	United States
ICE	Iceland	WAL	Wales
IT	Italy	WG	West Germany
LUX	Luxembourg	YUG	Yugoslavia
NI	Northern Ireland (see below)	ZAI	Zaire

Note: Northern Ireland. Ireland was divided into Northern Ireland and the Republic of Ireland in 1922, and therefore up to then there was only one international team representing the whole island. From 1922 until about 1954, Northern Ireland included Republic players in British Championship matches only, the two parts of Ireland fielding separate sides against other opponents. Since 1954, only Northern Irish players have represented Northern Ireland in the British Championship or elsewhere. In this book, NI has been used to represent the combined Irish teams that played in the British Championship up to 1954 and also the Northern Ireland teams since 1922, while EIR represents teams exclusively from the Republic of Ireland.

For League Internationals, the abbreviations designate the opposing country rather than the league itself as follows:

DEN	Danish League
EIR	League of Ireland
ENG	Football League
NI	Irish League
STH LGE	(English) Southern League

Index